FICTION, FAMINE, AND THE RISE OF ECONOMICS IN VICTORIAN BRITAIN AND IRELAND

We now think of economic theory as a scientific speciality accessible only to experts, but Victorian writers commented on economic subjects with great interest. Gordon Bigelow focuses on novelists Charles Dickens and Elizabeth Gaskell and compares their work with commentaries on the Irish Famine (1845–52). Bigelow argues that, at this moment of crisis, the rise of economics depended substantially on concepts developed in literature. These works all criticized the systematized approach to economic life that the prevailing political economy proposed. Gradually, the romantic views of human subjectivity, described in the novels, provided the foundation for a new theory of capitalism based on the desires of the individual consumer. Bigelow's argument stands out by showing how the discussion of capitalism in these works had significant influence not just on public opinion, but on the rise of economic theory itself.

GORDON BIGELOW is Assistant Professor of English at Rhodes College in Memphis, Tennessee. His work has appeared in the journals *ELH*, *New Orleans Review*, and *Research in African Literatures*, and in the volume *Reclaiming Gender: Transgressive Identities in Modern Ireland* (1999).

FICTION, FAMINE, AND THE RISE OF ECONOMICS IN VICTORIAN BRITAIN AND IRELAND

GORDON BIGELOW

Rhodes College, Memphis, Tennessee

CAMBRIDGE
UNIVERSITY PRESS

PUBLISHED BY THE PRESS SYNDICATE OF THE UNIVERSITY OF CAMBRIDGE
The Pitt Building, Trumpington Street, Cambridge, United Kingdom

CAMBRIDGE UNIVERSITY PRESS
The Edinburgh Building, Cambridge, CB2 2RU, UK
40 West 20th Street, New York, NY 10011–4211, USA
477 Williamstown Road, Port Melbourne, VIC 3207, Australia
Ruiz de Alarcón 13, 28014 Madrid, Spain
Dock House, The Waterfront, Cape Town 8001, South Africa

http://www.cambridge.org

First published 2003

Printed in the United Kingdom at the University Press, Cambridge

Typeface Adobe Garamond 11/12.5 pt.   *System* LATEX 2$_\varepsilon$ [TB]

A catalogue record for this book is available from the British Library

Library of Congress Cataloguing in Publication data
Bigelow, Gordon, 1963–
Fiction, famine, and the rise of economics in Victorian Britain and Ireland / Gordon Bigelow.
p.   cm. – (Cambridge studies in nineteenth-century literature and culture; 40)
Includes bibliographical references and index.
ISBN 0 521 82848 1
1. English fiction – 19th century – History and criticism.   2. Economics in literature.
3. Gaskell, Elizabeth Cleghorn, 1810–1865 – Knowledge – Economics.
4. Ireland – History – Famine, 1845–1852 – Historiography.   5. Dickens, Charles,
1812–1870 – Knowledge – Economics.   6. Economics – Great Britain – History – 19th century.
7. Dickens, Charles, 1812–1870. Bleak House.   I. Title.   II. Series.
PR868.E37B54   2003
820.9′355 – dc21   2003048558

ISBN 0 521 82848 1 hardback

Contents

Acknowledgments

The work that became this book owes its beginning to four extraordinary teachers: Thomas Vogler, John Jordan, Hilary Schor, and David Lloyd. It was in a series of lectures by John Jordan on Dickens and the social history of the 1840s that these ideas first began to take shape. Tom Vogler, a generous mentor and inspiring example of intellectual life, offered passionate encouragement and consistent insight. Hilary Schor gave nuanced and detailed responses to any number of false starts; the first overall outline of what follows was drawn up by her on a paper napkin. David Lloyd contributed generous advice and support at critical stages during the project. I thank these four for the remarkable insights of their own research, and for their guidance and encouragement.

Many people have read, and reread, significant portions of what follows. Among these are James Clifford, Joseph Childers, Kristin Ross, Richard Terdiman, Christopher Breu, J. Hillis Miller, and Cynthia Marshall; I thank them all for excellent suggestions and criticisms. Kevin Whelan and Stephen Heath, at different stages of the project, steered me toward important texts. Susan Kus and Lynn Zastoupil responded thoughtfully to new ideas at a formative stage in the revision process. Murray Baumgarten, Regenia Gagnier, and Christopher Connery provided important advice and help of various kinds, without which the project could not have developed. Catherine Newman and Michael Millner shared insightful responses to chapter 4 and provided on other occasions many restorative evenings of wine and conversation. Catherine John has been a rare intellectual companion, helping me make sense of my reasons for doing this work. The open-handed encouragement of Tadhg Foley and Luke Gibbons helped to sustain me through many long months of isolated work. The interest which Heather Miller took in this project, and the work she dedicated to it, were also crucial to its completion. Judith Haas gave more than one reading to each section of the book, and her interest and support has made all that follows possible.

My colleagues in the Department of English at Rhodes College have created the welcoming and stimulating intellectual environment that one hopes for in academic life, but rarely finds. In particular I thank Robert Entzminger, Marshall Boswell, Jennifer Brady, Rob Canfield, John Hilgart, Michael Leslie, Cynthia Marshall, Sandra McEntire, and Brian Shaffer for their friendship and advice.

Research and travel during two summers was supported by grants from Rhodes College, and I thank the College for these opportunities. Funding from Rhodes College also supported research assistance for this project by Meredith Cain; I thank her for her good-humored and careful work. The Center for Cultural Studies at the University of California, Santa Cruz fostered the work of several research clusters and conferences that helped this book evolve, and I thank the Center for its tradition of innovative work. The Department of Literature at the University of California, Santa Cruz provided extensive research and travel assistance. I am very grateful as well to The Dickens Project, a research consortium based at UC Santa Cruz, for providing a forum that brought me into contact with a variety of scholars and students of nineteenth-century literature and culture.

Parts of chapters 1 and 2 appeared in the *New Orleans Review* (1998), and I thank the journal for use of that material.

My parents, Gordon and Beverly Bigelow, deserve all my gratitude. They have provided constant support, sympathy, and an inspiring example. Finally, I owe everything my work has become to Judith Haas; her delicate sensibility, her stubborn advocacy, and her scrupulous intelligence have made my path in life.

Introduction

In the world of the twenty-first century, the study of economics has taken over the burden that once fell to the concept of empire. In contemporary global relations, power and privilege are thought primarily within an economic rhetoric; empire's frank assertions of hierarchy in race, class, and gender have been replaced in foreign policy by the sanitized terms of development, growth, and free trade. Public discourse on social and political policy, liberal and conservative, rests at every turn on an economic imperative of one form or another.[1] At the same time, the last decade has brought an expansion of financial institutions, consumer credit instruments, and capital investment programs, which can make citizenship appear only a matter of personal investment strategy and wealth creation. As an academic discipline and as a practice of public policy, economics is a crucial tool for sustaining the view that distribution of resources, either at the level of the household or of the international agreement, is today nonviolent and non-coercive. The discipline's explanatory power, its ability to theorize the expansion of markets as a form of social progress, was consolidated in the middle decades of the nineteenth century. This book studies that process of consolidation, examining the cultural and philosophical preconditions of the discipline's difficult birth.

The nineteenth century witnessed the failure of one set of economic concepts, known today as classical political economy, and the birth of a new one, now called "neoclassical" economics. The period between the demise of the first and the rise of the second was remarkably short, consisting roughly of the twenty years between 1850 and 1870. In this period the concepts provided by political economists to explain the functioning of capitalism, its force in history, and its impact on society, were in turmoil, and this turmoil is visible not only in debates among theorists themselves, but in governmental policy, and in popular discussions of factories, wages, agriculture, and stock shares.

What enabled the reemergence of economic theory as a widely accepted justification of capitalism, by the end of the nineteenth century, was the figure of the consumer. The consumer is a "figure" in that it represents an idealized and schematized model of human subjectivity, an outline of a universal human character. A particular modern avatar of *homo economicus*, rational economic man, the consumer is a rational actor, but one whose primary motivations are understood in metaphysical, even occult terms. But it is also correct to say that the consumer is a "figure of speech," since the model of consumer behavior neoclassical economics adopted derives significantly from the study of language in the Victorian period. While eighteenth-century philosophers of language were often interested in systems of writing and their history, Victorian philology focused on the spoken word as the paradigmatic form of human communication, and it sketched its model of human perception and human community based on this focus. In neoclassical economics, the consumer "speaks" in the language of commodities. Purchases are understood as expressive acts, in which the commodity forms a perfect representation of the consumer's desire; consumer behavior in the market, charted over the long term and in aggregate, is interpreted as the expression of popular will.

The philological approach to language gained influence in England in the 1830s. Its roots were in German idealist philosophy, and in the broad artistic and cultural movement we now call romanticism. The English writers of the romantic period, as currently understood in literary history, are a somewhat disparate group, from Blake to Keats, writing from roughly 1790 to 1820. But the assumptions and attitudes associated in English culture with these writers reverberated powerfully in the early Victorian novel of society, and they continued to exert a belated influence in other arenas of modern life: education, work, leisure, gender, politics, and, I will argue in this book, economics.[2] In chapters that follow on Charles Dickens and Elizabeth Gaskell, I trace an emerging romantic vision of markets and market factors which would ultimately become part of modern economic theory. To argue that economic theory is romantic, however, requires us not only to look beyond the rationalist paradigm of modern economics, it requires us to revise long-held assumptions about the literary and intellectual history of the nineteenth century.

The most important of these assumptions is that with the growth of industrial and market society over the course of the nineteenth century, there arose an increasing division between the economic and cultural spheres of human life. This assumed separation is perhaps nowhere more clearly to be

seen than in the modern history of the word "economics" itself. For most of
the nineteenth century, writers interested in what we now call "economics"
used the term "political economy" to designate their field of study. By the
1840s and 1850s, however, political economists had been drawn into bitter
disputes over government economic policy and had emerged the worse for
it. In 1879, writing in the preface to a new edition of his epochal *Theory of
Political Economy*, William Stanley Jevons urged "the substitution for the
name Political Economy of the single convenient term Economics."[3] A
growing consensus on this name-change eventually cleansed the discipline
of its original involvement with "politics" – that is, with moral philosophy
and social theory – and restricted it to the positive description of market behaviors alone. Jevons wrote in the same preface that "the Theory of
Economy thus treated presents a close analogy to the science of Statical
Mechanics, and the Laws of Exchange are found to resemble the Laws of
Equilibrium."[4] Following Jevons and others of his generation, economists
patterned their work increasingly after emerging theories in optics and ther-
modynamics, believing that the phenomena of production and exchange
conformed to clear mechanical laws, which functioned apart from cultural
or psychological or political considerations.[5]

The emergence of economics as a social science was in this way predi-
cated on the separateness of a thing called "the economy" from other forms
of human judgment. This economy must have its own laws and ordering
principles, which could be isolated and studied in themselves. But it is
important to recognize here that Jevons's retreat into the laboratory, and
out of the drawing rooms of culture and politics, in fact represents a concession to the romantic critique of political economy in the first half of
the nineteenth century. It was the romantic reconstruction of the social
landscape which, in Raymond Williams's famous formulation, posited a
"practical separation of certain moral and intellectual activities from the
driven impetus of a new kind of society."[6] These "moral and intellectual
activities" – poetry, philosophy, religion – were distinct from commercial
life and could not be understood in commercial terms. Wealth was not life,
and its pursuit was not the pursuit of truth. It was this plane of ethical
and aesthetic considerations, superior to the calculations of the marketplace, which the word "culture" would come to denote. And "culture"
in this sense would function "as a court of human appeal, to be set over
the processes of practical social judgment and yet to offer itself as a mit-
igating and rallying alternative."[7] Jevons's name-change represents then a
belated victory of the romantic critique, conceding a field of inquiry called

"culture" and confining itself to one called "economy." From this perspective the object of study which modern economics developed was itself a
product of a romantic hegemony.

Part of the crisis of political economy in the 1840s was its narrow political
and sectarian base. Political economy was the terrain of liberals and evangelicals almost exclusively. Linked not with Adam Smith but now with the
work of Malthus, this narrow vision amounted to what Boyd Hilton has
called "soteriological economics," a popular theory of poverty as atonement
for sin and wealth as a sign of personal rectitude.[8] In this evangelical system,
work and profit were understood as spiritual duties, steps toward salvation
rather than signs of social good. The politics of this early Victorian position were Whig and radical: freedom of trade, and abolition of all public
relief to the poor. This was the political economy Coleridge, Carlyle, and
Ruskin loved to hate. The antipathy between the advocates of culture and
those of political economy was deep and lasting; a highly partisan Arnold
Toynbee, looking back from as late as 1884, characterized the debate as "a
bitter argument between economists and human beings."[9] However, by the
point when Toynbee was writing, the "human beings" already controlled
the terms and premises of this debate. By the end of the century, a romantic
understanding of culture had already been accepted and absorbed by the
economists, as Jevons's example makes clear. Indeed, this book will argue
that the earliest glimpses of the neoclassical approach in English economic
thought originated from the harshest critics of liberal political economy
in the early Victorian period – romantics and Tory traditionalists. Although
Thomas De Quincey had parted company from his Lake Poet friends by
the time he began to write on political economy, his essays on Ricardo
apply a Coleridgean and quasi-Kantian sensibility to the theory of value.
These essays of De Quincey's date from the 1820s and 1830s, but, as I argue
in chapter 2 below, the metaphysical reorientation he proposes for political
economy would form the foundation of the system Jevons would eventually
call economics.

The other odd precursor of neoclassical economics in the early Victorian
period is the so-called Dublin School, a coterie of Anglo-Irish intellectuals
including Mountifort Longfield, Issac Butt, and Archbishop of Dublin
Richard Whately. The former two were organic intellectuals not of the
English commercial classes (like Ricardo) but of an Irish colonial settler
class.[10] The latter, Whately, was appointed Archbishop of Dublin in 1831
and left a chaired position in political economy at Oxford to accept the
post. Dependent as they were upon the traditional distinctions of church
and class, they were at best ambivalent to the liberal and radical strains of

English political economy, often deeply opposed. Out of their defense of the paternalist state and the established church, these thinkers developed a theoretical stance close to De Quincey's.

The extraordinary durability of economics in the twentieth and twenty-first centuries can be traced to its complex origins in the nineteenth century, origins that can be found partly within the history of positivism and the experimental sciences, but partly within the romantic reconception of human subjective experience. The romantic roots of neoclassical economics are what I set out to examine here, both within the central tradition of British economic thought, and in early Victorian fiction and non-fiction prose. The hegemonic staying power of economics can be clarified through such an approach; so can its particular limitations and blindnesses.

Serious students of economics today learn that the discipline offers them a model not of how the world should be, but a model of how it is. That is, neoclassical economics attempts only a positive description of the capitalist market, without presuming to evaluate the injustices that the marketplace may permit, or foster. In popular discourse, however, in the rhetoric of politics and journalism, the modern theory of market expansion amounts to a total vision of the good. Economics provides a relatively stable vocabulary for describing social processes, limiting the historical narrative that explains contemporary arrangements of power, and offering a range of solutions to social ills. But while neoclassical economics and its popular avatars hold sway in the academy and in public rhetoric, there is an increasing body of scholarship which questions the universality of the neoclassical categories and advances alternatives. Though a distinct minority among academics, and virtually invisible in government and commerce, there are subsets of economists determined to question the neoclassical theory of market behavior. Their work falls into three general and overlapping categories.

Those economists interested in language and rhetoric stress the always metaphorical nature of economic reasoning and economic discourse, challenging the realist assumptions of economics as a quantitative discipline. This is an approach pioneered by Deirdre McCloskey in her *The Rhetoric of Economics* (1985),[11] a book which borrows from structural linguistics and continental philosophy to foreground the narrative and figurative aspects of economic arguments.[12] Alternatively, feminist economists have begun to investigate the normative masculinity of the discipline's analytical tools, pointing out its blindness to unwaged work (like childrearing) and to the impact of cultural codes (like gender) on economic behavior. Since 1995 the journal *Feminist Economics* has provided a forum for debates in this field.[13] Finally, an ongoing tradition of Marxian political economy has continued

to subject the neoclassical paradigm to rigorous critique, sometimes borrowing tools from other disciplines in the humanities and social sciences.
The journal *Rethinking Marxism*, centered at the Economics Department
of the University of Massachusetts, Amherst, has been especially important
in encouraging this sort of interdisciplinary work, especially for dialogue
between Marxist economists and poststructuralist scholars in other fields.[14]

The current debate over the globalization of capital and international
free trade has also been the occasion for a good deal of critical work on
contemporary economic theory and discourse. There is a variety of popular
press literature that questions the ascendancy of neoliberal trade theory
around the globe.[15] The most innovative academic work on globalization
issues, however, has come from the discipline of anthropology. Following on
from the work of figures like Clifford Geertz, James Clifford, and Michael
Taussig, the gaze of anthropologists has turned back to examine its own
institutional locations, producing critical work on urbanity, modernity, and
"whiteness," for example. As a result of this new set of interests, the attention
anthropologists have always given to systems of exchange and codes of
value has evolved into a critique of economic concepts like "development"
and "debt," which structure the First World's perception of the Third as
powerfully as the lingering tropes of nineteenth-century orientalism.[16]

Much of the interdisciplinary work in literature and economics can
be traced in some way back to a set of provocative theoretical statements
in the 1970s from two writers: Jean-Joseph Goux and Marc Shell. Both
Goux and Shell posit a formal similarity between money, as a medium for
the exchange of resources, and language, as a medium for the exchange of
concepts.[17] Literary scholars operating in the wake of these arguments have
shown relatively little interest in economic thought and its history since,
for Shell and Goux, money and language exist not so much as objects of
culture but as concrete phenomena of human cognition.[18]

My approach in this study views the homology between language and
money less as a concrete feature of human consciousness than as the product of a certain historical experience. In the eighteenth and nineteenth
centuries, European economic thought developed in close connection with
the philosophy of language. I attempt to describe some of these connections in Part 1 below. However, I compare the similar approaches taken
by early linguists and political economists in order to reveal the historical
trends at work in the shaping of knowledge. To put the issue another way,
I am interested here not in a structural link between money and language,
but in what people in a given place and time *wrote* about both money and
language, markets and texts, commodities and words, values and meanings.

A trend toward historical approaches of this sort, where literary texts, market conditions, and economic theories from a given era are considered together, can be seen in a number of recent studies. Significant new work has appeared on the literary marketplace, the publishing industry, and the question of intellectual property.[19] Other critics trace the treatment of economic concepts like value, exchange, and debt within literary texts, often in connection with changes in market infrastructure and shifting conceptions of wealth and capital. The best work of this kind in nineteenth-century studies has focused on the connection between Victorian narrative and the commodity form. Jeff Nunokawa's *The Afterlife of Property* (1994) begins with the premise that, within the worlds of Victorian fiction, property only exists in an imaginary circuit of capital that moves inevitably between profit and loss. In the age of capital, the possession of a thing indicates always the possibility of dispossession, and Nunokawa watches this double logic at work in a series of elegant readings.[20] In *Novels Under Glass* (1995), Andrew Miller begins by noticing a new logic of display that emerges with the exhibition of goods behind broad shop windows, and he traces this changing status of objects in the work of novelists from Thackeray to Eliot.[21]

The greatest concentration of scholarship linking economic and literary discourse has emerged in eighteenth-century studies, where, in the careers of polymaths like Defoe, Swift, or indeed Adam Smith, it is clear to see that the marketplace was certainly not understood as a distinct and self-contained field of inquiry. Most notable here is James Thompson's book *Models of Value* (1996), which aims at an unusually careful reconstruction of the relationship between eighteenth-century fiction and the emerging theory of political economy itself. Rather than focusing on a particular economic concept – like exchange, the general equivalent, or the commodity – Thompson is interested in political economy as a historical and cultural phenomenon, and he argues that political economy and the novel grew in parallel, as interpretive tools for the analysis of new social landscapes.[22]

Still, interest in the history of economic theory itself is relatively uncommon among literary scholars. Perhaps because of the continuing influence of Shell's and Goux's innovative work, current interdisciplinary studies in economics and literature can tend toward a particular application of poststructuralism and semiotics, one that emphasizes the arbitrariness of signs and the limitlessness of their circulation. Christopher Herbert's *Culture and Anomie* (1991) remains an instructive example of this sort of work, where any non-immanent conception of economic value (from Smith to Milton Friedman) is equated with the Saussurian theory of the signifier.[23] The risks inherent in this particular application of poststructuralist thought to economics, which arises from the money–language comparison, can be best illustrated in a recent exchange between economists and cultural critics in the anthology *New Economic Criticism*. In a shrewd and far-reaching essay, radical economists David Ruccio and Jack Amariglio argue that an economics which borrows from poststructuralist theories of language might loosen the hold of the neoclassical school and open the way for more inclusive and potentially democratic ways to understand the distribution of resources in a given society. They offer a case for broadening the categories of economic thought, in order to conceive value, commodities, and prices, in conjunction with other forms of social and symbolic capital. "While symbolic economy, libidinal economy, and some of the other formulations [of poststructuralist theory] have little direct connection to academic economics," write Ruccio and Amariglio, "... they are indeed productive of economic knowledge and, as such, provide yet additional ideas and theoretical formulations that are largely alternatives, self-consciously or not, to the neoclassical orthodoxy that rules the academic economic roost."[24] They suggest that "for economists who are dissatisfied with the standard neoclassical dictum that the determinants of taste (culture, for example) have no importance for economic theory, such investigations into the deep ways in which symbols and meanings are produced, represented, and/or performed in economic transactions are potentially of great importance."[25]

In a lucid response to this article, literary critic Regenia Gagnier and philosopher John Dupré remind us that a poststructuralist emphasis on the endless circulation of the signifier and the lack at the center of the desiring subject can, when transplanted into economics, end up paradoxically affirming the subjectivist and radically individualist stance of neoclassicalism.[26] Signifiers that wander unhindered (by indexical relation to the signified) should not be confused with commodities and capital that move unfettered (by government regulation). It may be the case that in a deregulated market certain consumers are more free to make certain choices. However, as Gagnier and Dupré put it, "the *desire* to consume or to express one's individuality through consumption is not the same thing as the power to consume."[27]

My aim in this book is to understand the relationship between economics and other forms of social discourse and description in the nineteenth century. It is for this reason that I stress not the similarity of words and coins, but the similar projection of a subjectivity within nineteenth-century economic thought and nineteenth-century linguistics. Indeed, my argument in Part I begins with the observation that throughout the modern period, money and language have been understood as fundamentally and crucially *dissimilar*. In European philosophy, the phonetic alphabet has been seen as the standard and normative form of written communication; written words always represent sounds produced by the human body. But since the first financial institutions of the seventeenth and eighteenth centuries, money has been understood as a language of numbers, a *non-phonetic* system of writing. Numbers are signs not of the human voice but of abstract concepts themselves. Europe's focus on the phonetic alphabet as the most advanced and civilized form of writing has resulted in a peculiar fixation on spoken language as the immediate expression of human intentionality. The rise of a non-phonetic world of financial information in the last 300 years reverses this established order of things: in the mathematical language of money, writing comes before speech, and the subject of European history is obscured.

The inhuman agency of money has been a central problem of the modern period, and the history of European economic thought can be understood as a long effort to resolve this problem. The most secure resolution – one that is, however, still imperfect – came with the theory of marginal utility of the 1870s. This is the theory of economic value that placed the consumer at its very center. But the problem of the subject, the question of its immunity to the material agency of signs, is also at the center of European romanticism, with its emphasis on the organic over the mechanical, the expressive over the imitative. It is an organic and expressive subject – mysteriously whole, behaviorly fragmented – that still inhabits neoclassical economics today.

The anomaly of non-phonetic writing in the early eighteenth century is the starting point of Part I below. Caught up in the writing of financial numbers, I argue, are all the real and symbolic dangers of an emerging financial system. It was the romantic approach to language, philology, that eventually offered a way for economists to represent capitalism not as an autonomous and potentially threatening machine, but as a neutral medium to express human wishes.

Part I of the book begins in the 1740s, charting Adam Smith's early encounters with the philosophy of language, and moves rapidly to the 1870s, when the theory of marginal utility emerged. Part II returns to a pivotal era in this long transition, the 1840s and 1850s. Chapter 3 focuses on the work of Charles Dickens in the early 1850s. While outrage against the cold rationality of political economists is often discussed in relation to Scrooge in *A Christmas Carol* (1843) and to Mr. Gradgrind in *Hard Times* (1854),

I argue that Dickens's most sustained consideration of economic questions comes in *Bleak House* (serialized 1852–53). Rather than punishing cruel men of business, or mocking the practical ignorance of scholarly pedants, *Bleak House* offers a complex response to the commercial crises of the 1840s. The encounter of the individual consumer with the marketplace is retold in this novel as the struggle of the main characters with the English courts. Where the court represents a threatening and shifting system of meanings and values – like the stock market and currency systems in the 1840s – home and family connections seem to offer the solidity and self-identity of things which the court cannot provide. I argue, however, that in the novel "home" serves the same metaphorical function that the Bank of England serves in the financial discourse of this period: both promise an end to circulation, an immanence of meaning, a stilling of value.

The writing of the Irish Famine (1845–52) is the subject of chapter 4, which deals with newspaper accounts, review essays, polemical pamphlets, and travel narratives. The critique of British economic policy in these texts relies, as with *Bleak House*, on an image of home. But home in the Irish debate is the spiritual homeland of the nation. These commentaries stress the uniqueness of the Irish race, in order to critique the free-trade theory that had justified such widespread starvation. However, while these books and pamphlets protest against the cruel excesses of the free market, they each share the same fundamental assumptions of the later Victorian economists. They see character as essential and desire as occult, in the same way that economists after Jevons would see each consumer's choice of commodities as a secret expression of selfhood.

The romantic linking of language, economy, and national character, which is everywhere visible in commentaries on the Irish disaster, is the starting point for Elizabeth Gaskell's first novel, *Mary Barton* (1848), and it is Gaskell's work I turn to in the book's final section. *Mary Barton* takes a philological approach to the problems of industrial poverty. Gaskell transcribes the Manchester dialect of her working-class characters and compares it in a series of footnotes to the language of Chaucer and Wyclif. The book's narrative of class reconciliation thus springs from a theory of the linguistic, and therefore racial, unity of all Britons. However, I argue that in later work Gaskell, alone among writers of the 1850s, identifies the limitations of an economics based on identity and self-expression. *North and South* (1854–55) critiques the liberal assumptions inherent in the emerging figure of the consumer, and it presciently indicates the particular blindnesses of the modern economic paradigm.

Taken together, these texts offer a set of coordinates with which to chart an emerging redefinition of human experience in the world. This rethinking of human life responded to and attempted to compensate for the perceived injuries of modern financial and industrial capitalism. But the new categories of this early Victorian reaction would gradually be reabsorbed into the mainstream of British economic thought, until they formed its very heart.

PART I

Origin stories and political economy, 1740–1870

In order to understand the power economic theory has exercised in the twentieth century, it is necessary to understand the origins of its precursor, political economy, in eighteenth-century thought. This eighteenth-century context is one itself absorbed with the question of origins, not only the origins of wealth, but of human language, philosophy, and civilization. What I propose in this chapter is that Adam Smith's theory of wealth and poverty developed out of his engagement with the philosophy of language, in debates about the role of signs in human history, and about the significance of different forms of writing. From the work of Adam Smith, I go on to trace the development of economic thought, from "political economy" to twentieth-century "economics," in relation to trends in the philosophy of language in the same periods. What emerges from this particular tracing of historical change is that modern economics is a science of representation, one that has attempted since its inception to understand the way outward signs of wealth – that is, commodities – present, correspond to, or occult inner states of mind, thought, desire, or being. The rise of modern, neo-classical economics in the nineteenth century turned upon a new way of understanding commodities as signs, and it is the gradual development of that new understanding that I will try to follow in this section of the book.

While it is true that all human activity is constrained by the forms imposed by what Kant calls the "faculty of representation," or what Derrida more recently calls "arche-writing," it is also true that human interpretation of the representational process, and human deployment of the concept of representation, changes in response to historical pressures.[1] It is such a historical change that Derrida tracks in *Of Grammatology*. This work opens by arguing that the seventeenth- and eighteenth-century controversy over the origin of languages was provoked in part by examples of Chinese script and Egyptian hieroglyphic writing, which were made widely available to European scholars for the first time in this period. Chinese and Egyptian writing were both considered to be models for a perfect universal language, a language based on a written system of "real characters,"[2] where each letter, rather than representing a vocal sound, would convey some fundamental philosophic principle. Theorists of "real characters" seized onto Chinese and Egyptian texts as possible clues to a perfect form of writing, one which could transcend variations in spoken language. Leibniz, for example, concluded (basically incorrectly) that Chinese characters were "philosophical" in nature and based "on intellectual considerations" rather than on the representation of speech.[3] He proposed that Chinese writing would be "a model of philosophic language thus removed from history."[4] In other words, Leibniz imagined a writing with direct relation to the forms of thought themselves, unmediated by reference to spoken language or material things. Leibniz's dream was one of many, in a century during which, as Russell Fraser writes, "the forging of an exact correspondence between names and things becomes a matter of impatient concern."[5] However, this dream threatened the understanding common in European cultures of the very possibility of truth.

In this dominant European conception, truth resides in the mind of the thinking subject prior to its representation. We know what we mean to say before we say it, and the words available to us have no bearing on the original idea in our mind. This mental "signified" is privileged as an authentic intention of the subject, before its only slightly debased articulation in speech. As Derrida writes then, "the voice, producer of the first symbols, has a relationship of essential and immediate proximity with the mind." Thus while spoken signifiers seem to possess an original closeness to the mind, "the written signifier is always technical and representative," associated with a fall from an interior truth to an exterior of earthly deceit and materiality.[6] A non-phonetic writing system would suggest the possibility of communicating without reference to the voice and thus, metaphorically, without reference to the truth.[7] In this way the idea of a universal writing opened a gap which a tremendous amount of ideological work was needed to close. First, in its enthusiasm over Chinese, Egyptian, and in some cases South American scripts, it threatened to decenter Europe in world history, placing Asian, or African, or New World writing closer to God's original language and higher on the scale of intellectual precision.[8] Second, it threatened the dominant conception of the human subject. If writing could exist without being a representation of speech, then it was possible that the essential being of the subject was actually not in control of the signs it chose. It opened the possibility that the "self," the intentional being, was itself "written," a representational or "grammatological" construct. Early eighteenth-century theories of the origin of language addressed these threats by trying to prove that phonetic writing was the most perfect and most highly developed system of script.

William Warburton's prototypical history of writing (1737–41), for example, argues that human script progresses in linear fashion from pictographic signs, to hieroglyphics, and finally to its most "advanced" stage, the phonetic alphabet.[9] Such a historical narrative, which Warburton imposes rather arbitrarily on the evidence of world languages he assembles, contains the threat of a decentered Europe by establishing a hierarchy of civilizations.[10] This sorting out of the history of writing occurred, of course, in the take-off period of European colonial trade and plantation slavery, when colonists and missionaries made foreign-language texts more consistently available to European scholarship. The linear histories of writing ground the violence of empire in a myth of cultural superiority, and its attendant responsibilities. But while Warburton's hierarchy of scripts managed to recenter Europe in global history, it did not address the more fundamental threat to the "voice" that seemed to be posed by "real characters." The terms of the origin-of-language debate change over the course of the eighteenth century, until the generation of Rousseau and Herder gives rise to a philosophy of language – philology – that contains this threat as well.

But while "truth" and "power" are threatened in the eighteenth century by the decentering of the "voice," they are also challenged by a radically new and comparatively unstable form of money. This challenge arose also as a result of Europe's struggle for empire, in response to the need for the centralization of power, and its exercise across great distances. The Bank of England was founded in 1694 in order to manage the Crown's significant debt, incurred in the military suppression of Ireland and in continuing war with Ireland's Catholic ally, France. The Bank did this by distributing government debt in shares, which were themselves bought and sold on an open stock market. This system of government finance institutionalized the possibility of amazingly rapid creation and destruction of personal wealth; share prices could fluctuate widely according to the degree of public confidence in government policies, and with these price shifts thousands of pounds could appear or vanish overnight. The instability of this system of national debt and stock investment seemed compounded by the increasing use of unguaranteed paper money, which any bank could issue in this period in any amount it saw fit.[11]

This ratcheting up of the power of economic signs – often called the "financial revolution" – presents a slightly different assault on the metaphysics of truth and the justification of European conquest.[12] Social power in this period begins to stem less from traditional observances than from the calculation of financial numbers. On a formal level, mathematics is akin to a language of "real characters" (or, as far as Leibniz was concerned, with Chinese) in that it is a non-phonetic system of writing. It represents quantitative truths without reference to the voice. Indeed, Leibniz's idea of an universal language was one that would combine mathematical and logical reasoning. It was for this reason that he ultimately settled on Chinese as the perfect model, after he was persuaded by Jesuit missionary Joachim Bouvet that the origin of the Chinese characters was in the ancient numerical patterns of the *I Ching*.[13] For this reason, however, mathematics functions as "the place where the practice of scientific language challenges intrinsically and with increasing profundity the ideal of phonetic writing and all its implicit metaphysics."[14]

Whereas numerals in Greek and Latin relied on abbreviations of phonetic names for quantities, the Hindu-Arabic numerals of modern mathematics have no connection to the words or phonetic alphabet of European vernacular.[15] The Hindu-Arabic system was largely unknown in Europe until championed by tenth-century Pope Sylvester II, who studied it as a young man in Spain, but the traditional system of Roman numeral counting was only displaced much later, when Northern Italian merchants in the late fifteenth century found the new system better adapted to the needs of more advanced accounting.[16] Hindu-Arabic numeracy in England is belated by these Italian standards, but by 1600 an English instructional manual could claim, in a prefatory poem, that learning numbers was a foundation of all knowledge:

> No state, no age, no man, nor child, but here may wisdom win
> For numbers teach the parts of speech, wher children first begin.[17]

This perhaps hyperbolic advertisement suggests to readers that numbers offer a kind of perfect mental vocabulary, a foundation both for language ("the parts of speech") and for human thought ("wher children first begin").

However, even as the mercantile use of the new Hindu-Arabic system grew more widespread, numbers initially failed to live up to the promise held out in the verse above: a short-cut to the fundamental building blocks of thought, and power. This is a nuance Mary Poovey makes clear in her discussion of the early use of double-entry bookkeeping in seventeenth-century England. While the double-entry system seemed to offer numbers as "transparent" representations of truth, in fact Poovey shows that as a "system of writing," double-entry bookkeeping still functioned very much within the traditional epistemology of language.[18] In the merchant's books, Poovey argues, "the precision of arithmetic replaced the eloquence of speech [in classical rhetoric] as the instrument that produced both truth and virtue."[19] The numbers used in the double-entry practice, balancing columns of credits and debits, had no strict "referential accuracy."[20] Rather, in their elegant arrangement and precision, they proclaimed the character of the merchant to be precise, forthright, and honest. In early English mercantile use, numbers were treated as if they were phonetic signs. That is, numbers were understood exactly the way words were: not as direct or universal links to true concepts, but as signs controlled by the mind of the person manipulating the numbers.

It was not mercantile numbers that threatened the epistemological order of the period; it was financial numbers. The financial instruments of the 1690s – equity shares of joint-stock companies or of government debt – rely on the calculation of probabilities, a science that still carried with it its original association with gambling and numerological prognostication.[21] Unlike the rhetorical numbers of the merchant's books, numbers in the probabilistic sciences refer explicitly to potential events, to things that will or will not happen, regardless of human cause. Stock market numbers are not intentional; they are the expression or rhetorical presentation of no person; they have no author. Financial numbers thus reveal for the first time the threat that non-phonetic representation could pose.

This threat to the formal properties of "truth" is paralleled on the level of politics, as a new class of speculators and calculators, brought into being by the new trade in stock shares, was seen as poised to usurp the power of the landed classes, traditional guarantors of intrinsic or essential value.[22] However, the attack of "rationality" against "property" is figured by the landed classes in this period as a familiar kind of irrationalism. This slippage is accomplished through the metaphor of gender. The veering stock market and the fickle stock speculator appear as a feminine disruption of masculine authority, traditionally associated with property and political power. The metaphor of masculine "virtue" – the qualities associated with the landowning citizen, in a tradition going back to the Roman conception of the *vir* – is deployed by the propertied classes in this period, who want to portray the Bank and the national debt as eroding the masculine substance of English power.[23] The rational calculation of speculative wealth threatens severely to limit the transmission of power through patriarchal inheritance, just as the form of mathematical signs interrupts the phonetic transmission of the substance of the mind. The greed of the speculator – a kind of wild, excessive desire – is seen to correspond to the female consumer's supposed desire for luxury commodities. In the Tory order, these private desires appear to be dangerous, leading both to individual and state bankruptcy; in the new Whig financial establishment, however, these two figures, the investor and the consumer, must be vindicated, and their potentially disastrous private desires must be shown to produce a corresponding public restraint. This vindication is the function the concept of the market serves in economic thought.

It becomes the project of political economy, and eventually of economics per se, to posit this calculating and "rational" male subject as the agent of world history and the motive force of all change. To underwrite the emergent system of financial capital, the Whig interest (with Adam Smith eventually at its forefront) had to write a world history that would prove financial capitalism to be the key to European superiority, and to refigure the investor within the gender-appropriate terms of masculine "virtue."[24] Smith does both of these things, drawing on emerging notions of race and gender to argue that industrial capitalism will not spell the end of white male supremacy as the landed interest constantly warned. However, he accomplishes this by arguing that language and signs play a primary, material, and constructive role in the formation of the human mind. Smith's scheme recenters Europe, but it fails to settle the dangerous question of representation, of how wealth does or does not represent a subject of intrinsic or essential qualities.

It will take the next hundred years for political economy to develop an explicit theory of the subject that will counter the threat introduced by the math-machine speculator. By the publication of Jevons's work in 1871, the subversive desire of the speculator will have been corralled successfully into an orientalized femininity – the impulsive shopper, the hoarding peasant – while the capital investor will emerge as a figure of cool restraint.

This is the milieu out of which the discipline of economics emerges: an era when debates about the practice of finance and the politics of wealth overlapped with debates about Divine power in human history. Political economy's origins are in Europe's struggle not only to clarify the role of capitalism in its own history, but to claim the authority of God in its colonization of the globe. Modern ways of understanding poverty, wealth, and progress arose in connection with these debates about the significance of nationality – that is, what the nineteenth century would call "national character" and what the twentieth century would call "race." It is only by re-linking economic texts with their cultural contexts that we can begin to study the cultural and ideological work taken on by the discipline of economics today.

CHAPTER I

History as abstraction

CONDILLAC'S PHILOSOPHY OF SIGNS

Among Adam Smith's early works are an essay "Concerning the First Formation of Languages" (1761) and a piece in the early *Edinburgh Review* (1755)
largely concerned with Rousseau's *Discourse on the Origin and Foundations
of Inequality*.[1] While Warburton's *Divine Legation of Moses* inaugurates the
origin of language debate in England, his influence is less apparent in
Smith's early work than that of Etienne Bonnot, Abbé de Condillac, a key
figure in eighteenth-century philosophy, though little read today. Though
Condillac's major works were among the books in Smith's library, he does
not refer to Condillac in any extant writings; at the very least, Smith would
have known of Condillac's work from Rousseau's liberal use of it in the *Discourse on Inequality*.[2] Whether Smith had access to these ideas through the
work of Rousseau or through some other source, it is clear that the theory
of language which Condillac described, in particular his understanding of
the role of what he calls abstraction, functioned as a founding principle in
all of Smith's work.

Condillac worked in the empiricist tradition of Locke, and his first book,
Essay on the Origin of Human Knowledge (1746), attempted to correct the
errors he saw in Locke's theory of sensations. Condillac was persuaded by
Locke's strictly empirical account of human consciousness, but he argued
that Locke was imprecise in demonstrating that higher mental activities
could have developed from sensations alone. Condillac's signal innovation
is his argument that it is through the operation of language itself that the
human capacity for knowledge develops. "I am convinced," he writes in
his introduction, "that the use of signs is the principle that develops the
seed of all our ideas."[3] Condillac's task in the remainder of the book is
to demonstrate how the capacity for complex ideas develops in the individual consciousness, and to trace the history of early human language
use.

He begins with the synchronic element of his argument, describing the psychological development of a single mind in the present, and then uses this as a model for the diachronic development of human consciousness in history.

Let us consider a man at the first moment of his existence. His soul [*âme*] first has different sensations, such as light, colors, pain, pleasure, motion, rest – those are his first thoughts . . . [W]hen he begins to reflect on what these sensations occasion in him . . . we shall find that he forms ideas of the different operations of his soul, such as perceiving and imagining – those are his second thoughts.[4]

It is in the process of "reflecting" on initial sense impressions, what Condillac calls "perceptions," that more complex thought develops. The first and simplest form of reflection is "reminiscence." This is the awareness, when confronted with a particular perception of an object, phenomenon, sound, etc., that we have perceived it before. It is this potential to remember a perception that forms the basis of what we call experience. "Experience tells us," however, "that the first effect of attention is to make the mind retain its perceptions in the absence of the objects that occasioned them."[5] To retain and recall to the mind a perception when absent from its object, or cause, is the power of "imagination."

But for Condillac, imagination is a difficult and taxing mental operation, requiring the mind to reproduce a total sensory "image" of the object. There is, however, another operation that can recall some aspects of an object without imagining its total sensory impact; this is "memory." "[W]e are not always able to revive the perceptions we have had. It can happen that we manage only to recall the name, some of the circumstances that accompanied the perceptions, and an abstract idea of perception . . . The operation that produces this effect I call 'memory.'"[6] Memory is a simpler and more efficient means of recalling an absent object, and thus "we see why the imagination at our command evokes certain figures of simple composition, while we can distinguish others only by the names that memory brings to mind."[7]

As this passage indicates, what is necessary for this more efficient form of reflection is a sign, a marker that can hold the place of the object in our memory without requiring the imagination to reproduce each aspect of its full perception. It is on this basis that Condillac declares that "the use of signs is the true cause of the progress" of the mind from imagination to memory.[8] As long as the imagination operates on its own, "we cannot by ourselves govern our attention."[9] However, "the beginning of memory is sufficient to begin making us the masters of the exercise of our imagination.

A single arbitrary sign is enough for a person to revive an idea by himself, and there we certainly have the first and the least degree of memory and of the power we can acquire over the imagination."[10] The passage from a passive imagination – where mental activity is limited by immediate sensory perception of present objects – to an active memory is the key transition in human psychological development for Condillac; the key principle of the transition is an increasingly efficient use of the perceiving power, through the tool of the arbitrary sign.

Once the habit of using signs is established, the mind is increasingly freed to conceive of abstract and general ideas, which are not connected to any single sensory perception but to the common properties of a whole class of objects. Only through the sign-using power can the mind consider a number of objects simultaneously and weigh their similarities and differences. And this operation will produce new signs to mark these general or transferable qualities a number of objects share. It is this process of mental generalization, which can only occur in retreat from the specific properties of objects, that Condillac calls "abstraction," and it is the process responsible both for the development of language and higher mental functioning.

Condillac is quite careful to point out, however, that the categories and ideas which this process of abstraction produces are themselves creations of human thought, rather than properties inherent in nature. In his central chapter "Of Abstraction," he writes, "it is less by reference to the nature of things than to our manner of knowing them that we determine the genera and species, or to speak a more familiar language, that we distribute them in classes by subordination of some to others."[11] He argues that earlier metaphysical philosophy, "vain and ambitious, wants to search into every mystery; into the nature and essence of beings, and the most hidden causes; all these she promises to discover to her admirers, who are pleased with the flattering idea."[12] But when philosophers talk about "essences" in this way, he argues, they refer not just to "certain collections of simple ideas that come from sensation and reflection; they intend to go deeper by finding specific realities in each of them."[13]

When they ask "whether ice and snow are water"; "whether a monstrous fetus is a human being"; "whether God, minds, bodies, or even the vacuum are substances," then it is obvious that the question is not whether these things agree with the simple ideas collected under these words, "water," "human being," "substance," for that question would resolve itself. The point is to know whether these things include certain essences, certain realities which, it is supposed, are signified by the words "water," "human being," "substance."[14]

For Condillac abstract ideas are products of linguistic combination, not natural truth. But once the construction of an abstraction from a number of simple ideas is accomplished, once the abstraction is encoded in a sign, its construction is forgotten, and that sign seems to represent a natural essence instead of a bit of human shorthand.

This theory of human mental development leads to and justifies Condillac's theory of world history. Since his notion of the progress of the human mind is the story of the "mastery" that language gradually lends, he portrays the progress of civilization through the story of the origin of languages. The first humans' mental operations, he argues, were limited to the perceptions of their immediate surroundings and needs from moment to moment. Condillac uses as models of the first humans two children, left by God to wander alone and untutored, in the time following the great flood. He imagines that:

the sensation of hunger made these children call to mind a tree loaded with fruit which they had seen the day before. The next day the tree was forgotten, the same sensation called to mind some other object. Thus the exercise of the imagination was not within their power. It was no more than the effect of the circumstances in which they found themselves.[15]

Gradually, after much repetition, the children begin to connect their "cries of each passion" – sounds produced in fear, hunger, surprise – with the sensations that provoked them. Their cries may accompany "some motion, gesture, or action" to indicate them more completely to the other.[16] Still at this point, the cries and gestures are produced only when suggested by immediate perceptions – of hunger, cold, etc. Gradually the cries and gestures become so strongly associated with familiar perceptions that they could be used to recall those perceptions at any time. The cries and gestures pass from being what Condillac calls "natural" or "accidental" signs into "instituted signs," which allow human "mastery" over the power of the mind. From this point, abstract thought begins: "The use of [instituted] signs extended the exercise of the operations of the soul, and they in turn, as they gained more exercise, improved the signs and made them more familiar. Our experience shows that those two things mutually assist each other."[17] Signs compound each other, as they increase the mind's power to use signs of greater abstraction and complexity.

While Condillac argues that gestures – the "language of action" – were more commonly used for the first instituted signs, "articulate sounds" eventually became more common. But "when speech succeeded the language of action, it retained the character of its predecessor." Thus "to take the place of the violent bodily movements, the voice was raised and lowered by strongly marked intervals."[18] This expressive power of intonation gave rise to music; the coded bodily language of action "the ancients called . . . dance."[19] These arts were originally integrated with language: "If prosody at the origin of languages was close to chant, then, in order to copy the sensible images of the language of action, the style was a virtual painting, adopting all sorts of figures and metaphors."[20] Condillac argues that "the most abstract terms derive from the first names that were given to sensible objects," and concludes, "at its origin, style was poetic."[21] Thus poetry, dance, and music all emerged from the expressive fullness of early language. As language grew more efficient, these arts were codified and separated from the expressive power of linguistic signs, cultivated as mere ornaments or entertainments.

Seen in the context of the ideological pressures on language-study in Condillac's day, Condillac's theory places European civilization at the leading edge of global history. European society represents the height of "efficiency" and "mastery," in Condillac's history, exercising a business-like dominion over the rest of the world, which remains mired in its inefficient sign systems. However, Condillac's very emphasis on language as a tool, a material technique, threatens to undermine this deliberate ethnocentrism, for Condillac's underlying critique of metaphysical essences renders any distinction between civilizations radically contingent. His work nostalgically assumes a unity of speech and poetry in early languages. But within Condillac's theory, there can be no permanent and essential differences between human societies, only different modes of conventional practice, encoded in "instituted signs."[22]

Condillac's theory of an increasing "efficiency" in human mental evolution becomes, eventually, the cornerstone of Smith's political economy, and the critique of a metaphysical philosophy in Condillac's work produces similar instabilities and radical potentials in Smith's. Condillac's theory of history is also taken up by Rousseau, but with crucial alterations. For Rousseau the increasing capacity for abstraction is the story not of the rise of civilization, but of its tragic decline away from the natural principles of the human heart. The instabilities in Condillac's work are addressed substantially in Rousseau's, as he crafts the more durable romantic mythology of an essential human nature, which distinguishes one nation from another and marks it indelibly with its own "national character." These two opposite adaptations of Condillac's theory of language, Smith's and Rousseau's, will form the two major streams of economic thought in the modern period.

Their dialectical movement through the nineteenth century will produce economics as it is practiced today.

Rousseau's 1755 *Discourse on the Origin and Foundations of Inequality among Men* (hereafter the second *Discourse*) borrows from but revises Condillac's theory of language and history. Rousseau opens by arguing that there are two different kinds of inequalities that mar contemporary European society. The first are "natural" and stem from differences of "age, health, bodily strengths, and qualities of mind." The second are "artificial" and "depend upon a sort of convention and are established, or at least authorized, by the consent of men."[23] These two categories support a two-stage theory of human history which corresponds substantially with Condillac's. The first humans lived in a direct world of sensation, and mental awareness of sensation. At some point, however, human thought became abstract, connected to no particular object, no specific sensuous experience. In the new abstract world, concepts and signs are purely conventional, established through use and habit.

However, where Condillac accepts that the first humans, in their fallen state, begin life with no received ideas, Rousseau claims that the mind begins with "two principles."

Leaving aside therefore all scientific books which teach us only to see men as they have made themselves, and meditating on the first and simplistic operation of the human soul, I believe I perceive in it two principles anterior to reason [*antérieurs à la raison*[24]], of which one interests us ardently in our well-being and our self-preservation, and the other inspires in us a natural repugnance to see any sensitive being perish or suffer. (*DO* 95)

The "conjunction and combination" of these two principles – each presumably limiting the other – shape early human history. Much like Condillac's two children, the early human exists without the capacity to control the objects of their thoughts, to conceive time or space beyond the present: "His imagination suggests nothing to him: his heart asks nothing of him. His modest needs are so easily found at hand, and he is so far from the degree of knowledge necessary for desiring to acquire greater knowledge, that he can have neither foresight nor curiosity" (*DO* 117). However, it is the belief in these forces which precede language, impulses *antérieurs à la raison*, which ultimately defines the difference between Condillac's materialist model of cognition and Rousseau's revision of it. Identifying these principles provides

Rousseau with a ground he can call "nature," an unquestioned point of authenticity, an anchor of social value.

In the second stage of society, the directness of self-love and pity is replaced by sociability, reason, and convention. The mark of this transition for Rousseau is the multiplication of what he calls "desire." For early "man": "his desires do not exceed his physical needs, the only goods he knows in the universe are nourishment, a female, and repose; the only evils he feels are pain and hunger" (*DO* 116). But in the second stage, desire is unlinked from physical need and can expand limitlessly. This artificial appetite Rousseau calls "moral desire," and his defining example of the difference between moral and physical desire is, of course, sexuality. Rousseau writes, "the moral element of love [*le moral de l'amour*[25]] is an artificial sentiment born of the usage of society and extolled with much skill and care by women in order to establish their ascendancy and make dominant the sex that ought to obey" (*DO* 135). For Rousseau, a primary masculinity gets subverted here in the second stage of history, where the presumed vanity of women establishes the foundation of the higher orders of civilization.[26]

Rousseau's aim in this foundational essay is to recover what he has identified as the primary and original principles of human social organization and to cancel the contemporary order of artificial inequality. But this larger goal requires that Rousseau show how those original principles were lost to begin with. The difficulty for Rousseau is thus to explain the transition from the period of pure physicality to the stage where humans act by imitating conventions. "The more one meditates on this subject," he writes, "the more the distance from pure sensations to the simplest knowledge increases before our eyes; and it is impossible to conceive how a man, by his strength alone, without the aid of communication, without the stimulus of necessity, could have bridged so great a gap" (*DO* 118). To approach this perplexing question, Rousseau launches an extended digression on the origin and history of human language, and he draws directly on Condillac. But where Condillac sees the rise of human knowledge as a single continuity, a more or less unified progression from "natural" to "instituted" signs, Rousseau sees an "impossible" history, involving an unimaginable leap from ignorance to knowledge.

Rousseau argues that language begins with the "cry of nature" (*DO* 122), and these "cries" correspond to Condillac's "natural signs." At some later point "when the ideas of men began to spread and multiply, and when closer communication was established among them, they sought more numerous signs and a more extensive language" (*DO* 122). But while he suggests that new signs spread only with new ideas, he also argues (again following

Condillac) that new ideas are produced by words: "General ideas can come into the mind only with the aid of words, and the understanding grasps them only through propositions" (*DO* 124). General ideas (what Condillac called abstractions) are pure products of language, produced as categories of objects come to be remembered, compared, and labeled with a sign. But while Condillac conceives the progress from "natural" to "instituted" signs as more or less linear, Rousseau sees it as an insoluble paradox. "For myself," he writes, "I leave to whomever would undertake it the discussion of the following difficult problem: which was most necessary, previously formed society for the institution of languages; or previously invented languages for the establishment of society?" (*DO* 126). It is this quandary that guides Rousseau throughout the second *Discourse*: How can language exist when it requires language itself to generate it?

In Rousseau's first stage, the stage without language, there is a direct physicality of desire and a harmonious balance of the first principles of human nature – pity and self-love. These first principles are figured as the voice or will of God, uncluttered by the artificial abstractions of linguistic categories. On the other hand, however, while early human beings are tied like animals to the moment-by-moment perceptions of their senses, sign-users are freed to develop ideas and describe objects not within their immediate presence. This capacity of human beings to improve the very substance of their own thought is, for Rousseau, the greatest advantage of the human condition. But it is also its ultimate curse, since the expansion of abstract thought, with the multiplication of arbitrary signs, leads to the inequality in contemporary society that Rousseau sets out to critique. The two-stage system Rousseau establishes can thus be shown to disintegrate completely: human beings before language possess in one way the ultimate freedom, yet are in another way the ultimate slaves; human beings in linguistic society demonstrate the freedom of the capacity for improvement, but by choosing to live in a world of injustice they are ultimately prisoners as well. Each of Rousseau's categories threatens always to flip over into its opposite.

It is at this point that Derrida famously intervenes into Rousseau's discussion. Derrida argues that one can only understand these contradictions in Rousseau's theory according to the logic of what he calls "the supplement": a seemingly minor addition to a larger category which takes over or takes the place of the larger category.[27] The common interpretation of Rousseau argues that his primary focus is on the "savage" as a "noble" creature, motivated by the Godly influence of self-love and pity, while the more minor disadvantages of this primary state, like the inability to think abstractly, are ranked as secondary or "supplementary." For Derrida, however, these two sets of attributes – the "liberty" and the "slavery" of the early human – exist side by side, revolving with each other, each taking primacy in a moment of ideological necessity.

From this position Derrida argues that in Rousseau's work "the concept of nature and the entire system it commands may not be thought except under the irreducible category of the supplement." Nature in Rousseau's text is that principle of paradise which is caught up in the idea of direct expression; it is also that principle of stagnation or symbolic death in the inability to use one thing to substitute for another. The passage into the second stage of civilization, marked, according to Rousseau's appropriation of Condillac, by the emergence of abstract symbolization in language, is figured as the birth of human potential for freedom, as well as its ultimate death. Nature is thus not a definable category in Rousseau's thought, since the attributes that describe "nature" always seem to slide toward their opposites; rather, nature occupies a space of "regulated contradiction." Nature for Rousseau "is the ground, the inferior step: it must be crossed, exceeded, but also rejoined."[28] Nature, as the state of primitive inanition, must be killed to bring about the progress of human intellection and sociability. But nature is also that first principle of pity, which can mediate the evils brought about by human self-love and thus prevent the rise of artificial social inequalities.

It is only by understanding Rousseau's idea of nature in this way that we can begin to see in fullest terms the break Rousseau represents from the earlier scholarship on the origin of languages. For Condillac and his tradition, human history was linear. Human consciousness had moved from the cumbersome expression of immediate perceptions to an increasingly efficient system of symbolic codes. Language moved from its original physical and then "poetic" modes, to an increasing use of abstract signs. In this model of progressive efficiency, history is figured as the continual "abbreviation of signs," "the becoming-prose of the world."[29] Rousseau's historiography represents a major break from this tradition: not a straight line of technological progress but a circular return to spiritual beginnings. The divine origins of the human soul were not questioned by Condillac, Warburton, or Locke. But for them human beings' earthly existence was one of total alienation from divine influence, where the purely material influence of sense data provided the only origin point one could locate for human intellection. Writers in this tradition perceived human history as the advancement toward an increasingly powerful mode of human thought, but not necessarily toward the manifestation of divine will. For Rousseau however, the narrative of the fall from grace and return to heaven is transposed onto global history. "Nature" in Rousseau stands for the divine origin of the soul, and the end point of human civilization is a kind of circular reappropriation of divine will. Rousseau's conception of nature, and the powerful romantic conceptions of childhood, femininity, and "the primitive" it eventually supported, thus functioned by inventing what was in the eighteenth century a new way of imagining history.

Rousseau's version of human history and the human subject proved a more effective and long-wearing response to the eighteenth-century crisis than Condillac and his generation were able to provide. If human character originates prior to language, *antérieurs à la raison*, then it can resist the threat posed by the modern marketplace. The notion of a wholly integrated human subject, which precedes and in some fundamental way survives the social process and shapes individual character, is still the dominant one in European and American culture. With the gradual spread of this particular ideology of the self, through the course of the nineteenth century, literature becomes increasingly dominated by the narrative of self-development and the struggle of "the individual" to resist social influences in an attempt to discover the primary characteristics of its own nature. Individual actions and collective customs, within this Romantic psychology, are understood as expressions of essential character, personal or national. As I will try to show, Adam Smith belonged to the world of Condillac. The history of political economy after Adam Smith, and particularly after Ricardo, is the history of its gradual acceptance of Rousseau's conception of nature, history, and an expressive subjectivity. The blindnesses and limitations of contemporary economics can be substantially traced to these Rousseauist categories.

ADAM SMITH ON THE ORIGIN OF LANGUAGE

With these aspects of Condillac and Rousseau's work in mind, we can begin to understand Adam Smith's position in the debate on the origin of language. In Condillac and Rousseau the question of the origin of language leads to their most fundamental arguments. In a similar way, a theory of the origin of languages occupies a central position in Adam Smith's work. Smith addressed the origin of languages problem perhaps as early as the late 1740s, as part of his series of lectures on rhetoric and *belles lettres* at the University of Edinburgh.[30] He published a short essay on the subject in 1761, "Considerations Concerning the First Formation of Languages," an essay that was later attached to the third edition of Smith's *Theory of Moral Sentiments* in 1767. Smith's exposure to the French philosophy of language is thought to have come from his reading of Diderot's encyclopedia, and from various other French works.[31] That he was familiar with Rousseau's second *Discourse* we know from his 1755 review of that work in the *Edinburgh Review*. But this review confines itself to a comparison of Rousseau and Mandeville, and it is not until the 1759 "Considerations" that we find Smith taking a clear position on Rousseau's theory of language. Here in a mere thirty pages Smith dismisses the problems that were so perplexing for Rousseau. Smith produces what linguistic historian Steven K. Land describes as the simplest answer to the language question in his period, a theory which "traces a line of continuous development from the primal name to modern language structures."[32]

Like Condillac and like the Rousseau of the second *Discourse*, Adam Smith argues that the first human communication arose from physical needs. Early human beings "endeavor to make their mutual wants intelligible to each other, by uttering certain sounds, whenever they meant to denote certain objects."[33] Sidestepping the question of gestures, Smith argues that these sounds quickly functioned as proper nouns. "The particular cave," he writes, "whose covering sheltered them from the weather, the particular tree whose fruit relieved their hunger, the particular fountain whose water allayed their thirst, would first be denominated by the words cave, tree, fountain" (FFL 203). Eventually, as "their necessary occasions obliged them to make mention of other caves, and other trees, and other fountains, they would naturally bestow, on each of these new objects, the same name, by which they had been accustomed to express the similar object they were first acquainted with" (FFL 203).

To illustrate the process through which these common nouns gradually emerged, Smith turns to a contemporary illustration: "I have known a clown, who did not know the proper name of the river which ran by his own door. It was *the river*, he said, and he never heard any other name for it. His experience, it seems, had not led him to observe any other river" (FFL 204). The "clown," because of his limited experience, can identify a particular river with the generalized common noun "river," given that no other rivers would be confused under this heading. Conversely, Smith argues, one can apply a proper name to a different but related object which shares certain characteristics with the bearer of the proper name. "An Englishman, describing any great river which he may have seen in some foreign country, naturally says, that it is another Thames" (FFL 204). This practice of borrowing a proper name to describe all objects in the same class as that which the proper name signifies is called, in rhetoric, antonomasia, and Smith argues that the prevalence of this rhetorical strategy in modern writing "demonstrates how much all mankind are naturally disposed to give to one object the name of any other, which nearly resembles it, and thus to denominate a multitude, by what originally was intended to express an individual" (FFL 203–04). Smith identifies then a continuity between the "clown" who, because of limited experience, can substitute the place of proper and common nouns, and the contemporary flourish of antonomasia. Here he follows the tradition of Warburton and Condillac in arguing that the internal principles of linguistic development in early human society become rhetorical ornaments and separate arts in later human culture. "Clown" in Smith's day would have signified most strongly a countrified or ignorant person: the Oxford English Dictionary cites Cowper's *The Task* (iv.623): "the clown, the child of nature, without guile."[34] In this way Smith's theory looks forward to the romantic conception of the rustic, the child, the "savage," as embodying the earliest and purest principles of human history. However, for Smith the principles of early language in the child or the "clown" are the same as those which appear in the sophisticated speech of modern orators. As linguist Frans Plank argues, Smith emphasizes "the mental operations which the language-formers are capable of performing, and which are essentially the same as those still performed, if more expertly, by present-day man."[35] There is no catastrophic break in the history of human language development, but rather a single principle of human communication that bridges any supposed gap between the state of nature and the state of culture.

This example in the first pages of Smith's essay illustrates the way Smith breaks with the historiography of Rousseau. For both, words and concepts together move away from concrete objects to classify the qualities that define objects. And Smith agrees that human history is characterized by increasing levels of abstraction in language and thought. But for Smith the growth of abstraction does not tear human society away from its natural roots; rather, the growth of abstraction fulfills human nature, multiplying and expanding the earliest and most fundamental principles of human behavior. This understanding of abstraction is a feature that unites all of Smith's work, from his abrupt intervention into the origin of language debates, to his *Theory of Moral Sentiments*, to his history of economic civilization in the *Wealth of Nations*. The key intellectual leap made by early human society, according to Rousseau's account, is between the cry of nature, which would signify an immediate objective threat, and the common noun, which would signify an entire class of objects. Conceiving of a common noun, Rousseau argues, would require the broad comparison of the similarities and differences of a variety of objects, considering their attributes in common. This is the transition in human thought which Rousseau finds "impossible to conceive," and it is the reason why he devotes so much space in his essay to "the obstacles to the origin of languages."[36] But what represents for Rousseau a cataclysmic fall from immediacy into abstraction is covered by Adam Smith in a mere paragraph, where he explains how the principle of antonomasia guided the development of common nouns.

It is this application of the name of an individual to a great multitude of objects, whose resemblance naturally recalls the idea of that individual, and of the name which expresses it, that seems originally to have given occasion to the formation of those classes and assortments, which, in the schools, are called genera and species, and of which the ingenious and eloquent M. Rousseau of Geneva finds himself so much at a loss to account for the origin. (FFL 204–05)

A footnote here refers the reader to the second *Discourse* as the site of Rousseau's unimaginable confusion. For Smith, antonomasia identifies the simple operation of comparison and observation which must have allowed language to spread in a uniform and consistent manner.

Having dispensed with Rousseau's questions, Smith spends more time explaining the modern diversity of languages, and, in accordance with his strictly linear theory, he argues that the most advanced of the contemporary languages are those containing the highest number of abstract words; the most primitive are the most proper. After every class of objects came to be denoted by its own common noun, Smith argues, it became necessary for speakers to theorize the differences and peculiar qualities of individual objects in order that they might not be confused with each other. This contemplation of particular qualities gave rise to two sorts of words: adjectives, which would indicate the qualities of a given object, and prepositions, which would express relations between objects. In this first period all nouns would be substantives, referring to concrete objects. The spread of adjectives, to denote particular qualities, however, would bring about the rise of abstract nouns to label these qualities, which are themselves divorced from any particular object. Smith writes,

the words *green* and *blue* would, in all probability, be sooner invented than the words *greenness* and *blueness*; the words *above* and *below*, than the words *superiority* and *inferiority*. To invent words of the latter kind requires a much greater effort of abstraction than to invent those of the former. It is probable, therefore, that such abstract terms would be of much later institution. Accordingly, their etymologies generally show that they are so, they being generally derived from others that are concrete. (FFL 206)

Smith's history of verbs conforms to this same pattern. The first were what Smith calls impersonal verbs: sounds used to designate a specific event. When a word which originally signified an event came to represent a whole class of similar events, it became necessary to identify a specific event by some particular quality. At this point impersonal verbs, which would express "the whole of an event, with that perfect simplicity and unity with which the mind conceives it in nature" (FFL 216), would give way to those that break down events into constitutive elements of actor and action. Personal verbs lend specificity, but in them "the simple event, or matter of fact, is artificially split and divided" (FFL 216). Through this operation particular actions are separated from individual actors and freed from any particular instance. Actions take on abstract qualities which can be applied interchangeably to any actor.

Because of the linearity of Smith's history, he has no trouble affirming that the most abstract languages are the best. Early languages, Smith argues, used inflection to express the abstract qualities with which a particular object or event needed to be labeled in order to separate it from other similar objects or events named by the same common noun or impersonal verb. Variation of nouns by case contained the operation of prepositions (FFL 210); variation by gender, though now highly conventionalized, originally contained some of the qualitative differences expressed by adjectives (FFL 207). Variation of verbs by person and number likewise contained in a single word the separation of actor and object necessary to identify events. Modern languages rely much less on inflection and much more on adjectives, prepositions, and pronouns to express abstract qualities. This renders the syntax of modern languages much less flexible and also requires the use of more words to express the same concept. This process, Smith notes, is most exaggerated in English, and from this Smith concludes that English is the most advanced of the modern languages. His anglocentric family tree of European languages thus runs as follows: Greek in combination with Tuscan vernaculars produced Latin, which in combination with Lombard variations produced Italian and French. The latter in conjunction with the Saxon languages produced English (FFL 222–23). English is the most complex language, its syntax the least flexible, its nouns and verbs the least inflected. Smith concludes:

language becomes more simple in its rudiments and principles, just in proportion as it grows more complex in its composition, and the same thing has happened in it, which commonly happens with regard to mechanical engines. All machines are generally, when first invented, extremely complex in their principles, and there is often a particular principle of motion for every particular movement which it is intended they should perform . . . In language, in the same manner, every case of every noun, and every tense of every verb, was originally expressed by a particular distinct word, which served for this purpose and for no other. But succeeding observation discovered that one set of words was capable of supplying the place of all that infinite number, and that four or five prepositions, and a half a dozen auxiliary verbs, were capable of answering the end of all the declensions, and of all the conjugations in all the ancient languages. (FFL 223–24)

But while the modern languages increase in precision and efficiency, like an increasingly refined machine, they also lose some advantages of the earliest languages. Smith argues that the proliferation of helping verbs, prepositions, and adjectives in modern language results in a "prolixness" which "must enervate the eloquence of all modern languages" (FFL 224). The varied sonority of the inflected languages made them more "agreeable to the ear" (FFL 224) and more suitable to poetic expression.

There is a clear sense of nostalgia in this account: Smith's idea of a lost sonority and poetry in human speech, and an increasingly "mechanical" mode of modern expression, narrates world history as the transition from an age of idyllic speech to an age of bureaucratic writing. The role of the sign is constrained within a narrative of the decay of proper meaning and the loss of a primitive concreteness.[37] But while Smith posits the integrity of the "voice" in these ways, he breaks with Rousseau in portraying this progression as an absolutely linear one, marked by the progressive and consistent unfolding of increasingly abstract mechanisms in language and thought. There is no qualitative separation between the function of language in contemporary society, in ancient society, or in the supposed language of earliest humans. There is no qualitative separation between the "voice" of nature and the "inscription" of culture.

The contrast between this historiography and that of Rousseau will become clearest if we examine Rousseau's theory of the history of writing. This is a theory he works out not in the second *Discourse*, which we know Smith was familiar with, but in the "Essay on the Origin of Languages." The date of composition of this essay is unknown; it was only published after Rousseau's death. But it is in this essay most explicitly that Rousseau introduces another element of Romantic historiography vital to the history of political economy, and that is the relationship between language and national culture.

ROUSSEAU: WRITING AND NATIONAL CHARACTER

Interest in the character of nations is not unique to Rousseau. Condillac argues that climate and the quality of land will influence the character of a people and the structure of their language.[38] But Condillac's emphasis falls much more strongly on the way that the expanding structure of a language itself influences culture. For Condillac, humans before language are simply screens for immediate sense perceptions. Within this system one can ascribe no "character," no particular emotional temperament to humans prior to language. "If we recollect," Condillac writes, "that the habit of the imagination and memory depends entirely on the connection of ideas, and that the latter is formed by the relation and analogy of signs, we shall be convinced that the less a language abounds in analogous expressions, the less assistance it gives to the memory and the imagination." "The arts and sciences" will tend to flourish when language has reached the sufficient degree of reflection or abstraction to enable the function of the imagination. "It is with languages as is with geometrical signs; they give a new insight into things, and dilate the mind in proportion as they are more perfect."[39]

In this way the operation of language itself on the mind ends up being more important than the particular characteristics of a people derived from climate or location. Language in Condillac's scheme is not the gauge of temperament; there is only one measure Condillac posits with which to compare languages, and that is the degree of their abstract signification. Within Condillac's scheme it would be impossible to say that language is formed by the collective personality of a group; rather this collective personality is a function of language. On the other hand, Rousseau proceeds from very different assumptions in the "Essay on the Origin of Languages," which opens as follows:

Speech distinguishes man among the animals; language distinguishes nations from each other; one does not know where a man comes from until he has spoken. Out of usage and necessity, each learns the language of his own country. But what determines that this language is that of his country and not of another? In order to tell, it is necessary to go back to some principle that belongs to the locality itself and antedates its customs, for speech, being the first social institution, owes its form to natural causes alone.[40]

Rousseau looks to some principle of "locality itself" to explain the differences between national groups, and in its locality speech emerges not through artificial convention but by "natural causes alone." Nature in this essay turns out to leave an essential imprint on the language of each national group, and this imprint becomes the most fundamental indicator of national character.

In order to understand how the "Essay" weaves this argument, we need to begin with Rousseau's basic claim – strikingly different from that of the second *Discourse* – that early humans were "naturally indolent."[41] In the second *Discourse* he argues that early humans are motivated by self-love and pity; in the "Essay" he assumes that human beings are naturally passive, lazy. Whereas in the second *Discourse* Rousseau is interested in that transition from a primary stage of human society to a secondary, purely conventional stage, in the "Essay" Rousseau looks more closely at the primary stage and attempts to explain the emergence of the ability to pity others, out of an original torpor. This he links to the operation of the imagination. But while Condillac sees imagination as being progressively enlarged throughout human history, through the increasing use of signs, Rousseau suggests that imagination was most strongly present at the origin point of language, and that it has declined drastically since then.

"Although pity is native to the human heart it would remain eternally quiescent unless it were activated by imagination. How are we moved to pity? By getting outside ourselves and identifying with the being who suffers." The capacity to "identify" is one of imagination, and Rousseau argues that without an exposure to different human beings – without the opportunity to imagine the suffering or desire of the other – the capacity to imagine will not develop: "He who imagines nothing is aware only of himself; he is isolated in the midst of mankind." It is clear in one way that Rousseau's notion of imagination is drawn from Condillac: Rousseau writes, "reflection is born of the comparison of ideas, and it is the plurality of ideas that leads to their comparison."[42] But where for Condillac presumably a small glimmer of imagination might emerge with the first comparison of ideas in the mind, for Rousseau a veritable riot of imagination, pity, and "desire" bursts all at once on the scene of early human history, at the single moment when the first comparison takes place. Where "the first rendezvous of the two sexes" would take place, "there too, the original festivals developed. Feet skipped with joy, earnest gestures no longer sufficed, being accompanied by an impassioned voice; pleasure and desire were mingled and were felt together."[43] The birth of the sign is the birth of desire; the rise of reflection as a linguistic principle is the reflection of desire in the desire of the other.

However, once Rousseau finishes laying out this theory, we find that this origin point characterizes not all human beings but only those in "the South." In the following chapter, "Formation of the Languages of the North," Rousseau offers a different story: "In southern climes, where nature is bountiful, needs are born of passion. In cold countries where she is miserly, passions are born of need, and the languages, sad daughters of necessity, reflect their austere origin."[44] In "the North" humans would have been brought together earlier in their history, out of physical need, and their collection would have brought about the operation of "difference" and "comparison" in the mind necessary for the birth of abstract thought. But while humans in early northern civilizations were presumably just as "indolent" as those in the south, Rousseau suggests they were forced into action by the harshness of the climate and thus produced a language not of "passion" but of "necessity." This early influence of the climate on character is imprinted through the function of language, and carries through every following stage of the development of human knowledge and government. In this way world languages are not, as they were for Condillac, gradients on a scale of the progressive unfolding of abstract thought. For Condillac the linear history of abstraction is encapsulated by the history of writing, from pictography to alphabetic script. For Rousseau the difference between national languages is not the gradient of abstraction or efficiency. Rather this difference is the measure of national character, the godchild of "nature"; character is unalterable, after its natural birth, and it exerts its influence in terms of a gradient of passion. In this text an innocent speech is ambushed by a street-wise writing. "[O]ur tongues," he writes, of the northern languages, "are better suited to writing than speaking, and there is more pleasure in reading us than in listening to us."[45]

In these texts by Rousseau we can identify the necessary tensions of a given ideological system, struggling to maintain Europe as both endpoint and center of global history. From a twentieth-century standpoint we might easily argue that Rousseau's texts are in this way fundamentally unreadable, caught in a set of undecidable differences. One might also say that these texts are incomplete in the way that any ideological production must be. But the cult of national identity in the nineteenth century, with its reliance on studies in poetry and language, will build directly on Rousseau's fundamental assumptions.

THE ABSTRACTION OF DESIRE: SMITH'S *THEORY OF MORAL SENTIMENTS*

At this point I have laid out what can generally be called Enlightenment and romantic conceptions of the origin of language, conceptions which always imply both a global historiography and a contemporary cultural geography. These are conceptions of world history, through the model of language, which share a great deal, but which differ also in fundamental ways. And we have seen Adam Smith's involvement in these debates.

What it remains to show now is that Smith's allegiance to Condillac and what I have roughly called the Enlightenment side of the language debate has importance in Smith's major works. I do not argue that the language debates play a central role in Adam Smith's thought over the course of his life; that Smith devoted only one essay to this subject, one which formed only an appendix to a late edition of his work on moral philosophy, would suggest that they did not. Nor have I provided the full philosophical context for Adam Smith's thought. This would require a much broader examination of early eighteenth-century philosophy in both England and France, encompassing the work of Hume, Mandeville, Montesquieu, and Hutcheson. However, I contend that understanding Smith's intervention into the language debates will highlight important aspects of his work in moral philosophy and political economy.

In *The Theory of Moral Sentiments* (1759) Smith refuses the Rousseauist idea of an absolute split between nature and culture. With Condillac, Smith argues that the principles that guide the development of individual thought, social interaction, and political organization are present in human society from the very first. The principles he identifies, however, are borrowed directly from Rousseau. Smith opens the first chapter of the volume, "Of Sympathy," as follows: "How selfish soever man may be supposed, there are evidently some principles in his nature, which interest him in the fortune of others, and render their happiness necessary to him, though he derives nothing from it except the pleasure of seeing it."[46] Like Rousseau in the second *Discourse*, Smith suggests that human nature is equipped with two unchanging characteristics: selfishness and sympathy. But for Rousseau the operation of sympathy, or what he calls pity, is an equivocal one; pity seems to be the thing which makes humans good in the first stage of civilization, as well as the thing which pulls human beings into more complex social relationships and corrupts them in the second stage. For Smith, however, the capacity for sympathy to mediate the effects of selfishness is a constant principle in human history.

Sympathy, Smith argues, allows us to understand suffering in others, giving us the ability of "changing places in fancy"; understanding the pain of the other will tend to dampen actions spurred by selfish pleasure that might injure other people. But much more importantly, Smith argues that human beings derive pleasure not only through the gratification of their selfish desires, but also through the knowledge that other people sympathize with them. "Nothing pleases us more," Smith writes, "than to observe in other men a fellow-feeling with all the emotions of our own breast." The injured person, "longs for that relief which nothing can afford him but the entire concord of the affections of the spectators with his own." At the same time, however, the sympathy of spectators enables them to identify only imperfectly with the feelings of the injured person. Thus it is necessary that the injured person learn to moderate the expression of "his" passion, to soften "his" cries if injured, such that a spectator, given "his" shrunken sense of the injured person's passion, will not feel that the injured person is reacting excessively. Desiring the pleasure of sympathy, the spectator "can only hope to obtain this by lowering his passion to that pitch, in which the spectators are capable of going along with him. He must flatten, if I may be allowed to say so, the sharpness of its natural tone, in order to reduce it to harmony and concord with the emotions of those who are about him" (*TMS* 10, 13, 22).

Thus the subject learns to feel by imagining the feelings of the other; the experience of passion is educated through the circuit of the spectator. And while it may seem that Smith conceives the direct experience of passion as a natural and unchanging response that exists prior to the moderating influence of the spectator, he makes it clear that feelings themselves are altered by the way they are performed and reflected, according to the codes of spectatorship. "As the reflected passion, which [the original subject] thus conceives, is much weaker than the original one, it necessarily abates the violence of what he felt before he came into their presence, before he began to recollect in what manner they would be affected by it, and to view his situation in this candid and impartial light" (*TMS* 22).

Smith's theory of the affective life here escapes from a number of romantic preconceptions about the autonomy of passions or desires and the simplicity of individual perception. Perception in every instance, for Smith, is triangulated between the object perceived and the consciousness of an "impartial spectator" which exerts that reflecting influence on a subject. The desire of the subject for any given object is mediated through the spectator; the feeling of the spectator for the subject is mediated through the consciousness of the object of passion. And the feelings experienced in this perpetual triangle are constructed in the mode of their expression. The feeling subject is inconceivable without the feelings of other subjects; desire is social, and feelings are performative.

But while aspects of this theory of intersubjectivity might make it possible to reevaluate the formation of subjects into a given sexual and political order, Smith uses these ideas, laid out in his first chapters, to mount a defense of the existing social order. To understand why a potentially radical theory of the subject activates an explicit defense of capitalism, it is necessary to consider some aspects of Smith's theory in its eighteenth-century context. This context can be best approached through the gender categories at work in this text. "Men of retirement and speculation," Smith writes "who are apt to sit brooding at home over either grief or resentment, though they may often have more humanity, more generosity, and a nicer sense of honor, yet seldom possess that equality of temper which is so common among men of the world" (*TMS* 23). The danger of the individual isolated from society is that the wildness of selfish passions will not be moderated by the effect of reflection. This is conceived as a danger here for the philosophical speculator, but would certainly apply to that other sort of "speculator" who alienates himself from "men of the world" – that is, established and prudent men of business and property – in order to gamble for his own individual interest on the wild and unpredictable fluctuations of the stock market.

Eighteenth-century writers, including Smith as we shall see, argued that the prudent codes of the business man, conceived in terms of masculine virtue and restraint, would tame the excessive desire of the effeminate speculator.[47] In a similar way here, the play of feelings in "reflection" is conceived as an arena of exchange: metaphorically, a market of human feeling. The effective circulation of desire in this market of sympathy will have the effect of moderating the wild desire of the isolated individual. Again the contrast with Rousseau is helpful. While Rousseau conceives of human nature as a primary set of masculine characteristics – phallic presence, immediate physical need, and its direct expression – the development of complex forms of social interaction are figured as castration, the effeminate absence of physicality. For Smith, however, society has the opposite influence. The isolated person who gives the fullest and most direct expression of the most deeply felt passions is prone to an effeminate wildness, a lack of substance, while the complex operation of the intersubjective comparison of thoughts and feelings will restrain the effeminate expenditure of the individual.

In this figure we can begin to see links between language theory and political economy in this period. For Condillac and Smith an increasing level of abstraction in language yields an increased capacity for complex thought. The rise of abstraction here exerts a civilizing force. Though Smith's *Moral Sentiments* is less concerned with historiography than his essay on languages, an increasing level of complexity in social interaction would presumably accompany the increasing level of abstraction in language, exerting also a civilizing effect as it dampens the extreme pursuit of self-interest and the excessive indulgence of passion. In this passage, we see the glimmerings of a similar historiography of capitalism, where an expanding arena of free exchange would exert a civilizing influence.

The misogyny that grounds this figure is even more plainly visible in Section Two, where Smith contrasts "passion from the body" with "passions from the imagination." It is more difficult, Smith argues, to sympathize with bodily feelings than it is with the imagination. Thus "to cry out with bodily pain, however intolerable soever, appears always unmanly and unbecoming." Again the self-indulgent expression of passion – here bodily pain – is understood as a kind of feminine excess. The correct operation of sympathy on the mind, where the person experiencing bodily pain is able to sympathize with the spectator's inability to sympathize completely with them, will exert a force of masculine restraint. But while the spectator is only imperfectly able to understand the passions of the body, Smith writes, the "imagination is more ductile" (*TMS* 29). This interesting metallic metaphor suggests again something about the fungibility of imagination in the "marketplace" of sympathy.

Of all the passions of the imagination, however, the one which Smith's theory fails to encompass is "love." He calls this one of the passions "which are . . . extravagantly disproportional to the value of their objects." And yet he recognizes that the expression of love, even while so excessive, is likely to excite complete sympathy on the part of an impartial spectator.

The sympathy which we feel with [the lover], renders the passion which they accompany less disagreeable, and supports it in our imagination . . . notwithstanding all the vices which commonly go along with it; though in the one sex it necessarily leads to the last ruin and infamy; and though in the other, where it is apprehended to be least fatal, it is almost always attended with an incapacity for labor, a neglect for duty, a contempt of fame, and even of common reputation. (*TMS* 33)

In the defiance of "reputation" and "duty," the man in love may fall completely out of the circuit of sympathy, caring nothing for the reflection of his excessive passion in the mind of the spectator. Thus the male subject of Smith's theory is tempted always by an excessive indulgence of self-interest, represented here by the allure of women.

Assuming that the system of society will always tend to balance the forces of self-interest with those of sympathy, Smith writes: "man, who can subsist only in society, was fitted by nature to that situation for which he was made" (*TMS* 85). Self-interest and sympathy seem to function for Smith like the Newtonian laws of physics, providing limits and checks for every movement in what Smith calls at one point "the great machine of the universe" (*TMS* 19).[48]

In later sections of the book Smith goes on to show how these laws function explicitly in economic history. He begins this process in answer to Rousseau's question about the origin of inequality. Smith's chapter "Of the Origin of Ambition, and of the Distinction of Ranks" argues that "it is because mankind are disposed to sympathize more entirely with our joy than with our sorrow, that we make parade of our riches, and conceal our poverty" (*TMS* 50). The desire for wealth is thus, for Smith, based completely on a misidentification of the power of wealth. We wish to be rich only to experience the pleasure of the more complete sympathy of the society around us. In some ways Smith here anticipates Marx's theory of the fetishism of commodities, where the desire for the commodity is mediated through the other's desire, and where the possession of commodities provides not the direct satisfaction of needs or natural desires, but the mediated expression of social relations.

But for Marx the "language" of commodities,[49] as it constructs human desire, has led to vast immiseration; for Smith the social craving for wealth will end up having universally beneficial effects. First, Smith argues that since the pursuit of wealth is in reality the pursuit of approbation, the pursuer will naturally be disinclined to do injury to others, or to behave in a way that might turn any impartial spectator against him. For most men, Smith writes, "real and solid professional abilities, joined to prudent, just, firm and temperate conduct, can very seldom fail of success," and thus "the road to virtue and that to fortune . . . are, happily in most cases, very nearly the same" (*TMS* 63). This formula, where the misguided pursuit of fortune leads to the cultivation of "solid" masculine "virtues," brings Smith eventually to the celebrated theory of the invisible hand. While this phrase has been popularly associated with the *Wealth of Nations*, and interpreted largely as a metaphor for the operation of price within the deregulated market, the phrase figures prominently in Smith's first book, and it refers to Smith's idea that the seemingly selfish pursuit of wealth will, through the law of social reflection, produce an enlargement of social "virtues."

The produce of the soil maintains at all times nearly that number of inhabitants which it is capable of maintaining. The rich only select from the heap what is most precious and agreeable. They consume little more than the poor, and in spite of their natural selfishness and rapacity, though they mean only their own conveniency, though the sole end which they propose from the labours of all the thousands whom they employ, be the gratification of their own vain and insatiable desires, they divide with the poor the produce of all their improvements. They are led by an invisible hand to make nearly the same distribution of the necessaries of life, which would have been made, had the earth been divided into equal proportions among all its inhabitants, and thus, without intending it, without knowing it, advance the interest of the society, and afford means to the multiplication of the species. (*TMS* 184–85)[50]

Again the operation of reflected desire, in producing the mirage-like goal of personal wealth, in the end provides for the economic progress of civilization. Smith insists that humans desire wealth not "to supply the necessities of nature," since "the wages of the meanest laborer can supply them," but rather to attract the approbation of those around them. This leads Smith to argue that the rich in reality "consume little more than the poor," and that their greed in fact leads to the wider distribution of the necessities of life among the poor, who provide them with their "baubles and trinkets," while the rich must guard their wealth and power "with the most anxious attention." From here Smith proceeds to the outrageous conclusion that "in ease of body and peace of mind, all the different ranks of life are nearly upon a level, and the beggar, who suns himself by the side of the highway, possesses that security which kings are fighting for" (*TMS* 150, 184, 183, 185).

We should note the influence of Rousseau in this claim, one which seems to have been brewing since the opening chapter, in which Smith argues that "the pangs of a mother, when she hears the moaning of her infant" are in fact worse than the pain a suffering child feels.

The infant . . . feels only the uneasiness of the present instant, which can never be great. With regard to the future, it is perfectly secure, and in its thoughtlessness and want of foresight, possesses an antidote against fear and anxiety, the great tormentors of the human breast, from which reason and philosophy will, in vain, attempt to defend it, when it grows up to be a man. (*TMS* 12)

Here the youthful (male) subject of history, like the beggar, who has advanced little upon the road of socialized desire, is assigned the characteristics of primitive man: contentment, and immediacy of present experience. While the beggar is bathed with the golden light of nature, the chilly and artificial clink of gold buys the modern businessman only an early death.

THE ABSTRACTION OF LABOR: THE *WEALTH OF NATIONS*

In the *Wealth of Nations* Smith returns explicitly to the historiographical questions that occupied him in the essay on languages. He frames the entire work, in his introduction, with the question of how "civilization" rose out of the conditions of "savagery." "Among the savage nations of hunters and fishers," Smith writes,

every individual who is able to work, is more or less employed in useful labour . . . Such nations, however, are so miserably poor that, from mere want, they are frequently reduced, or, at least, think themselves reduced, to the necessity sometimes of directly destroying, and sometimes of abandoning their infants ... Among civilized and thriving nations, on the contrary, though a great number of people do not labour ... yet the produce of the whole labour of society is so great, that all are often abundantly supplied, and a workman, even of the lowest and poorest order, if he is frugal and industrious, may enjoy a greater share of the necessaries and conveniences of life than it is possible for any savage to acquire.[51]

Smith here proposes to answer the question of the "origins of inequality." In the *Moral Sentiments* Smith considers the history of human feeling as it develops progressively with the reflection of desire in society; in the essay on languages he tries to describe the history of knowledge through the stages of the development of the sign. In his last major work he considers similar questions about the origin of civilization, here in relation to the multiplication of material goods and the differences between nations in this process.

In *Wealth of Nations* the engine of material progress in world civilization is the division of labor, which Smith describes in a series of famous passages in his opening chapter, and which turns out to be an application of the same principle of abstraction which he outlined in his history of languages.[52] For Smith the first linguistic signs, either proper nouns or impersonal verbs, would denote each aspect or attribute of any given object or event, but the range of objects and events contained in the language was quite limited; with the rise of a diversity of signs, language becomes efficient enough to refer to any combination of objects and any series of events, and it does this by dividing signs until they refer to smaller and more precise ideas. The history of human productive power works for Smith in precisely the same way. The first labor was "unified," both in that one person would perform each task necessary to create a given object or process, and in that each person would perform every aspect of the labor necessary to sustain life. Labor becomes more and more "efficient" when its steps are divided into smaller and smaller operations.

This principle of divisibility, as it contributes to social abstraction, is made clear in chapter 2, on water transport. Smith argues that the first "civilized" societies arose because of their proximity to the Mediterranean Sea, which is "by far the greatest inlet that is known in the world, having no tides, nor consequently any waves except such as are caused by the wind only" (*WN* 34). This is a misunderstanding of the history of navigation, as anyone who has read any account of Mediterranean storms will attest, but the importance of the Mediterranean for Smith seems to be its status as an "inlet." Inlets, like rivers and canals, have the effect of dividing land into smaller and more easily accessible units. Since water transport is so much more efficient than overland transport, which Smith demonstrates in detail (*WN* 32–33), trade between those locations accessible by water will be transacted more efficiently.

The development of the division of labor, Smith argues, will be limited by the extent of any market. Here, just as in the *Moral Sentiments*, Smith suggests that the principle of abstraction in society will only operate to the extent that society is built around unlimited interchange; in the *Moral Sentiments* this interchange is the psychological one of sentiment, in *Wealth of Nations* it is an exchange of material goods. Those parts of the world, Smith argues, which are undivided by inlets or rivers, left as great chunks of land on which the principle of subdivision into smaller units cannot operate, will develop the most slowly.

There are in Africa none of those great inlets, such as the Baltic and Adriatic Seas in Europe, the Mediterranean and Euxine Seas in both Europe and Asia, and the gulphs of Arabia, Persia, India, Bengal, and Siam, in Asia, to carry maritime commerce into the interior parts of that great continent: and the great rivers of Africa are at too great a distance from one another to give occasion to any considerable inland navigation. (*WN* 36)

The same principle is at work in Smith's story of the origin of commodities and money. "When the division of labor has been once thoroughly established" (*WN* 37), humans live not by producing to satisfy all their needs but by exchanging their produce for some other. This exchange in early times would have often been "clogged and embarrassed," imposing much inconvenience on early society (*WN* 37). Under these circumstances each person would be likely to maintain a stock of one commodity which was held to be universally desirable, such that they might always be able to exchange for what they needed. Metals eventually take the place of all such commodities, not only because they are not perishable, but because "they can likewise, without any loss, be divided into any number of parts, as by fusion those parts can easily be re-united again" (*WN* 39). Metal is the ultimate commodity because it is the most divisible, capable of being drawn into the smallest possible quantities and then reunited into larger ones; metal is thus the ultimate tool of the principle of abstraction. Just as the passions of the imagination are more "ductile" than those of the body, and thus better able to circulate in the "market" of abstract desire, so metal, being the most divisible commodity, enables the freest possible exchange in the market, and thus the most highly abstract and precise mode of the division of labor.

Smith's theory of the division of labor and its operation in history seems to be shaped by his understanding of the principle of abstraction in the history of language. But while Smith's account of abstraction, sympathy, and the division of labor all correspond in a general way to the position I have assigned to Condillac, the *Wealth of Nations* contains a number of undigested contradictions arising out of the debate between Rousseau and Condillac. While Book One treats money as the final abstraction of production, facilitating the complex exchanges necessary to maintain an increasingly elaborate market, Book Two discusses the role of the accumulation of capital ("stock") in the rise of the productive power of any society. Here Smith considers money as part of his discussion of the relationship between fixed and circulating capital. Fixed capital is comprised of anything which increases the productive powers of labor, including buildings, improvements to agricultural land, and machines. Circulating capital is made up of those things which must be either exchanged or consumed to continue the process of production: raw materials, finished commodities, provisions, and money. Smith argues that, unlike the other three forms of circulating capital, money is never consumed in the process of its exchange, and thus in effect it behaves much more like fixed capital than circulating, since it must be maintained, either at public or private expense, in order to continue its role in facilitating other exchanges. This leads Smith to declare, in a number of well-known passages, that money is not part of the wealth of any nation, but merely one of the tools by which nations create wealth. As the "great wheel of circulation," money "is altogether different from the goods which are circulated by means of it. The revenue of the society consists altogether in those goods, and not in the wheel which circulates them" (*WN* 289).

This is an understanding of money consistent with Condillac's theory of signs. Money here functions in the market in the same way that Condillac's "instituted sign" functions in the process of human intellection. It is a tool of abstract thought, a wholly artificial construct which works as a tool promoting the increased efficiency of association and exchange. As an "instituted" or artificial sign, money bears no intrinsic relation to the object it signifies. Thus money functions by common consensus, by its status as an "institution," rather than through the function of an inherent quality. When Smith writes then that money functions as "a sort of waggon-way through the air" (*WN* 321), he seems to be pointing to the artificiality of money as sign, in the tradition of Condillac.

But Condillac goes to the extent of arguing that abstract signs are the result of purely human mental operations. Abstract signs are derived not from humans' noticing categories that exist in natural surroundings, but by constructing categories, and by imposing them on an unordered sensorium. Smith seems to violate this logic, which has structured his general understanding of money all along, when he comes to discuss the modern operation of banking and the use of paper money.

On the one hand, when he introduces this subject, he seems to consider paper money as simply a more refined degree of abstraction in the process which created money to begin with. "The substitution of paper in the room of gold and silver money," he writes, "replaces a very expensive instrument of commerce with one much less costly, and sometimes equally convenient. Circulation comes to be carried on by a new wheel, which it costs less both to erect and to maintain than the old one" (*WN* 292). Paper notes can accomplish this, Smith argues, by taking the place of gold and silver money in domestic circulation, and freeing gold and silver to be invested in foreign trade, where locally issued paper notes have no value.[53]

But on the other hand, Smith proposes that

the whole paper money of every kind which can easily circulate in any country never can exceed the value of gold and silver, of which it supplies the place . . . Should the circulating paper at any time exceed that sum, as the excess could neither be sent abroad nor be employed in the circulation of the country, it must immediately return upon the banks to be exchanged for gold and silver. (*WN* 300–01)

Smith assumes that when the amount of money in circulation exceeds the value of the aggregate wealth – in goods – of any country, those extra notes will somehow be unemployed, and that their owners will be anxious to exchange them for gold, which can be invested abroad. This is a fairly limited understanding of the operation of paper money, but it leads Smith to argue that there is, in effect, a natural relationship between paper and the object it represents. Smith here appears to abandon the linguistic metaphor he seems to follow in his larger discussion.

Rather than following Condillac in arguing that human categories are artificial, bearing no natural relation to the objects they represent, Smith creeps toward the position that signs represent natural categories of objects that appear in the world prior to human conception. Perhaps because of the authority Smith's theory of paper money borrows from the Rousseauist metaphysics of essences, his views were influential. They informed the nineteenth-century argument for the free issue of bank notes, public and private. Proponents of this view, called the "Banking School," held that given a natural tendency for paper notes to correspond exactly to the amount of metallic money they represented, banks should not be legally restrained from issuing notes in any amount. As it emerges in Smith's text, the position appears again to result from an odd mixture of incompatible premises about "nature" and "culture," criss-crossing their way through Rousseau and deriving from Smith's earlier work in historical psychology and linguistics. His conception of paper money as representational sign both follows from and is marked by the entanglements and double binds of Rousseau's historiography.

But although Smith's defense of unregulated banking relies on his sense of a natural order which limits the issue of paper currency, it also relies on the general argument for freedom of trade and free competition which Smith makes throughout. He ends the chapter by saying that among banks, "free competition . . . obliges all bankers to be more liberal in their dealings with their customers, lest their rivals should carry them away. In general, if any branch of trade, or any division of labour, be advantageous to the publick, the freer and more general the competition, it will always be the more so" (*WN* 329). This general defense of free trade and competition is repeated many times throughout the book. Perhaps most famously at the end of Book Four, after his critique of various systems of economic administration, Smith argues that any system which either restricts or protects any given industry "retards, instead of accelerating, the progress of the society towards real wealth and greatness; and diminishes, instead of increasing, the real value of the annual produce of its land and labour. All systems either of preference or of restraint, therefore, being thus completely taken away, the obvious and simple system of natural liberty establishes itself of its own accord" (*WN* 687). But Smith's conviction that "natural liberty" will lead to an increasingly productive and wealthy society is only understandable in the context of his earlier work. Smith, to recap, borrows Condillac's model of human history moving in a self-perpetuating development of abstract signs. Where for Rousseau increasing levels of abstraction are evil, for Smith they result in an increasing capacity for thought, and an increase in the powers of material production. Given that Smith begins his argument on the history of human productive labor with this claim, derived from a theory of historical linguistics, he concludes that every obstruction to the progressive rise of abstraction amounts to a retardation of human potential.

However, this central aspect of Smith's thought is again marked by certain contradictions that span the work of Rousseau and Condillac. Rousseau conceives of the rise of abstraction as a kind of emasculation, where the originary solidity and immediacy of primitive human passion is refracted and weakened by an order of desire associated with vanity and feminine sexuality. History for Rousseau is the history of effeminization. In general Smith takes the opposite position, arguing with Condillac that human perception begins as a feeble and "embarrassed" power, dominated by the random events of the physical universe, while the rise of human mental powers enables the increase of "mastery" and substance. The universal man of this history emerges only latterly, and he is the man in whom the powers of reason, language, and social convention enable the control of effeminate passions.

While this is the general scheme Smith follows, in Book Five he laments that while "in . . . barbarous societies, as they are called, every man . . . is a warrior" (*WN* 783), for the specialized worker in a society with an advanced division of labor, "his dexterity at his own particular trade seems . . . to be acquired at the expense of his intellectual, social, and martial virtues" (*WN* 782). Smith seems to regret extremely the loss of the martial spirit that would characterize society before the division of labor, arguing that as martial virtues fall out of use, when they are cultivated only among professional soldiers, men in other trades inevitably become "cowards." This condition Smith figures explicitly as a kind of castration:

A coward, a man incapable either of defending or of revenging himself, evidently wants one of the most essential parts of the character of a man. He is as much mutilated and deformed in his mind, as another is in his body, who is either deprived of some of his most essential members, or has lost the use of them. (*WN* 787)

Here abstraction is vital loss, and human history is a record of gradual effeminization. Smith uses the point to argue that one of the few responsibilities of the state is to provide the sort of male education that would cultivate military discipline. Thus while Smith's conception of abstraction leads him in general to a linear model of history, the nostalgic misogyny he borrows here leads him into a Rousseauist circularity, whereby the responsibility of contemporary (i.e. feminized) society is to guide its members in their behavior back toward society's (masculine) point of origin.

In certain of its elements, then, Smith's linear view of history is no less focused on lost origins than Rousseau's. The important differences between these two views of history, however, can be seen in each writer's attitude toward the idea of national character, an idea which will have a place of growing importance in the development of political economy. In Smith's work national character does not even achieve the somewhat confused status it has in Condillac's. Smith does not directly address the idea anywhere. In Book One his discussion of the varying extent of markets and the various stages of development of the division of labor does not mention land or climate, but only the access to navigable rivers. His account in Book Three of the growth of European wealth and power refers only to the way European societies adhered to or deviated from a "natural" course of the development of the division of labor. In Smith's political economy, the rate of "progress of opulence in different nations" (*WN* 376) is a function simply of the linear unfolding of the division of labor. Where the division of labor is complex, wealth will multiply; where it is simple, it will stagnate. Underdevelopment is a result only of a nation's position along a one-way time line of the abstraction of productive tasks.

For Rousseau, however, the concept of passion within his historiography leads to a theory of foundational differences in the character of humans of different nations. Smith makes no distinction between need and passion; it is all the same, leading even in the case of excessive or selfish desires toward an aggregate improvement in society. Rousseau's "supplementary" understanding of the fall from direct need to triangulated passion – where both can represent either the best or worst qualities of early society – leads to other consequences. Need becomes for him the principle that structured the formation of "northern" languages, while passion structured the "southern" ones. The language developed in this northern scene would be one of practicality and commerce. The first scene of human cooperation in the south was the amorous encounter of young people, that is, the first scene of "moral" desire.

Underdevelopment for Smith is simply a function of the division of labor; for Rousseau it is a function of being "southern." As with Condillac's linguistics then, it is important to recognize a certain radical potential in Smith's economic historiography. His understanding of poverty is grossly distorted by his progressivism. But the *Wealth of Nations* explains varying levels of global wealth as a simple function of material and technical means. Efficient techniques, including transport and financial infrastructure, will produce wealth. For Rousseau, nations are limited in their economic development by inalterable qualities of character.

CHAPTER 2

Value as signification

In chapter 1 I traced central elements of Adam Smith's political economy from founding assumptions in Smith's work on the origin of languages. Smith's linear historiography, but perhaps more importantly, his conception of human agency and character, seem to have been worked out in his early conjectural history of language and then applied to the question of wealth and poverty. Because of his historiographical and psychological assumptions, the central category in Smith's political economy is the division of labor: the principle of gradually increasing abstraction and efficiency which corresponds to the generation of signs in the history of language.

In nineteenth-century political economy, and in modern economics, the cornerstone concept is no longer the division of labor, it is value. The discussion of value takes up little space in Adam Smith's work. It takes on more prominence in David Ricardo's 1817 *Principles of Political Economy*, but as the century goes on, the question of value becomes the subject of an epoch-making debate. The sea-change in the understanding of value that takes place between the work of Ricardo and that of Jevons, in 1871, reveals a great deal about the cultural and political orientation of economic thought in the period. The rising prominence of the theory of value indicates a movement away from Condillac and Smith's theory of history as abstraction and toward the historiographical and philosophical assumptions I have located in Rousseau. The human subject at the center of this theory shifts radically: from the fabricator of sign-technology to the naturally expressive subject of desire.

Smith considers value early on in Book One of the *Wealth of Nations*, but he introduces the discussion as follows: "what are the rules which men naturally observe in exchanging [goods] either for money or for one another, I shall now proceed to examine. These rules determine what may be called the relative or exchangeable value of goods."[1] The passage occurs at the end of chapter 4, after Smith has already discussed the origin and development of the division of labor, exchange, and money. Value for Smith is a secondary principle, governed by the "rules" of a much larger and more interesting game, and as such it seems to deserve relatively little attention. Perhaps as a result then, Smith's statements in the following chapter are somewhat confused, and have led to a number of confusions. He writes in his first paragraph, "the value of any commodity, therefore, to the person who possesses it, and who means not to use or consume it himself, but to exchange it for other commodities, is equal to the quantity of labour which it enables him to purchase or command. Labour, therefore, is the real measure of the exchangeable value of all commodities." From this statement Smith is often assumed to have argued for a "labor theory of value." He does go on to argue that "it was not by gold or by silver, but by labour, that all the wealth of the world was originally purchased."[2] This is the sort of passage that made Smith such a worthy figure in Marx's eyes, for here Smith places the productive power of human labor at the center of things. To say that it was by a certain quantity of labor that any good was originally "purchased" seems to argue that the value of any good involves the amount of labor required to produce it.

However, in the first passage, and throughout the rest of the chapter, Smith insists that it is not the quantity of labor involved in a commodity's production which controls its value, but rather the quantity of labor one might exchange for it in the market. Labor is thus in Smith's theory not the origin of value but simply the most accurate way to measure it. This is because, in Mark Blaug's words, Smith assumes that "the disutility per unit of common labor is constant for everyone":[3]

Equal quantities of labour, at all times and places, may be said to be of equal value to the labourer. In his ordinary state of health, strengths and spirits; in the ordinary degree of his skill and dexterity, he must always lay down the same portion of his ease, his liberty, and his happiness. The price which he pays must always be the same.[4]

Smith argues that all commodities will naturally fluctuate in price in any given market, thus no commodity can provide an accurate measure of the value of any other commodity, given that its own value is always in motion. But he suggests that labor is an exception to this rule, given the fixed and invariable "cost" to the laborer for any given task. This emphasis on the wear and pain of labor as the real measure of value again seems to look forward to Marx. But of course here Smith understands this pain and sacrifice of health simply as an expenditure, strictly equivalent to the expenditure of money within any market exchange. This bracing logical inconsistency is covered in a mere four pages, which themselves form the basis of innumerable later commentaries and critiques. The inconsistencies in these passages, however, demonstrate the relatively minor position of the concept within Smith's larger theory. The division of labor for Smith is not a "fallen" or alienated state. Complex markets do not divide commodities from themselves, they simply create more of them; wage labor does not separate the laborer from "himself," it simply makes "him" a little sore. Thus the theory of value in Smith's work involves no complex isolation of essential and original principles; it is simply a system of measurements which allows the market to operate efficiently, and this seems to be why Smith wastes so little time on it.

VALUE AND CHARACTER IN RICARDO

While it is clear that Smith speaks of value in more than one way, it is important to notice that his treatment of the question of value is guided by and results from a larger description of human economic activity as a system. The same is true for David Ricardo, whose 1817 *Principles of Political Economy* opens with the long chapter "On Value." The broader defining questions of the work, however, those which allow us to position him in relation to Smith, are found in his preface, which begins as follows:

The produce of the earth – all that is derived from its surface by the united application of labor, machinery, and capital, is divided among the three classes of the community; namely the proprietor of the land, the owner of the stock or capital necessary for its cultivation, and the laborers by whose industry it is cultivated. But in different stages of society, the proportions of the whole produce of the earth which will be allotted to each of these classes, under the names of rent, profit, and wages, will be essentially different . . . To determine the laws which regulate this distribution is the principle problem in political economy.[5]

Thus while for Smith the driving question of political economy was the difference between the wealth and poverty of different nations – a question which Smith answers with a theory of the historical development of wealth – Ricardo assumes an advanced division of labor, and a state of production where society is already divided into "classes." The function of political economy for Smith is to define the rules which allow the division of labor to make history; political economy for Ricardo involves not the diachronic principle of development, but the synchronic principle of the distribution of wealth.

Perhaps because Ricardo does not deliberately set out to explain the differences between rich and poor nations, but simply the difference between rich and poor classes within a single highly differentiated economy, he takes no direct interest in the subject of national character. His comments on this subject seem incidental and off-hand, as in his remarks in the first edition of the *Principles* on the laziness of the Irish. Even this quality, he argued, was not permanent or inevitable but could be altered by the incentives of the market: "Give to the Irish laborer a taste for the comforts and enjoyments which habit has made essential to the English laborer, and he would be then content to devote a further portion of his time to industry, that he might be enabled to obtain them."[6]

Here Ricardo suggests, in a manner reminiscent of Smith, that the Irish are "idle" not because of any fundamental disposition but because of "the facility with which the wants of the Irish are supplied."[7] This indeed is the dominant perspective held by political economists until the middle of the nineteenth century. National character is not a solid foothold in the argument; rather Irish workers are seen as eminently pliable, subject to market forces which could be manipulated from London. While this view led to the most notorious blunders of political economy at the time of the Irish Famine, it is important to recognize that these views proceed from what I have been calling here an Enlightenment conception of the subject. Desire and motivation here are produced by experience, just as abstract concepts are produced by the "grammatological" process of their writing. In practice, however, this assumption about the nature of desire was filtered through a number of other religious and political doctrines and produced a disastrous set of policies.[8] The resulting crisis at the time of the Famine contributed to the decisive turn economic thought took in the nineteenth century.

Where Ricardo's work does lead in a different direction from Smith's is in the theory of value. Ricardo's emphasis on the distribution of wealth among the three classes grew not from a prior conception of history, as in the case of Smith, but rather from a practical debate in 1814–16 over the corn laws.[9] The interested parties here were the owners of land, those who rented it for profit, and those who worked it, and Ricardo's theory of value rests on his understanding of the economic relation between these classes.

This relation, he suggests, is governed by the law of diminishing marginal utility of land: the idea that as the demand for arable land increases with population, land of increasingly poor quality will be brought into use. From this premise Ricardo develops his theory of rent, which, he writes, "invariably proceeds from the employment of an additional quantity of labor with a proportionally less return."[10] That is, when competition drives people to cultivate poor land, which will require an extra amount of labor to produce good yield, other people will be willing to pay for the privilege of cultivating the good land, just in the exact amount that would be required to hire the extra labor necessary to cultivate the poor land. Thus "when in the progress of society, land of the second degree of fertility is taken into cultivation, rent immediately commences on that of the first quality, and the amount of that rent will depend on the difference in the quality of these two portions of land."[11]

As the amount of land under cultivation increases, so the amount of labor expended on the production of agricultural goods must increase. Agricultural goods, Ricardo argues, form the greatest part of the wage expenditures of the laboring class, and the long-term rate of wages will be whatever sum is necessary for laborers to maintain themselves and their families. As agriculture continues to operate with decreasing efficiency – as more resources of the agricultural capitalist must go to rent and to wages of extra laborers – the price of subsistence foods must rise, and with them must rise the average wage of the laborer. The result of Ricardo's theory of agricultural rent is thus that over time wages must tend to increase while the rate of profit must decline.

According to Ricardo, within such a system of diminishing agricultural returns, the exchange value of any commodity in the market will be equal to the quantity of labor required to produce it. This is not because labor has any special status within Ricardo's thought. He argues, first of all, quite carefully in his long opening chapter, that value has no fixed standard of measure: not corn, not labor, nor gold. "Of such a measure it is impossible to be possessed, because there is no commodity which is not itself exposed to the same variations as the things, the value of which is to be ascertained."[12] The only fixed standard, for Ricardo, is that natural one – the amount of good land – which limits the efficient production of subsistence food, and thus the rate of wages and of profits. At any given stage of the progress of agriculture, the value of labor in relation to all other commodities on the market will correspond to the value of resources the laborer needs. When this food is easily produced, labor absorbs a relatively small amount of the complete productive energy of the society. As more labor must be devoted to the production of food, more of the total output of social energy must be devoted to the wages of labor, and labor-intensive commodities must increase in exchange value relative to others.

The exchangeable value of all commodities, whether they be manufactured, or the produce of the mines, or the produce of land, is always regulated, not by the less quantity of labor that will suffice for their production under circumstances highly favorable, and exclusively enjoyed by those who have peculiar facilities of production; but by the greater quantity of labor necessarily bestowed on their production by those who have no such facilities."[13]

While Ricardo devotes the opening of his book to the theory of value, value turns out only to be important as a way of understanding the natural limits of all economic production. Ricardo does claim that, given conditions of scarcity, "all things [are] more or less valuable in proportion as more or less labor [is] bestowed on their production."[14] However, for him, as with Smith, the theory of value is not yet a theory of representation. Labor is not the "signified" of the commodity, in its outward form; labor is not the "secret" of the commodity, as in Marx. For Ricardo and Smith, value is an axiom which helps us trace the quasi-mechanical, Newtonian laws of wealth. Their understanding of these underlying laws is different: Smith's comes from his philosophical assumptions, Ricardo's from his role in the political debate between manufacturers and land owners. But for both the calculation of exchange value is a direct indicator of a society's stage of economic development within an assumed developmental model: for Smith the extension of the market through the division of labor, for Ricardo the decreasing marginal utility of land. The value of a commodity is not understood by either thinker as the expression of some lost and hidden original quality.

This understanding of the early theory of value should lead us to be somewhat suspicious of Foucault's periodization of "the Human Sciences" in *The Order of Things*. Foucault argues here that for Smith labor functions as "an irreducible, absolute unit of measurement."[15] The contrast Foucault stresses is between an earlier characterization of value as fungibility – exchangeability with gold or other useful things – and value as representation of labor, which is the universal principle of value. As such then, for Foucault,

Adam Smith's analysis represents an essential hiatus; it distinguishes between the reason for exchange and the measurement of that which is exchangeable, between the nature of what is exchanged and the units that enable it to be broken down . . . As men experience things – at the level of what will soon be called psychology – what they are exchanging is what is "indispensable, commodious, or pleasurable" to them, but for the economist, what is actually circulating in the form of things is labour – not objects of need representing one another, but time and toil, transformed, concealed, forgotten.[16]

This view assumes a "labor theory of value" as the central facet of Smith's thought, which it was not, and it assumes Smith treated labor as a "signified," a hidden interior of the commodity, as outward "sign." It is at this level that Foucault aligns Smith with the nineteenth-century philologists, who read modern languages as the faded outward signs of a hidden national character. Smith, however, clearly belongs to the pre-philological, pre-Rousseau/Herder epoch of linguistic thought; his work is structured not by the fixation on lost essences, characteristic of romantic – or what Foucault calls "modern" – thought, but rather on human constructions. It is important to understand Smith and Ricardo within this eighteenth-century context in order to see the way modern economic thought arises in relation to global conditions, indeed to "globalization" itself in the era of early imperial capitalism. Changes in economic thought move dialectically, in connection to material conditions, like any of the symbolic systems that structure human representations of the material. My approach to this history, in looking for common conditions of possibility shared by seemingly disparate modes of knowledge, is much indebted to Foucault. But Foucault's sense of how change in economic thought should be periodized might lead us, as Gayatri Spivak once argued in another context, to conclude wrongly that the rest of the world was irrelevant to the development of European thought.[17]

This might be the place to pause again, long enough to consider another recent treatment of Adam Smith, Christopher Herbert's *Culture and Anomie*. This is an accomplished and careful work in many ways, one which traces conceptions of "culture" throughout the nineteenth century. Herbert argues that early nineteenth-century notions were essentially Hobbesian, viewing culture as a set of laws that prohibit anarchic or violent human desire; this view was supplanted, he suggests, by a "holistic and ethnographic" one, in which culture is conceived as a complex system of affinities and signs which themselves produce the desiring subject.[18] This is a compelling frame for understanding many aspects of the nineteenth century, and Herbert is surely right in asserting, as he does in his long chapter on economic thought, that political economy dealt more directly with the question of culture than any other discipline in the era before the codification of anthropology.[19] But Herbert's readings in political economy, focused as they are on demonstrating this nineteenth-century shift, depart from any eighteenth-century context. He argues correctly that Smith theorized culture as a productive system, not a law of restraints. For Smith, he writes, "value does not inhere in objects of commerce at all, but purely in *the institutionalized system of relations which enables exchange to occur.*"[20] But since Herbert does not look to the philosophical context of Smith's thought, he does not see that this view was a commonplace of European linguistics and epistemology in the middle of the eighteenth century. Given this state of things, Herbert can only identify Smith's work as a kind of uncanny anticipation of the "ethnographic" conception of culture as a semiotic system. He refers to this as "the deconstructive turn" in Smith's work, and he asserts that "the *Wealth of Nations* closely anticipates in these respects the philosophical theory of exchange propounded by Georg Simmel," who argued that "value . . . refers purely to desire, and desire itself is fundamentally a function of the exchange-system."[21] After giving both Smith and Simmel the "deconstructive" seal of approval, he sums up the consequences of their theory of value as follows: "Value always depends on one's point of vantage and is impossible to grasp except as a conventionalized fiction of a particular social system – which is to say that it becomes identical after all to its price in money."[22] This will become the fantasy of contemporary economics: that actors in the market differ only in the "desires" they "express" in their earning or purchasing behavior. It is a perspective established by the so-called marginalists in the late nineteenth century, one of whom, W. S. Jevons, I will discuss in more detail below. But the theory of value in their work is fundamentally different from Smith's and is not in the least "deconstructive."

It is true that neither the late nineteenth-century marginalist conception of value, nor Smith's theory, conceives value as an immanent or positive quality. And both think of value as functioning roughly like a sign. But while Smith sees the subject as (deconstructively) "written" by the sign, marginalism sees the subject's desires as reified, a stable point of agency that pre-exists and authors the market's "meanings" (i.e. production and distribution). Though Herbert's survey of ethnographic writing extends well into the twentieth century, he does not trace the theory of value any farther than Simmel (whose impact is in any case in sociology, not economics). Because of this, Herbert does not recognize that the relativism in twentieth-century definitions of value is explicitly a positivist theory, based on a stable subject whose impulses are represented in quantitative terms by their earning and purchasing behavior. Herbert does make it clear that no such stable subject exists in Smith's work. But at the same time, he seems essentially to declare that the price=value formula is the outcome of any correct poststructuralist approach to the question of the commodity. As a result then, he ends up naturalizing "free" market economics, suggesting that the relativism of values under global free trade, which we see trumpeted regularly in the business journals, is just another way of understanding the celebrated "indeterminacy of the sign."

Such are the dangers then of any attempt to place money and language in a strictly structural comparison. One risks excluding the global dimension of these systems, and celebrating, with the language of a vulgar deconstructionism, the "freedom" of economic signification. In the final section of this chapter, I try to understand how this theory of value as desire became established, up to one founding text in this tradition, Jevons's *Theory of*

Political Economy of 1871. In this process I attempt to keep the question of the subject at the center of things, in order to avoid the trap of a naive money/language homology.

KANT AND THE PHILOLOGISTS

As we have seen, the concerns of eighteenth-century political economists emerged in close connection with philosophy, especially the study of language. The same is true in the nineteenth century, as radically new conceptions of value and character emerge alongside new approaches to the philosophy of language. Against Smith's interest in language as clue to subject-formation, the nineteenth-century spirit of "inductive" or "positive" inquiry focused on documenting language as actually spoken. Ignoring the eighteenth-century concern with the observing subject, the nineteenth century simply assumed (as a matter of what Thomas Reid called "common sense") that the speaker of language was a coherent entity, whose thought preceded in an ideal sense the process of its casting into words. Nineteenth-century language study moves toward the concept of a stable pre-linguistic subject, a user of language rather than a linguistic construct. The idea of this a priori subject – emergent in Rousseau – turns language from a potentially dangerous agency to a more or less debased representation of human thought. And while *parole* was a representation of individual character, *langue* and its history could be traced as the representation of a (lost or debased) national character. As I will suggest below, one indication of this shifting ground in English thought is the reception of Kant's critical philosophy in the first half of the nineteenth century.

In England the study of language in the late eighteenth century was dominated by the approach outlined in Horne Tooke's *Diversions of Purley* (1786–1805), a faithful adaptation of principles found in Condillac and Smith. Tooke follows their idea that the increase of mental efficiency is the motive force in the history of language. As Hans Aarsleff puts it, Tooke "makes abbreviation the cornerstone of his theory."[23] This Smithian view was gradually displaced in a philosophical movement Aarsleff traces to Scottish philosopher Thomas Reid and his student Dugald Stewart, friend and critic of Adam Smith.[24] Reid's *Inquiry into the Human Mind on the Principles of Common Sense* (1764) criticizes Locke, Hume, and the French materialists for an "absurd" questioning of modes of perception that were simply matters of common sense.[25] This critique leads him to the position that the mind is "an independent entity," and that "language is an imperfect vehicle of mental intercourse."[26]

Reid's position came only gradually to dominate the study of language in England, through the work of English students who returned home from apprenticeships with German and Danish philologists to spread their craft.[27] With its idealist conception of subject-formation, Aarsleff writes, philology reacted "against what was considered the deplorable and shallow philosophy of the eighteenth century. This reaction . . . is a reminder that the quarrel between the nineteenth century and its predecessor was waged on philosophical and ideological grounds, with Locke, the Philosophes, and the Utilitarians pitted against the Victorian or rather the European Sage."[28]

It is this nineteenth-century revision of Enlightenment materialism that has relegated Condillac to the status of a minor thinker and subordinated his reputation to that of Rousseau. Even John Stuart Mill, loyal though he was to Locke, refers to "the ideology of Condillac and his school" as "the shallowest set of doctrines which perhaps were ever passed off upon a cultivated age as a complete psychological system."[29] The continuing power of this nineteenth-century version of things, embracing the study of language and economy, also makes it very difficult now to read the work of Adam Smith. Championed by neoclassical economists as a prescient advocate of free trade, Smith's work seems to appear – as in both Foucault's and Herbert's periodization – at the dawn of a modern age of social science. The philosophical foundations of Smith's economics, the potentially disruptive epistemology that would in fact undermine the claims of twentieth-century economists, are available only if we can see past the nineteenth-century's trashing of Condillac.

One of the first public manifestations of the philological perspective came with the formation in 1842 of the Philological Society of London. Its initial meetings took place in rooms borrowed from the London Statistical Society, and the connection between the organizations makes sense, given the common assumptions that shaped the two fields in this period.[30] As philologists sought to observe and analyze the speech of already socialized speakers, the science of statistics sought methods to record and analyze just such observational data. Both follow a positivist methodology, avoiding diachronic speculation in favor of synchronic observation, recording current phenomena rather than inquiring into how they came to be. The "common sense" affirmation of a coherent, perceiving agent, essentially impervious to social systems, entered political economy in the early nineteenth century, most noticeably in the debate over the theory of value. And it is only in this period that value becomes a central theoretical issue in the field.

A number of writers in the 1820s argued, against Smith and Ricardo, that exchange value was wholly unconnected with the larger system of production and exchange, and was a function only of consumer demand. The central figure of this reaction was Malthus. His 1820 *Principles of Political Economy* argues that in the early stages of society before the invention of money, "the rate at which [an] exchange is made, or the portion of one commodity which is given for an assigned portion of the other, will depend upon the relative estimation in which they are held by the parties, founded on the desire to possess, and the difficulty or facility of procuring possession."[31] Malthus extrapolates from this bit of "speculative history" to argue that the "intensity of demand" within particular conditions of scarcity will also regulate exchange value in the market, after the division of labor. Samuel Bailey's 1825 *Critical Dissertation on the Nature, Measure, and Causes of Value* argues likewise that "the ultimate cause of value is not labor but rather the esteem in which a commodity is held."[32] "Value," Bailey writes, "denotes, strictly speaking, an effect produced on the mind."[33] To base a theory of exchange value on the "esteem" of the consumer is to posit a consumer whose "sense" of value exists prior to the system of social evaluation. If, for philology, speakers exist before language, consumers in this new theory of value exist before their contact with the market.

We should notice in both the study of language and political economy in this period the effect of the English reception of the critical philosophy of Kant. Writing in 1931, René Wellek estimated Kant's impact as follows: "The history of Kant's introduction, reception and influence in England . . . sheds a flood of light on the peculiar intellectual condition of England in the early nineteenth century. It helps us understand the momentous change which took place in the mental atmosphere of England during those decisive 50 years."[34] While Kant scrupulously outlined the limitations on the reasoning subject imposed by the form of sense perception itself, his British readers cast him as the great opponent of Locke and Hume, upholding a reasoning subject prior to sense perception. For Coleridge Kant seemed to offer a way of affirming an "original unity of consciousness," which all humans shared in.[35] As Crabb Robinson put it, Kant provided a "refutation of Locke's . . . famous principle, that there is nothing in the intellect which was not before in sense, or that all our conceptions (ideas) are derived from sensation. According to the empirical system, as stated in its utmost consistency by Horne Tooke, man has but one faculty, that of receiving sensation from external objects."[36] In fact one could argue Kant also sees humans as possessing just this sole "faculty" – what he calls "the faculty of representation."[37] While Kant warned against "the subreption of the hypostatized consciousness" – i.e. counting the effect of the mental representation "I think" as its own cause – he was taken by a generation of English students as an enemy of Locke, and thus a proponent of innate ideas, or even, in the hands of Whewell, of Divinely implanted knowledge.[38] This reception in England of Kant's critical interventions provided a philosophical position from which to assert a subject that values, prior to the social structure of value, a subject that intends, prior to the acquisition of a transitive syntax.

LONGFIELD AND WHATELY: VALUE IN IRISH ECONOMIC THOUGHT

The decade of the 1820s, when the demand theory of value made its appearance, also witnessed the appearance of a series of texts seeking to explain political economy in popular terms to widespread audiences. These texts, although they recognized the authority of Ricardo, generally share the assumptions, if not the outright positions, of the anti-Ricardian theory of value. They portray political economy as describing a system of natural or Divine law, which uneducated working-class people and uneducated middle-class women ought to learn, in order to understand and maximize their position in the universe of wealth and poverty.[39] The subject again, in these models, is static, existing in all its desires and predilections prior to the iron laws of the marketplace.

The implications of these popular texts for English domestic economic policy have received a good deal of attention elsewhere. A striking example of the colonial dimension of this literature can be found in Archbishop Richard Whately's 1832 *Easy Lessons on Money Matters*, a text written for use in the system of Irish free national schools, created the year before, in 1831. It was in 1831 that Whately left the Drummond Chair in political economy at Oxford to serve as Archbishop of Dublin, the leader of the Church of Ireland, and he used his authority in this post to support the new school system and to encourage instruction in the science of political economy. Ireland in the 1830s was the dubious beneficiary both of the first public elementary schools and the first state-organized police force in modern history; both institutions were created in the wake of the 1829 "emancipation," which moderated a century and a half of anti-Catholic legislation. Ireland in the 1820s was in a nearly constant state of unrest, with agrarian peasant groups enforcing demands on the Anglo-Irish land-owning class through secret violence. S. J. Connolly calculates that in 1825, 25,000 of the total 30,000 standing British troops were stationed either in Ireland or on the west coast of Wales and England, where they would be available for deployment.[40] Education and a partially native police force were designed to assimilate unruly Irish-speaking children into an Anglophone empire.

Whately's school text attempts to speed this process of assimilation by teaching them the demand theory of value. "Scarcity alone," he writes,

[will] not make a thing valuable, if there were no reason why any one should desire to possess it. There are some kinds of stones which are scarce, but of no value, because they have neither use nor beauty. You would not give anything in exchange for such a stone; not because you can easily get it, but because you have no wish for it.[41]

Whately does concede that "scarcity" amounts to a measurement of the labor required to produce a commodity: "It costs only as much in labour and other expenses, to obtain about fifteen pounds of silver, as to obtain one pound of gold; and this is the cause that one pound of gold will exchange for about fifteen pounds of silver."[42] But labor itself is repeatedly dismissed as having any direct connection to value. Labor quantity is rendered as "scarcity," and the focus of the chapter becomes the role of desire itself in the creation of value. Whately concludes finally:

It is not, therefore, labour that makes things valuable, but their being valuable that makes them worth labouring for. And God, having judged in his wisdom that it is not good for man to be idle, has so appointed things by his Providence, that few of the things that are most desirable can be obtained without labour. It is ordained for man to eat bread in the sweat of his face; and almost all the necessaries, comforts, and luxuries of life, are obtained by labour.[43]

In this Nietzschean reversal of cause and effect, labor here becomes a Divine rule, suffered equally by all humans. And as a universal in human behavior, labor represents another Divinely implanted human quality – the desire for commodities. This desire is, in Whately's model, inborn and precedes the division of labor, or any process of production or exchange. In this passage, an object is bestowed with value because it is evaluated by the desiring subject. The estimation of value within the discrete subject fixes the system as a whole.

Whately's *Easy Lessons* proved an extremely popular text, going through sixteen editions by 1862.[44] It was used in schools throughout the United Kingdom and the empire and appeared in a number of foreign languages. Whately noted in a letter that a Maori-language edition produced for schools in New Zealand had been found "highly acceptable to the natives."[45] Whately's example demonstrates again the centrality of the colonial process worldwide in the European history of ideas. Colonial school systems appear in the ideological vanguard of consumer capitalism here, proposing some decades before its acceptance in professional circles a theory of supply and demand that would come to dominate the modern discipline of economics.

Whately's other major educational initiative was to endow a professorship in political economy at Trinity College. The first occupant of the Whately Chair – and thus the first professor of political economy in Ireland – was Mountifort Longfield, who held the position from 1832 to 1836. In a series of lectures delivered in 1833, Longfield attempted to further refine a theory of value regulated by a prior conception of consumer demand, extending this principle to a theory of wages. Where Ricardo argued that wages were always determined in relation to the cost of subsistence goods in the market, Longfield argues "that the wages of the laborer depend upon the value of his labor, and not upon his wants, whether natural or acquired, and that if his wants and necessities exercise, as they do, some influence upon the wages of his labor, it is indirect and secondary."[46] The value of labor in this model is a function solely of the willingness of an employer to pay, within a given environment of supply. The value of labor here is connected only to the level of desire felt by the consumer of that labor, that is, the capitalist.

The focus on desire in early nineteenth-century political economy represents a major shift in the understanding of the market. Where Smith and Ricardo posit models of development based on the expansion of production, here consumer demand influences the aggregate level and distribution of wealth as much as any principle of production. In this transition one can argue that the work of Adam Smith is ultimately abolished. Smith's work was conceived in reaction to the fear that, as financial markets grew more complex, with an expansion of credit mechanisms and the institutionalization of national debt, the value of all goods (and the system of social values) would become increasingly unstable. The idea that the value of a given stock share might rise or fall with the desire or repulsion of common consumers was interpreted in the eighteenth century through the metaphor of femininity. The professional speculator became the emblem of this abhorrent principle, which undermined earlier notions of wealth as a representation of intrinsic qualities of nobility. The masculine virtues deemed necessary for the successful management of an estate or a business could be ignored by the speculator, as he rode the fickle and inconstant swerves of the shares markets.

The work of Adam Smith throughout his career met this metaphorical threat associated with capitalist markets head on. In Smith's model of history, the increasing abstraction of exchange is a principle of progressive civilization, where the growing productivity enabled by the subdivision of tasks improves the conditions of each segment of society. Smith does represent the disadvantages of the division of labor as a kind of castration threat, where male laborers lose their capacity as warriors and are feminized by the specialization of their tasks. But for Smith this is a relatively minor problem, correctable by the limited intervention of the state, in providing a standing army and a system of male public education to counteract the erosion of masculine vigor. The demand theory of value, however, embraces the idea that markets are driven by affective responses, by desire. Thus the eighteenth-century threat against which Smith marshals his whole career becomes, in the nineteenth century, the central assumption of economic thought. Late nineteenth-century economists argued that they provided a more precise model of the way values fluctuated within the market, responding to the forces of supply and demand. But while it was gradually accepted that the demand or utility theory led to a more accurate model of market prices, the philosophical problems associated with this idea in the eighteenth century never disappeared. The market continued to be conceived as a fallen realm of hollow signs, a dance of absent presences, inconstant, insubstantial, or "castrated."

One result of this changing metaphorical landscape in economic thought was that the theory of value eventually developed into a theory of human expression. Commodities were conceived as signs not of any single measure – like labor, utility, or gold – but as the expression of prior desire in the consumer, in the same way the romantic philologists conceived language as a medium that expressed the prior intention of the speaker. Political economy thus gradually becomes in the nineteenth century what Derrida calls a "logocentric" theory of representation. That is, it posits an ideal desire or intention in the mind of the individual which is unaffected by the market. Just as Derrida demonstrates that a kind of "writing" precedes speech, critics of political economy since Marx have made it their aim to demonstrate that the commodity, and the whole system of social relations it implies, precedes and constructs the consumer's desire for it. The desire is a retroactive effect of the commodity system. As Marx puts it, "the mutual relations of the producers, within which the social character of their labour affirms itself, take the form of a social relation between the products."[47] The "logocentrism" of the theory of value becomes explicit in De Quincey's *Logic of Political Economy*, in the 1840s, which argues that the commodity's essence as a useful thing – what he calls its "intrinsic serviceability" – is measured by the intensity of consumer desire for it. For De Quincey the commodity, in its outward form, does not present its essential value directly, but the idea of the commodity, its "signified," in the mind of the buyer, is an exact measure of this inner essence.[48]

J. S. MILL'S POLITICAL ETHOLOGY

The ideological uses of political economy also become increasingly sharpened in the 1820s and 1830s. In its appeal to the working class, this consumption-centered version of political economy stressed, as we saw in the work of Whately above, the irrelevance of political or social systems of organization to the immutable laws of value and wealth. The status of Ricardo's work in this era became a matter of hot controversy. Ricardian socialists used Ricardo's emphasis on labor to argue that workers deserved an increasing share of national wealth.[49] The demand theory of value became a tool to demonstrate the bankruptcy of Ricardo's work, in "a more or less conscious effort to counter the spread of socialism."[50] As Marx put it in a well known passage:

With the year 1830 there came the crisis which was to be decisive, once and for all. In France and England the bourgeoisie had conquered political power. From that time on, the class struggle took on more and more explicit and threatening forms, both in practice and in theory. It sounded the knell of scientific bourgeois economics. It was thenceforth no longer a question whether this or that theorem was true, but whether it was useful to capital or harmful, expedient or inexpedient, in accordance with police regulations or contrary to them. In place of disinterested inquirers there stepped hired prize-fighters; in place of genuine scientific research, the bad conscience and evil intent of apologetics.[51]

By the 1840s the capitalist boosterism of the anti-Ricardians had brought political economy into an increasingly serious state of crisis. Widely perceived as cruel, or at least callously unconcerned with the suffering of the poor, political economy seemed a partisan tool of industrial capital.[52] The future discipline of economics was rescued at this point almost single-handedly by John Stuart Mill, whose 1848 *Principles of Political Economy* became the standard text for students throughout the next thirty years. As we might expect at this point, the solutions to the crisis come from philosophy, and move in parallel with the philosophy of language. The work of Mill does not alter the central aspect of the 1830s school – the theory of value – but it succeeds in cleaning up its messy association with narrow class interest and with the selfishness of the rich.

The methodological solution Mill provides at this juncture is the positivist philosophy of Auguste Comte. Comte advocates an inductive or empirical approach to knowledge, arguing, as Mill puts it in a later essay,

We know not the essence, nor the real mode of production, of any fact, but only its relations to other facts in the way of succession or similitude. These relations are constant; that is, always the same in the same circumstances. The constant resemblances which link phaenomena together, and the constant sequences which unite them as antecedent and consequent, are termed their laws. The laws of phaenomena are all we know respecting them. Their essential nature and their ultimate causes, either efficient or final, are unknown and inscrutable to us.[53]

The call for an inductive approach in the physical sciences at this point was nothing new. The original argument Comte makes, and which Mill takes up, is that positive principles of inquiry needed still to be applied to the study of human society, which Comte argued was still largely bound by atavistic theological and metaphysical precepts. "The human mind," Comte wrote in 1830, "has created celestial and terrestrial physics, mechanics and chemistry, vegetable and animal physics, we might say, but we have still to complete the system of the observational sciences with social physics."[54]

Mill makes the case for an application of Comte's positive method in his only full-length philosophical work, the *Logic* of 1842. Following the injunction in Comte to trace the relations of "succession and similitude" which unite phenomena in constant laws, Mill argues in this book that the positive study of society must lead ultimately to a "science of the formation of character," which Mill calls "ethology" – the science of peoples. "Although," Mill writes,

there is scarcely any mode of feeling or conduct which is, in the absolute sense, common to all mankind . . . yet all modes of feeling and conduct met with among mankind have causes which produce them; and in the propositions which assign those causes, will be found the explanation of the empirical laws, and the limiting principle of our reliance on them.[55]

These laws of the causes of character would seek to explain the "ethological consequences of particular circumstances of position" and "account for the characteristics of the type [of human society] by the peculiarities of the circumstances."[56] That is, as Mill describes it here, ethology would generalize about the types of collective identity produced by various conditions – presumably climate, technology, conflict, etc. The most important consequence Mill foresees for such a science is in political economy. In the *Logic* Mill actually suggests political economy could be replaced with a new discipline called "political ethology." This would amount to a "science of national character," "a theory of the causes which determine the type of character belonging to a people or to an age."[57] Mill's method works from the "social physics" of Comte but indeed can be seen more broadly as fitting with Mill's constant allegiance to the English empiricist school, "the school of Locke and Bentham," as he puts it in his famous critique of

Coleridge.[58] But while in the *Logic* Mill advocated a study of what today we might call subject-formation – of how certain material and ideological conditions produce and replicate cultural characteristics on an individual and social level – his application of this method in his economic work is more ambiguous.

By the 1840s "political economy" had become popularly associated with claims by wealthy capitalists and politicians that the poor suffered only because they refused to accommodate themselves to the "natural" laws of the market. To counter this perception – and largely at the insistence of Harriet Taylor – Mill argued in his 1848 *Principles of Political Economy* that laws of the market were of two sorts: "laws of the Production of wealth – which are real laws of nature, dependent on the properties of objects – and modes of its Distribution, which, subject to certain conditions, depend on human will."[59]

At the end of Book One of the *Principles*, on "Production," Mill sums up the "objective" laws of production as follows:

the limit to the increase to production is two-fold; from deficiency of capital or of land. Production comes to a pause, either because the effective desire of accumulation is not sufficient to give rise to any further increase of capital, or because, however disposed the possessors of surplus income may be to save a portion of it, the limited land at the disposal of the community does not permit additional capital to be employed with such a return as would be an equivalent to them for their abstinence.[60]

There are for Mill two kinds of factors influencing national wealth: natural resources, and human social institutions. The latter reduce ultimately to an "effective desire of accumulation," which Mill counts as one of the "moral attributes" of a nation.[61] In this concept, Mill's earlier idea for a study of the formation of economic "character" is narrowed to the location of any nation on a single scale of desire. And though Mill indicates that the desire to accumulate capital is a social institution, he treats this concept in Book One, "Production."

In general Mill describes desire as an aspect of character inculcated by environmental conditions:

In countries where the principle of accumulation is as weak as it is in the various nations of Asia; where people will neither save, nor work to obtain the means of saving, unless under the inducement of enormously high profits, nor even then if it is necessary to wait a considerable time for them; where either productions remain scanty, or drudgery great, because there is neither capital forthcoming nor forethought sufficient for the adoption of the contrivances by which natural agents are made to do the work of human labour; the desideratum for such a country, economically considered, is an increase of industry, and of the effective desire of accumulation.[62]

The means Mill offers for this transformation of desire are better government, "an improvement of the public intelligence" through education, and an "introduction of foreign arts" to provide new objects (commodities) for people to desire.[63] This is a familiar plan, which we have seen in Ricardo, one that holds with the eighteenth-century view of national character. But Mill's discussion of the importance of the "desire to accumulate" comes within the "laws" of production, which "partake of the character of physical truths."[64]

Thus he indicates that social institutions like government and education produce the economic "character" of a nation, but he seems to suggest likewise that character is an important cause of disparities in wealth, part of the "physics" of production that precedes human intervention: "There is, in different portions of the human race, a greater diversity than is usually adverted to, in the strength of the effective desire of accumulation. A backward state of general civilization is often more the *effect* of deficiency in this particular, than in many others which attract more attention."[65] National character seems to function as a "supplementary" category in Mill's economics. It is the human feature he wishes to add to what were popularly viewed as mechanistic and cruel systems of political economy, but it slides toward the possibility of an even more sweeping moral justification of poverty on the basis of character. Mill affirms, in his section on the distribution of wealth, that value is, as the utility theorists and De Quincey in particular had urged, a function of consumer demand within a given environment of scarcity. His focus on the level of aggregate "desire" then confirms the central role which the theory of value plays in Mill's system: what people desire is what has value; the more they desire, the more value (wealth) they, as a society, will produce.

This movement parallels the shift in language study quite precisely. Both philology and political economy work toward a positive, empirical, or inductive method of scientific inquiry, in order to overcome what were seen as metaphysical flaws of earlier systems. Both fields find, in their observation of the "physics" of social systems, evidence that the differences among vernacular national/racial groups are fundamental to any understanding of social phenomena. National/racial groups appear to be the only possible category of social analysis, and the Enlightenment concern for universally human dynamics of subject-formation and representation is discarded. Philologists in England argued that the fundamental roots of national languages revealed innate characteristics of a people. Some argued explicitly that these innate ideas were Divinely implanted, and represented the "final causes" of human history.[66] Mill worked strenuously against these premises, producing a ridiculing attack against them in his essay on Whewell. Writing on Famine conditions in Ireland, in a series of *Morning Chronicle* pieces in 1846–47, Mill was equally dismissive of the view that the Famine was caused by any innate characteristics of the Irish.[67] Where Mill and the philologists agree is in arguing that an empirical, scientific study of social forms must lead finally to national character, as the most basic level of social analysis.

JEVONS'S PERFECTED SPEECH

In twentieth-century economics the question of national or individual character goes underground. The positivist revolution Mill foresaw was largely completed in the work of William Stanley Jevons, whose mathematical reformulation of the theory of value set the program for twentieth-century economics. Jevons argued that political economy should not involve itself with moral, social, or characterological questions, believing that "every mind is inscrutable to every other mind."[68] He argued that political economy should confine itself to a numerical analysis of the positive behavior of individuals and groups in the marketplace, and that, to signal its narrowed emphasis on the calculation of relative value, the discipline ought to change its name from "political economy" to "economics" plain and simple.[69] The name change stuck, along with the general housekeeping operation Jevons imagined. "Economics" became increasingly distant from "politics" and cultivated a patina of scientific objectivity based in numerical analysis. It eschewed judgments – traditional in political economy since Adam Smith – about why certain people or nations were rich and others poor, focusing only on concrete actions of economic actors.

In order to avoid "prolixity" and "the inherent defects of the grammar and dictionary for expressing complex relations,"[70] Jevons proposed confining economic analysis to mathematics: "The symbols of mathematical books are not different in nature from language; they form *a perfected system of language*, adapted to the notions and relations which we need to express. They do not constitute the mode of reasoning they embody; they merely facilitate its exhibition and comprehension."[71] In this formulation we see the absolute triumph of a non-phonetic language which had plagued the era of finance capitalism from its first institutions. The "prolixness" of modern languages which Smith worried over is totally recouped here by a "perfected system" of numbers. Against the threat to the agency of thought – to a thinking that precedes its own symbolization – Jevons affirms that mathematical symbols (like any other in his view) simply aid in the "exhibition" of thoughts, the display of an already complete and autonomous will.

But this promise alone would not be enough to dispense with the threat to the subject posed by modern capitalist markets. The math-machine subject of economics is supported, as we have seen in economists since De Quincey, by a reified notion of desire. Jevons continues and completes this reification of subjective desire, and he accomplishes this by setting out a formula to calculate the "degree of utility" perceived by the consumer in any commodity, within its precise environment of supply. This degree of perceived utility – i.e. consumer demand – cannot be measured in any absolute way, he argues, but can be measured in relative terms by noting degrees of consumer preference for one commodity over another. When purchasers on average perceive no advantage in utility between two purchases, the market expresses this equality by giving the two commodities the same price. Thus "every such act of indifferent choice gives rise to an equation of degrees of utility."[72] Every such point of consumer "indifference" marks an equivalence of value; value can be measured by mapping these points in any market.

For Jevons then, the market gives direct evidence of human desire:

I hesitate to say that men will ever have the means of measuring directly the feelings of the human heart. A unit of pleasure or of pain is difficult even to conceive; but it is the amount of these feelings which is continually prompting us to buying and selling, borrowing and lending, labouring and resting, producing and consuming; and *it is from the quantitative effects of the feelings that we must estimate their comparative amounts*. We can no more know nor measure gravity in its own nature than we can measure a feeling; but, just as we measure gravity by its effects in the motion of a pendulum, so we may estimate the equality or inequality of feelings by the decisions of the human mind. The will is our pendulum, and its oscillations are minutely registered in the price lists of the markets.[73]

Rather than being constructed by natural or cultural systems of perception, the human subject in its private, literally unspoken desires, is understood here as a kind of natural force, like gravity, which pushes and pulls social institutions into the forms which most accurately reflect it.

Within this twentieth-century system, differences between individual economic actors, or between national economies, can only be understood as evidence of different forms of autonomous desire. Jevons refused to directly consider social and moral reasons for poverty, citing his belief in the "inscrutability" of motives and causes. But while he argued that the question of why people behave as they do in the market should be outside the scope of economics, a racial, characterological foundation of economic behavior still underlies his system. He argues that "in minds of much intelligence and foresight, the greatest force of feeling and motive arises from the anticipation of a long-continued future."[74] That is, the desire to accumulate – to save capital against future uses – varies according to the level of mental advancement. In this way Jevons suggests that wealth is an implicit measure of racial intelligence and economic prudence. Capitalist economic development can be interpreted as an index of mental and moral development. "That class or race of men who have the most foresight," Jevons writes, "will work most for the future. The untutored savage, like the child, is wholly occupied with the pleasures and the troubles of the moment; the morrow is dimly felt; the limit of his horizon is but a few days off."[75]

It is with this turn that the market as understood generally in twentieth-century economics emerges: a neutral arena where all street-level distinctions among economic actors are denied, and where each is seen simply as the agent of his or her desire. Since acts in the market are theorized as authentic acts of will, economic relations and contracts are considered always to be voluntary and non-coercive. History and material conditions are presumed irrelevant to economic acts, at the level of their psychological origin. Within this system, poverty – whether individual or national – can be explained implicitly as a matter of choice, merit, intelligence, or natural prudence. It is with this final turn that the metaphysical dangers of basing value on desire are finally reduced to acceptable levels. Imprudent, excessive, destructive, or selfish desires – which were seen in the eighteenth century as both dangerous and inevitable in finance capitalism – are completely marginalized here, contained with an orientalized femininity.

To understand this transformation, we have to see nineteenth-century political economy as increasingly structured by romantic modes of understanding. Gradually after Adam Smith, the materialist psychology emergent in Locke, and which I have described in relation to Condillac, became associated with the apology for capitalism. The materialist theory of the subject, from the point of view of the romantic generation, seems entirely consumed with what Wordsworth called "getting and spending" – the jealous economic activity which "lays waste our powers." In Carlyle's rhetoric materialist psychology is associated with the "cold rationality" of the machine. Against the theory that humans begin life as screens of sense perception, developing according to whatever linguistic and mental technologies they are exposed to, the romantic reaction against capitalism posits a subject replete with sentimental attachments and aesthetic responses, which capitalism gradually perverts.

This romantic reaction against the market and the machine has been one of the most enduring subjects of English literary history. What it is crucial to understand, however, is that the romantic theory of a human nature which underwrote the cultural critique of capitalism in this era also provided bourgeois political economists with the means to theorize the ultimate triumph of capitalism. This is the thesis I explore in the following chapters: that the defense of the market and the reaction against it in the mid-nineteenth century share the same fundamental assumptions. This was a formative era for the patterns of modern culture, establishing paradigmatic responses to the institutionalization of market capitalism, a process which, in its global dimensions, we continue to live out today. The expressive theory of the romantic subject, the artist who makes an internal quest to strip away the layers of acculturation and find his most natural responses and desires, and then represents them in language, corresponds exactly to the dominant theory of economic value which takes hold after the 1870s in England, where the desire of the individual economic agent is assumed to be inherent in the individual, an authentic indicator of selfhood, which finds its objective representation in the commodity.

Just as recent critical studies in language and literature have sought to displace the intentional subject of literary creation, so we need now to challenge the expressivist subject of economics. In the following chapters, I try to contribute to this project by tracing this subject-position of economic thought as it appears through the middle decades of the nineteenth century, in a variety of literary, journalistic, and political texts. Just as with the romantic conception of the artist, it took a great deal of cultural work to make the subjectivity of the consumer seem inevitable and universal, although today it is taken as the starting point for any conception of economic relations. It is the highly contested emergence of this subject, and of a world around it, which I try to understand in the texts I consider below.

PART II

Producing the consumer

My argument in this book is that modern economic theory was formed
not simply in the private studies of Victorian political economists, but in a
broad matrix of philosophical and literary debate. Out of this debate, across
the nineteenth century, emerged the figure of the consumer, as an abstract
and universal outline of human experience. I began in Part I by suggesting
that political economy was from the start riven by the tensions between a
new financial order and the European tradition of knowledge and authority.
The rapid movement of financial markets, since the earliest trading on Bank
of England shares at the turn of the eighteenth century, was seen as a threat
to the stable authority and secure self-knowledge of the property owner. I
argued that this threat can best be understood if we see the new financial
markets as a regime of non-phonetic writing. Hindu-arabic numerals are a
non-phonetic code; where alphabetic writing records the sounds of spoken
words, numbers represent abstract quantities. The financial revolution of
the early eighteenth century held out the threat that social power would
henceforth be negotiated in the language of numbers: price lists, discount
rates, interest. Numbers represent the potential demolition of everything
associated in the European tradition with phonetic writing. Writing here
is always at the service of speech, and speech itself is seen as a more or
less accurate representation of the secure and stable ideas produced within
the mind. Numbers referred to quantitative truths which seemed to exist
on their own, independent of any human agency. Financial numbers had
the power not only to influence but to undermine or destroy the secure
authority of the propertied citizen.

To resolve this tension, it would be necessary to rearrange the terms
of debate, in order to bring the capitalist marketplace and its language of
numbers under the big tent of European idealism. Defenders of financial
capitalism had to show that the language of numbers could be controlled
and tamed by individual market actors, that individuals could effectively

73

express their will through their actions in the marketplace. The final stage in this transformation is announced by William Stanley Jevons in 1871, when he writes that numbers and mathematical symbols "form a perfected system of language."[1] In Part I I laid out the starting and ending points of this enormous change within economic theory, a change which is indicated in the disappearance of "political economy" and the rise of the new discipline of "economics." The goal of Part II is to begin to understand how this massive shift occurred.

What I have asserted is that the rise of economics relied on a broad redefinition of individual life in capitalist societies. This redefined individual is what we now call a consumer. Neoclassical economics, in the twentieth and twenty-first centuries, only rarely confronts its assumptions about the nature of human perception and agency. Indeed the very durability of economics as a modern discipline derives in part from the fact that its assumptions about human subjects and communities appear to need no direct exposition or defense. That is, by the close of the nineteenth century, these assumptions were accepted as common sense, as a universal framework for human social existence. This consensus was built and contested in the popular press of the nineteenth century. In what follows I have chosen a number of test cases from this popular discourse: four major works of fiction, and a set of statements on the Irish economy during the time of the great Famine, 1845–52. In chapters on novels, I work with some texts which confront economic issues head on – Elizabeth Gaskell's *Mary Barton* (1848) and *North and South* (1854–55) – as well as those which, though they have long been understood as social problem novels, have generally not been considered in connection with economic activity or Victorian economic thought – Charles Dickens's *Bleak House* (1852–53), Gaskell's *Cranford* (1851–53). What I have aimed at is not a comprehensive survey of economic theory in Victorian fiction. Rather, I have focused on the novels which seem to me to address the most fundamental questions that plagued political economy in the mid-nineteenth century: the agency of individuals and the nature of their actions in the market. The readings below do not provide a catalogue of economic concepts or lessons in these texts but rather try to understand how each one addresses these fundamental issues in Victorian political economy.

My method here derives most centrally from recent work on the relationship between the novel and the social and natural sciences in the Victorian period. A number of studies in the 1990s offered new ways of understanding works of Victorian fiction as embedded in an emerging consumer economy, and I have described the approach these works take in my general introduction above. But most fundamentally it is not economic *context* I am concerned with here; it is economic *theory*. And in this way, my approach derives perhaps more importantly from the innovative work of Gillian Beer and George Levine. In two studies of Victorian fiction and the work of Charles Darwin, these authors assert a common discursive terrain for literature and the sciences, showing the potential for not just influence but subtle interdependence between the two.[2] I take this common terrain as a premise here. But indeed, as students of Victorian culture are already well aware, we need no abstract theoretical staging to support the idea that literature and, in particular, economic theory participate in a common dialogue during the nineteenth century. The figures I focus on below make this link quite evident: Walter Bagehot, financial journalist and prolific literary reviewer; Elizabeth Gaskell, who suggested in the preface to her first (anonymous) novel that she knew "nothing of Political Economy, or the theories of trade" and yet wrote with demonstrable insight on these subjects;[3] Thomas De Quincey, who forged a Coleridgean defense of Ricardo; and Charles Dickens, who tried to cure Malthus of his apparent grumpiness in *A Christmas Carol*.

I focus on specific works of these authors because they contributed centrally to the process of cultural change I have argued for. But there is a historical rationale for these choices as well. The major texts I treat were published between 1844 and 1855. If it is true that classical political economy died in the nineteenth century, then the date on its tombstone would fall somewhere within these years. Intellectual trends do not expire all at once, of course, and something still called "political economy" continued to be studied. But the chaotic events of the 1840s, the devastation of the Irish economy, the close of the railroad boom, and the market crash of 1847, threw political economy into a defensive and destabilized position. I explore the significance of these historical events at the start of chapter 3 below. Here I will only point out that, as Eric Hobsbawm suggested long ago, during the periodic crises of the 1830s and 1840s, and before the relative prosperity of the 1850s, it was by no means clear that the system that came to be called capitalism would be able to survive.[4] Even in the atmosphere of rising wages and productivity in the early 1850s, well-informed observers like Walter Bagehot were openly cautious. "That money is abundant," Bagehot wrote in 1852, "is a fact; why it is abundant, is a theory."[5] The novels I consider here were written and read during this era of crisis and tentative recovery, and they participate in a reconsideration of the market and its ideologies. Gaskell's *Mary Barton* and *North and South* have long been categorized as industrial novels and read as commentaries on the factory system. But in positioning these two novels alongside *Cranford* and Dickens's *Bleak House*, and in avoiding Dickens's self-consciously "industrial" novel *Hard Times*, I highlight the fact that these are novels not just about industrial build-up but about financial markets, and about the market as a mode of social organization.

The relevance of these texts to a broader rethinking of capitalism can be confirmed by comparing them to specific statements on economic policy during this time. This is the task of chapter 4, which examines pieces of the debate over the untold hundreds of thousands who died in Ireland between 1845 and 1852. What caused this extraordinary suffering, how it might be alleviated, what might result from it: These questions formed one heated center of economic debate in this era, and the terms of this debate, I will argue, correlate clearly with those employed by Dickens and Gaskell, as they think through related stories of human suffering.

A major cultural shift of the kind I am arguing for can only be understood to happen through a series of interdependent causes and instruments. If it is true that what I have called the figure of the consumer emerges in this era as a new model for understanding the human subject, then the causes of that change can only be seen as overdetermined. My claim is not that, some time around 1850, the novel created the consumer, nor that the Irish Famine killed Adam Smith. Rather, by triangulating works of fiction with examples of economic policy and arguments within economic theory, I try to understand one aspect of modern culture. If that element of modern thought, consumerism, has attained now to the status of common sense – in academic economics, in politics, and in popular culture – then it becomes only more important that we understand the heterogeneity of its origins.

CHAPTER 3

Market indicators: banking and housekeeping
in Bleak House

In 1858 Walter Bagehot, finance writer and editor of *The Economist*, published a review essay on Charles Dickens. In it he writes:

Mr. Dickens's genius is especially suited to the delineation of city life. London is like a newspaper. Everything is there, and everything is disconnected . . . As we change from the broad leader to the squalid police-report, we pass a corner and we are in a changed world. This is advantageous to Mr. Dickens's genius. His memory is full of instances of old buildings and curious people, and he does not care to piece them together.[1]

Bagehot argues here that Dickens's strength is in representing the discontinuity of modern urban life: the clashing juxtapositions, and the odd simultaneity of unrelated events in every second of the urban clock. This temporality of the "disconnected" ("we pass a corner and we are in a changed world") is what Walter Benjamin refers to in the famous formulation "homogeneous, empty time," the time of the newspaper, the telegraph, the crowd, a time that attenuates the telos of the Christian calendar.[2] But for Bagehot this discontinuity of simultaneous lives is merely a semblance, a surface effect that belies a hidden order. The "disconnectedness" of events and objects in Dickens becomes, as Bagehot's argument in the review develops, not a condition of history but rather a quirk of Dickens's imagination itself, a symptom of his "irregular genius" (CD 80). Thus the *seeming* disunity of the city is "advantageous" to Dickens's "irregular" mind. While Dickens exhibits a "detective ingenuity in microscopic detail," his works have no "mark of unity" (CD 84). It is not that the city has no "order" then, even though its life can appear quite random to the observer; it is just that Dickens is unable to perceive the "symmetry and unity" (CD 85) which binds this apparent chaos into a functioning whole ("he does not care to piece them together"). Bagehot's dissatisfaction with Dickens is a crucial one, for it illustrates two typical views of the process of capitalist modernization in this period. Is modern life, typified by the experience of

77

the city, in fact a chaotic patchwork of random and unrelated events, or is there, as Bagehot would argue, some underlying principle which organizes the systems of modern life in symmetrical fashion?

Bleak House deals with the lawsuit of Jarndyce and Jarndyce, a complex inheritance case that involves characters from every class of English society, from the homeless child, Jo, in the city, to Sir Leicester and Lady Honoria Dedlock in their Lincolnshire estate. As the novel opens the narrative flaunts its seeming fragmentation, as it depicts a bewildering number of new characters and scenes that seem related only through the various tangents of the lawsuit.

What connexion can there be, between the place in Lincolnshire, the house in town . . . the whereabouts of Jo the outlaw with the broom, who had the distant ray of light upon him when he swept the churchyard-step? What connexion can there have been between many people in the innumerable histories of this world, who, from opposite sides of great gulfs, have, nevertheless, been very curiously brought together![3]

The rhetorical questions serve to assure the reader that there is in fact some "connexion" which will be uncovered as the narrative progresses. But while in one way the novel wonders over the way the court can "bring together" all of English society, in another way it theorizes a fundamental discontinuity. The function of inheritance law is to insure that writing accurately transmits power and property, but in *Bleak House* the written documents of the Court of Chancery become endlessly confused. While the documents are meant to represent, and thus to guarantee, the circulation of property, the legal papers simply create a circulation of their own, one which moves chaotically, never progressing toward a solution to the case. In Chancery then, writing constantly *defers* judgment, rather than settling *differences*. When the one document that might solve the case – a definitive will – does finally come to light, its content proves wholly irrelevant because the case has already consumed the estate in legal fees. The omniscient narrator thus pronounces that "the one great principle of the English Law is, to make business for itself" (*BH* 603). But the failure of the law to do anything but continue its own procedures seems to threaten every other aspect of life depicted in the novel, as every social process seems increasingly governed by bureaucratic systems like the court's. The Jarndyce suit is like the unnavigable clutter in Krook's chandlery shop: one key piece of recycled junk could prove the solution to each of these great mazes, but both Krook and the Jarndyce suit consume themselves "spontaneously," before the key piece is found. The bureaucratic administration of charity in Mrs. Jellyby's house is also shown to consume its own object, as the engineering of charity abroad produces only neglect at home. Narrative "connexions" will indeed emerge, over the course of the novel's nineteen original monthly numbers, but in Chancery, nothing ever quite fits together. The court is a system of writing, and while its writing persists, its meaning never clarifies.

The most ambitious critical studies of *Bleak House* have understood the novel's account of Chancery as a model of other complex systems. In J. Hillis Miller's 1971 reading, Chancery is a figure for the radical impossibility of the linguistic sign, illustrating a universal "sickness in the sign-making power."[4] For D. A. Miller, systems in the novel enfold and discipline subjects in public networks even as they struggle most for private, domestic identities.[5] Bruce Robbins, in an argument about professions and professionalization in Victorian society, suggests that *Bleak House* theorizes the limitations of human action within bureaucratic systems of administration.[6] I will be interested here in the novel's relationship to the sort of systems Bagehot spent most of his time thinking about: markets. The Court's chaos of representation points most strongly toward the agentless and inhuman writing of market capitalism. Though it is the policeman who constantly enjoins Jo, the homeless crossing-sweeper, to "move on" in the novel (*BH* 319–20), it is the accelerated motion and increasing abstraction of value itself that is the novel's fundamental motive force. *Bleak House* depicts a circulation without end or essence. In its portrait of Chancery, the novel links the problem of economic value with the problem of linguistic representation, treating market circulation as a crisis of meaning. In this way the novel plays a part in the mid-nineteenth century realignment of both economic and linguistic paradigms. It experiments with the problems of agency, intention, and value at the center of both political economy and philology in the early Victorian period.

It may be true, as Karl Polanyi once wrote, that "there is nothing natural about *laissez-faire*"; it required intense administrative and legislative effort in the 1830s and 1840s to set up the procedures of free trade.[7] But by the middle of the nineteenth century, with this new state bureaucracy in place, it certainly *looked* as if all commodities were flowing in a self-sustaining and independent system. Polanyi's term for this condition is "the commodity fiction" – the appearance that all human and natural resources are equally interchangeable elements of the market.[8] However, the more exchangeable all things are (through legislative construct), the more the value of any particular thing is destabilized, as it becomes subject to any fluctuation of the market. In Dickens's terms, the more things are drawn into "connexion," the more chaotic and fragmented they will appear.

Anxiety about the instability of market prices is not new in this era; it had been a prevalent feature of public discourse in Britain at least since the earliest debates about the founding of the Bank of England in the 1690s.[9] This instability was often conceived through the metaphor of femininity. The lack of "substance" in paper money and stock shares, and the groundless plunge of prices in a market crash, were figured as castrating threats to the institutions of male authority, in property, inheritance, and the transmission of the family name. However, as I have tried to show in chapter 2, by the middle of the nineteenth century the strategies Smith and Ricardo had devised to keep the threat of the market's "fickleness" at bay had been gradually discredited. In political economy and in popular culture, these rhetorical strategies had to be reinvented, for the rapid build-up of rail and financial infrastructure in the 1840s only made value more difficult to fix.

Throughout Part I I argued that in the first half of the nineteenth century the theory of value within mainstream political economy became a theory of signification. This new theory, oriented around utility and consumer-demand, took its form from the philological theory of the speaking subject. Value is authored by the intentionality of the purchaser; value inhabits the mind of the consumer and is represented outwardly by the commodity. *Bleak House* presents a model of this kind of world, where value functions in representation, and the market is a semiotic system. However, whereas political economists like Whately and Longfield (and De Quincey, as I will argue here) saw commodities as neutral signs that could express human will, *Bleak House* portrays signs of value as deadly things, never quite within their user's control. In response to this dangerous instability, however, Dickens is just as eager as Bagehot himself to reground the market system with some sort of metaphysical principle of "unity." Each writer attempts rhetorically to pin value down within some more limited and orderly circuit. Two parallel metaphors emerge from this project of ordering the chaos of circulation: the central bank and the private home.

1847

Although an English historian once famously declared that "of all decades in our history, a wise man would choose the eighteen-fifties to be young in," there was reason for even the youth of 1850 to be uneasy.[10] Harvests were good at the start of this decade, and agricultural profits were high. It was in this context that Bagehot made the remark I mentioned above: "That money is abundant, is a fact; why it is abundant, is a theory."[11] The cause of the easy economic conditions was not clearly identifiable, and Bagehot warns against "a feverish and irrational excitement" for speculation.[12] The most recent period of crisis had been particularly devastating. Between 1845 and 1850, some million Irish had starved or died from common diseases in the workhouses.[13] In its human cost the Irish Famine of these years was one of the most devastating economic events of the nineteenth century. A British government aid campaign was mounted along lines dictated by liberal economic principles, but, as with the teaching of political economy in the Irish state school system in this era, economic principles were seen as a way to discipline the economically irrational or profligate Irish rather than a way to feed hungry people.[14] The fact that a whole generation died despite this scheme shook a number of political economy's confident assertions: that wealth and goods flowed according to Providential control; that economic hardship led to spiritually beneficial chastening of the soul; that hunger could spark a healthy drive toward self-advancement; that free trade principles, if strictly adhered to, would bring food to where the demand for it was highest.[15] But the crisis in English finance that coincided with the Famine's worst year, 1847, spread an even more appalling brand of economic uncertainty. As the prices of highly inflated railroad stocks plummeted during the course of this year, observers frequently argued that the crash was caused by the bad harvests in Ireland, which caused an unusual drain on English gold reserves, spent on purchases of foreign grain. But alongside these common explanations sat the uncomfortable perception that the wild fluctuation of share prices was caused not by any agricultural event, but by the structure of the market itself.

A debate over the causes of what was called "the commercial crisis of 1847" raged throughout the following year in the reports of three Parliamentary commissions and numerous books and reviews. Because of the large number of banks and firms that failed, the crisis was viewed by some as the worst of the century,[16] but there was another reason why its causes should be a source of such concern. Three years earlier, the monetary system of the country had been restructured in the Bank Charter Act of 1844, devised under the direction of then Prime Minister Robert Peel. The Act was conceived as a response to the financial crises of 1825, 1837, and 1839, which Peel and others felt had resulted from the reckless issue of bank notes. Paper notes could be issued by any private or joint-stock bank in this era, their worth guaranteed only by the assurance of each issuing bank. In 1825 in particular, there were runs on the currency of numerous small banks, many of which simply shut their doors for good, leaving worthless notes in the hands of their customers. The instability of unregulated paper could be corrected, according to Peel and his followers, by gradually centralizing note issues at a single state bank, the Bank of England, and by limiting the Bank's note issues strictly in proportion to its gold reserves and securities. This would stabilize the value of paper currency, and guarantee the convertibility of bank notes into gold. The Bank of England was restructured into two theoretically separate entities: an issue department responsible for currency, and a banking department to carry on the normal business of loans and deposits.[17] The new system was intended to prevent the loss of investments due to speculative or excessive issue of notes. The issue department at the Bank of England was strictly separated from the profit-making wing; its only responsibility was to monitor the amount of the paper circulation and to publish weekly accounts of gold and securities on deposit.

To understand why politicians would seek to stabilize prices by standardizing the currency system, we need first to understand the representative function that money serves. While commodities only realize their value by dropping out of circulation and being consumed, money circulates constantly. Money thus takes on an appearance of constancy and regular motion, an appearance of representing "the economy" itself. As Marx puts it, "the movement of the circulation process of commodities is . . . represented by the movement of money as the medium of circulation, *i.e.*, by the *circulation of money*."[18] Or more directly: "As a medium of circulation, [money] has a circulation of its own."[19] The misrecognition of money becomes total at the point where it appears self-producing, that is, when the bank loan becomes institutionalized, and it begins to look "as if interest is the specific fruit of capital."[20] Within this final "fetish form" of capital,[21] production and social labor seem irrelevant, supplementary by-products of the state of capital itself.[22] In the Charter Act of 1844 then, we see one phase in the development of a distinctly modern form of knowledge. Solutions to complex social problems are sought within a fetishized sphere of capital, what we now call "the economy."

When interest-bearing capital reaches this fetishized form, the circulation process of money appears to be total; the exchangeability of money has to be considered infinite in order for it to "represent" the circulation process itself. As an article in Bagehot's *Economist* put it in 1851, "Capital, with compound interest on every portion of capital saved, is so all-engrossing that all the wealth in the world from which income is derived, has long ago become the interest of capital."[23] But if everything is capital, then the frequent crashes in market prices seem to threaten everything; the fantasy of a total circulation brings with it the threat of total indeterminacy. If everything is just a price, what happens when all prices crash overnight?

The 1844 Bank Charter Act addressed the threat of market crashes on the level of the currency as a fetish – a historical effect which is invested with the power of natural causation. Peel's contingent, the so-called "Currency School," followed Ricardo's theory of currency, which argued that changes in the supply of paper money, without corresponding changes in gold reserves, would create a premium on gold and cause inflationary pressure.[24] They believed that prices would rise when too much money was issued and public confidence in paper notes dropped. This lag in confidence would cause a run on issuing banks, and a proportional decrease in the volume of currency available. To prevent this, Peel's Act tied paper money to specific quantities of gold in the vault of the Bank of England. Against the dangers of a total circulation, the Charter Act posited a circulation that was ordered and regular, where notes issued by the Bank would return in predictable and uniform circuits, so that the total amount of currency needed in the country at any one time could be accurately predicted.

Supporters of the Act soon discovered, however, that this was not enough to prevent a panic. Early in 1845, public demand for railway stocks began to rise, as the country embraced the optimistic predictions of a horde of railway developers. One commentator, writing from the near remove of 1848, characterized the incipient boom as follows: "The power of steam; the humanizing influence of a close connexion between the refinements of the city and the requirements of the hamlet were all eloquently announced. London was to receive the superfluities of the village; the village was to be gladdened with the civilization of London."[25] The "connexions" afforded by rail were thought capable of producing an even internal flow of trade, which would transfer wealth and strength to every corner of a recently and still uncomfortably "united" kingdom. Railroads, this same writer noted, were "emblems of internal confidence."[26] Between 1844 and 1848 more than six hundred new joint-stock rail companies sought investors.[27] In this atmosphere, the Banking Department of the Bank of England, eager to demonstrate that it was still out to compete vigorously with other lenders, offered loans at extremely low rates; interest rates stayed low throughout the country. Money was easily available to developers, and the boom was on.[28] A competing broker at a private bank described the Bank of England in these months as "canvassing for discounts and fomenting transactions."[29]

By the late fall of 1845, the extent of potato crop failures in Ireland was becoming known. Gradually convinced of the coming crisis, Peel initiated a plan to import North American maize, which the government would release cheaply into Irish wholesale markets to prevent food prices in Ireland becoming prohibitively high. This attempt to lower prices of food in Ireland made it unreasonable for Peel to support elevated food prices in England, the result of the import tariffs mandated by the Corn Laws.[30] With the backing of most of his cabinet, Peel abandoned the traditional position of his party and advocated for the Corn Laws' repeal. As foreign grain became cheaper, however, when these tariffs were abolished, and as demand for food in Ireland promised to become morbidly high, private corn merchants began importing grain on speculation. The resulting glut did little to help the Irish, but in August 1847 the price of corn fell by nearly one half, and large numbers of established corn merchants went bankrupt.[31] By this time investors had stopped buying railroad stocks, and, as the market dried up, the railroad companies and the banks that had loaned money to them were short of cash. The amount of paper in circulation at this point had spiked, according to evidence presented to one Parliamentary committee, by £4 million above normal levels; Members concluded that the public – gripped with fear that the Bank of England would fail and default on all its deposits – was hoarding notes, rather than investing them or placing them on deposit.[32] But with so much paper already out, it was impossible for the Issue Department to release notes to make new loans, which were in demand from businesses unable to pay their bills.

On October 25, 1847, the Treasury intervened by relaxing the limits of the Act of 1844 to allow the Bank to make new loans in paper currency, even if the notes with which new loans were paid out drove the volume of the circulation to previously illegal levels. The panic subsided almost instantly; demand for loans dropped. As one director of a private bank reported, "the effect was immediate. Those who had sent Notice for their Money in the Morning sent us Word that they did not want it – they had only ordered Payment by way of Precaution . . . From that day we had a market of comparative ease."[33]

In the House of Commons report of 1848, the first cause cited for the crisis of 1847 is the Irish Famine: "There has been a general concurrence of opinion amongst the witnesses examined before Your Committee, that the primary cause of the Distress was the deficient harvest, especially of the potato crop, in the year 1847, for the unprecedented importations of various descriptions of Food which took place in that year."[34] This committee, headed by Peel himself, largely supported the Act of 1844 and argued in its report that the Act had prevented a more devastating crash which might have resulted if banks had been allowed to issue notes indiscriminately. The House of Lords Committee, however, was stacked with Members who opposed a state monopoly in currency. They argued that the

1844 Act had actually exacerbated the panic, giving the business community and general public an exaggerated sense of the scarcity of money. Because it attempts to fix partial blame on the 1844 Act, the House of Lords' report is less absolute in its explanations of the crash:

A sudden and unexampled demand for foreign corn, produced by a Failure in many Descriptions of Agricultural produce throughout the United Kingdom, coincided with the unprecedented Extent of Speculation produced by increased Facilities of Credit and a low Rate of Interest [i.e., that caused by the Banking Department], and had for some Time occasioned Over-Trading in many Branches of Commerce.[35]

J. C. Clapham's often-cited economic history of this era also stresses over-speculation: "the gambling spirit of the railway mania had left the general trade of the country full of weak spots."[36]

As Peel's committee showed, however, it was still possible to fix the Irish situation as primary cause of the crisis. Disraeli also, in an 1848 speech, declared unequivocally that "the Famine in Ireland led to the Commercial crisis."[37] His address is excerpted at length in David Morier Evans's *The Commercial Crisis* (1848), a book-length description of the crash by a London financial journalist. Evans's account is a compilation of statements and statistics, not an overall analysis of the bankruptcies. However, this passage, quoted without comment, clashes with Evans's careful documentation in preceding pages of the extent of overspeculation by private investors, businesses, and banks, both on railways and, in a gruesome attempt to profit on hunger, through the purchase of foreign corn. The bulk of Evans's evidence indicates that the collapse of these markets had little to do with the infestation of fungus on Scottish and Irish potatoes; it had to do with the structure of the market that could create and destroy wealth out of nothing more solid than perceptions of public mood.

But even those who defended Peel's Act, and cited the potato blight as the real cause of the crisis, still assumed that the market was subject as much to the vicissitudes of consumer perception as to real fluctuations in the supply of vital commodities. Charles Wood, Chancellor of the Exchequer, for instance, said in defense of the Act that the government's decision to relax its limits in October of 1847 actually worked in accordance with the principles of the Act itself. The Act, he argued, had been designed to prevent the issue of notes as bogus substitutes for metallic currency, but the extra notes released at the height of the panic were merely needed to reassure public fears about the solidity of the currency. He argued that these extra notes were authorized "not to create capital – not to support credit, which had no security – but to quiet public fear and alarm."[38] The extra issues were not technically capital, according to Wood; they were issued to stand for something like persuasion, affect, or confidence.

Wood's twisted logic was probably not widely endorsed. But both extremes of opinion on the Charter Act demonstrate that in the wake of this crash it was generally recognized that price fluctuations could as easily be caused by the structure of markets themselves as by the supply or quality of real goods and services. That is to say, the thing markets were meant to negotiate – economic value – could be created as much by the markets themselves as by the essential qualities of the things they were designed to trade.

Another way to state the lesson of 1847 is to say that the more trade is systematized in exchange, the more unstable it becomes. As all objects are potentially linked by money (and the national standardization of bank notes begun in 1844 was a watershed in this process), other patterns among objects appear random. Rail development, as we saw above, was thought to establish profitable "connexions" between all parts of society, just as a standardized currency was thought to connect all markets with a reliable medium of exchange. But what resulted from this totally connected network was not the "symmetry and unity" Bagehot looked for, but rather the fragmented world he found in Dickens's novels: "everything is there, and everything is disconnected."

THE BLEAKNESS OF THE HOUSE: THE NOVEL'S SYSTEMS AND METAPHORS

Chancery as market

What the 1847 crash seems to have demonstrated was the danger that a system of total exchange would produce a chaotic circulation, and a final instability of value. This is precisely the problem *Bleak House* takes up, and the novel produces a fantastically detailed model of just such a total system, with all its symbolic dangers. The novel's opening chapter, "In Chancery," depicts one afternoon court session when Jarndyce and Jarndyce is being heard. The suit, we learn, "has, in course of time, become so complicated that no man alive knows what it means . . . Innumerable children have been born into the cause; innumerable young people have married into it; innumerable old people have died out of it" (*BH* 52). In its complexity, the case seems to have encompassed every possible nuance of the entire system of Chancery law; one of its solicitors is "supposed never to have read anything else since he left school" (*BH* 53), and another lawyer remarks that in Jarndyce and Jarndyce "every difficulty, every contingency, every masterly fiction, every form of procedure known in that court, is represented over and over again" (*BH* 68).

This never-ending process of representation is handled by a series of solicitors, Chizzle, Dizzle, and Mizzle, whose names are as interchangeable as machine parts. Along with the other solicitors in the case, they are "ranged in a line" (*BH* 50) before the court, and when called upon by the Lord Chancellor they, "each armed with a little summary of eighteen hundred sheets, bob up like eighteen hammers in a pianoforte" (*BH* 54). The machine-like court – a "slow mill" as it is later called (*BH* 102) – churns on smoothly, but it produces nothing but itself, training generations of new lawyers and clerks who use the case to "flesh[] their legal wit" (*BH* 52).

But while the court effectively blocks the process of patronymic trans-mission – the passage of symbolic and economic power between men – it does insure a patriarchy of its own. The case has spanned the careers of many of its solicitors, "some two of three of whom have inherited it from their fathers" (*BH* 50), and witnessed "a long procession of Lord Chan-cellors" (*BH* 52). The court thus preserves its own formal organization of power while failing to order its social content: the property cases it takes up. The novel's final pronouncement on this state of things seems to be the remark I quoted above: "The one great principle of the English law is, to make business for itself" (*BH* 603). Marx makes the same point about the currency system after 1844. He surveys reports from merchants and small bankers who claimed that the effect of the 1844 Act was to increase com-petition for loans and keep interest rates artificially high. "And this high rate of interest," Marx comments, "was precisely the aim of the Act."[39] In other words, the system designed to insure efficient transmission of value insured only its own enrichment.

In the course of the novel we see every level of legal work "from the master . . . down to the copying-clerk in the Six Clerks' Office, who has copied his tens of thousands of Chancery-folio-pages under that eternal heading" (*BH* 53). We see law offices of every quality, from the chambers of the Lord Chancellor to the garret of a copyist. The novel investigates every turn in this highly differentiated system and in every location points out the way the court functions as a material network, a vast circulation of paper and ink. The lawyers all carry their gigantic "summaries," and the registrars of the court sit beneath the Lord Chancellor, "with bills, cross-bills, answers, rejoinders, injunctions, affidavits, issues, references to masters, masters' reports, mountains of costly nonsense, piled before them" (*BH* 50). In a later chapter called "The Law Writer" we visit the shop of the legal stationer, Snagsby, who carries, along with every variety of paper and pen, "all sorts of blank forms of legal process" (*BH* 178); we move then to the decrepit bed-sit of a copyist named Nemo – just one, presumably, among thousands of such "nameless" law writers – his desk "a wilderness marked with a rain of ink" (*BH* 188). The papers of Chancery swirl throughout the text in similarly random storms, producing "mountains," "cartloads of paper" (*BH* 145), "wicked heaps of paper" (*BH* 146), "reams of dusty warrants" (*BH* 53). The case never comes to decision in the novel but is consumed by costs – that is, all its money goes to the legal system itself, rather than to any deserving suitor. This vast circulation of writing yields only, as the first chapter puts it, costly non-sense: a pure materiality of writing, an infinite semiosis, a language that does not signify, but only increases itself.

But while the legal system manages to sustain itself, the court's constant deferral causes panic and disaster for the men who appeal to the court to settle their inheritances. Hint of a potential inheritance has inspired suitors in the case with a manic desire for money, and Jarndyce and Jarndyce is so encompassing that possible beneficiaries are, as the first chapter says, "innumerable." They believe meaning will emerge from the "cartloads of paper" in the suit. But Chancery is a language network that observes only the pure circulation of the material sign. The piles of paper that comprise the suit signify nothing but piles of paper. They move in a circulation without rest, without profit, without closure. Thus "the little plaintiff or defendant, who was promised a new rocking-horse when Jarndyce and Jarndyce should be settled, has grown up, possessed himself of a real horse, and trotted away into the other world . . . the legion of bills in the suit have been transformed into mere bills of mortality" (*BH* 52). The money in the suit, far from building Adam Smith's "waggon-way through the air," is a conveyance only to death.[40]

In his famous reading of Balzac's 1830 "Sarrazine," Roland Barthes writes: "replacing the feudal index, the bourgeois sign is a metonymic confusion."[41] The events of late 1840s had the effect of eroding stable connections between the signs of wealth (bank notes, commodities) and any stable quantity of value (in gold or land), let alone any personal qualities of the wealthy class. In the case of bank notes, while the Bank Act of 1844 sought to guarantee in the mind of the commercial public the convertibility of notes to gold, the major positions in the debate demonstrate that convertibility is a legal fiction, not a metaphysical axiom. In the case of land, the controversy over the causes of the commercial crisis disputed any natural connection between the movement of the market and a natural order of values rising from rents or agricultural produce. Dickens's response to these conditions is to recast the relationship to the sign in the terms Barthes describes here. The unstoppable motion of exchangeable commodities in the market is a kind of infinite semiosis, pulling value into a constant and unfixed motion. The failing systems in *Bleak House* point to – more than the legendary ineffectuality of lawyers – the condition Barthes calls "metonymic confusion," a static horizontal circulation of the signifier, without transcendence to any principle of signification.

Thus the problem is not just that the suit itself ruins people; rather, Chancery's principle of "metonymic confusion" seems to be operating everywhere else in English society as well. The title of chapter 2 is "In Fashion," and it invites us to see that fashionable society "is not so unlike the Court of Chancery" (*BH* 55). Aristocratic society in the novel centers on Sir Leicester and Lady Honoria Dedlock. Before marriage, we are told, Lady Dedlock had no money of her own, but Sir Leicester's "wealth and station . . . soon floated her upward" (*BH* 57). Having found her own level, to use the metaphor of the free market that the text employs, she finds only that she is "bored to death" (*BH* 56). That is, the variety of houses and estates her husband owns, the elaborate and tasteful commodities they contain, and the round of fashionable companions she has at her disposal, have become interchangeable to her; none retains any inherent qualities that make it more desirable than any other.[42] Her boredom places her within a declining aristocratic tradition of feminine display and consumption of leisure entertainments.[43] Aristocratic, anti-domestic femininity in the text is an endless consumption without satisfaction, a Chancery-like movement of objects that voids their essential qualities. To consume in this way is to be "bored to death," and thus again the principle of an unlimited interchangeability carries with it the touch of mortality.

These definitive portraits of systems – in Chancery, and in Fashion – are reinforced and redrawn throughout the novel. Mr. Gridley, another Chancery suitor, enlarges the point with his constant railing against "the system" (*BH* 268). Representational government is shown to be another "grid-like" network; its interchangeable candidates Doodle, Coodle, and Boodle, like the solicitors of Jarndyce and Jarndyce, are equally ineffectual. Mrs. Jellyby's bureaucratic system for the administration of charity abroad is shown to produce only chaos and neglect at home. Her daughter and amanuensis, Caddy, works in a room "strewn with papers," and is herself blotted, like Nemo's desk, "in such a state of ink" (*BH* 85). Because of its unnavigable clutter, Mr. Krook's chandlery shop is nicknamed "Chancery," and himself "the Lord Chancellor" (*BH* 100). In Krook's enormous collection of used junk is eventually found the single document that all the parties in the Jarndyce suit are looking for: a definitive Jarndyce will. But, like the case that consumes its money in fees, Krook himself is found dead eventually of "spontaneous combustion" (*BH* 512). This much-discussed episode in the novel illustrates not the power of the particular sign Krook possesses – it is quite meaningless to him and, in the end, to the outcome of the suit – but the irrelevance of any particular sign within a vast system. Krook dies not because, as a common expression would have it, the sign "burns a hole in his pocket" – that is, not because the desire to deploy or spend its value consumes him – but rather because the market-system loathes a hoarder. Stoppage of circulation creates build-up, friction, heat.[44]

Chancery as Famine

We are introduced to Krook and his shop in the chapter called "The Law Writer." Krook's connection to the system of Chancery is advertised in the variety of signs posted on his front window. Most of these advertise his dealings in words: "Rag and Bottle Warehouse," "Dealer in Marine Stores" etc. But one offers a pictorial sign that represents Krook's business to the segment of his suppliers least likely to be able to read: "In one part of the window was a picture of a red paper mill, at which a cart was unloading a quantity of sacks of old rags" (*BH* 98). One of the shop's businesses is to buy waste rags from the street paupers who collect them – a profession extensively documented by Henry Mayhew. The pictorial sign in Krook's window has several meanings within the text. First, for readers accustomed to understanding paper only as part of an "immense collection of commodities,"[45] the image points out the intricate trail of labor involved in its production. But while this revelation of the labor required to produce paper, what Marx calls the "secret" of the fetishized commodity,[46] seems to gesture toward a demystification of the paper-and-writing regime of the court, the image itself fails to provide any more direct function of reference. In depicting the process of labor, the picture shows us an exchange that is one step removed from what happens in a rag shop like Krook's. If the picture is intended to advertise to illiterate rag collectors that this shop buys rags for money, then why would the image not depict this transaction specifically? Why not show a rag collector handing over a bundle and receiving coins in exchange?

The answer to this question requires that we notice the somewhat unusual references to Ireland that occur at the conclusion of this chapter, "The Law Writer." Here we see the small room that Nemo rents from Krook, where the lawyer Tulkinghorn discovers Nemo dead from an overdose of opium. It is in this scene that we find the description of his ink-stained desk I quoted above. In full, the passage reads:

In the corner by the chimney, stand a deal table and a broken desk; a wilderness marked with a rain of ink. In another corner, a ragged old portmanteau on one of the two chairs, serves for cabinet or wardrobe; no larger one is needed, for it collapses like the cheeks of a starved man. The floor is bare; except that one old mat, trodden to shreds of rope-yarn, lies perishing upon the hearth. No curtain veils the darkness of the night, but the discoloured shutters are drawn together; and through the two gaunt holes pierced in them, famine might be staring in – the Banshee of the man upon the bed. (*BH* 188)

The "broken desk" and the random marks of ink are further illustrations of the emptiness of legal writing. But here this undomesticated "wilderness" of writing is linked to the hollow cheeks of starvation, an image that would certainly recall the grisly descriptions of the dying that became a staple of *The Times'* Irish coverage. Nemo's room is also haunted by "famine," in the form of the banshee, the spirit of death in Irish folk tradition. The sunken cheeks of the case – a storage place for food, clothes, all household goods – presents his poverty as a kind of starvation for things, and the "famine" that threatens him seems offered as a description of the atmosphere of impoverishment that pervades the cheap lodging. But Nemo himself, though poor (Krook claims he was six weeks behind on his rent), does not die of starvation but of the effects of opium addiction, in a deliberate or inadvertent overdose. The reference to Ireland, then, as a metonym for poverty, is a little off center. It seems hard to dismiss, however, for later in the novel, after we are presented with Nemo's true identity, we learn that he was a deserted army officer, "(Officially) reported drowned, and assuredly went over the side of a transport-ship at night in an Irish harbour" (*BH* 907–08). Certainly by the early 1850s London had seen a large number of new and desperately impoverished Famine immigrants, and public awareness of the Irish disaster would have been high.[47] But nowhere else in the novel is Ireland evoked as an image of poverty. Why is the death of Nemo, in particular, described in terms of the starving Irish?

Nemo, we eventually find out, was the lover of Honoria Dedlock before her marriage and with her conceived a child. This child, called Esther Summerson, was raised as an orphan by Lady Dedlock's sister, who kept the child ignorant of her parents and told Lady Dedlock that the child was dead (*BH* 789). Because of his status outside the institution of the family, his work as a copyist, and his addiction, Nemo embodies more completely than any character in the novel the killing principle of static, horizontal circulation that Chancery represents. As a legal scribe, his connection to the sign is the most purely formal of any character, since his job involves simply the reproduction of legal documents without regard to their significance. Like the endless craving of addiction, law-writing is an endless repetition without transcendence. Having dropped out of the chain of patronymic transmission, the normative structure of power and sexuality, he is in this way also literally nameless, *nemo*, outside the organization of the proper name.

The image of Ireland associated with Nemo thus condenses all the anxieties over the failure of the representative sign. The linguistic failure that characterizes Chancery is depicted here as a total breakdown of all the analogous systems in the novel: the sign, the patronymic, the commodity. All crash in Nemo's writing without meaning, his affiliation without the proper name, his hollow housekeeping, his addictive eating (of opium) without nourishment. Ireland comes to stand for the chaos of circulation.

But the question this metaphor raises, given the contemporary debates about whether the failure of Irish potatoes caused the stock market crash, is whether Ireland can represent this idea of systems-failure because it is outside the signifying economies of metropolitan England. That is, does Ireland's starvation set off London's market crash, or does Ireland starve because it is part of London's market system? The former answer was favored by the Parliamentary committees, I have argued, precisely because it seemed to provide an explanation outside the market itself. This view seems to be the one favored by Dickens; two prominent mentions of the Irish in *Household Words* articles portray Irish characters as outside of and unable to comprehend the circulation of money.[48] It could be argued as well that Nemo's position as an unmarried father confirms this reading: by his own improvident and irresponsible action he drops out of the economy of paternity, just as the Irish have resisted incorporation into the United Kingdom, have failed to save for rainy days or bad harvests, and have starved as a result.

But in another way, the novel makes it clear that it is impossible to "drop out" of the market as represented by Chancery. The circulation of the sign "in Chancery" and the commodity "in fashion" pervades every corner of the novel and the experience of every character. As Marx puts it, in a more technical mode: "the exchange of commodities breaks through all the individual and local limitations of the direct exchange of products."[49] The stamp of meaning which the commodity form puts on objects once in circulation applies even where, for example, no mass-produced consumer goods are widely purchased. The problem of whether there is, or ought to be, an "outside" to circulation is a central question of the novel. But in this instance, it is clear that however much Nemo may die from being *outside* the system of the family, his writing of the law is very much *inside* the system of the court. In the Jarndyce case it is the bureaucratic administration of value and the family name that creates the crisis, not any willing or willful exclusion from that system. The system generates the crash, not anything outside it.

Krook's shop placard presents the same answer to this question. Krook himself is illiterate, as are presumably the rag-pickers the sign is meant to advertise to. In this way, like much of the peasant population of Ireland, Krook and his clients appear to be outside of the circulation of the written sign.[50] But Krook's sign presents another message. The sign, again, is not direct or autonomous in its reference, for as a signifier it points toward its signified (the fact that rags are bought in this shop) only indirectly, triangulating the signified by reference to another signifier (the rags being unloaded at the paper mill). Understanding the signified requires knowledge on the part of the interpreter of a network of other signs, in this case the stages in the process of making paper. The pictorial signifier refers not to the content of its own image, but to a network of other signifiers,[51] all moments in a complex system of commodity exchange and production. Being unable to understand written linguistic signs, thus, does not mean that you are "outside" the principle of endless substitution which governs them.[52] In *Bleak House* Chancery is a famine of significance, and Ireland is a sign of this famine.

Domesticity as finance

We should also see Jo, the homeless child crossing-sweeper, as a central figure for the terrors of an endless circulation, for the novel's symbolic answer to these fears seems, as the novel opens, to involve nothing more elaborate than the comforts of home. Whenever Jo rests in one place, he is prodded by a policeman to "move on"; his exposure causes him to become ill, and although he is taken in and cared for by Esther, he dies. In this way he is like the papers in Chancery, bound in motion by a bureaucratic network, prevented from ever coming to rest.

In its opening chapters the novel seems to present the ideology of domestic femininity as its solution, for the crisis of chapters 1 and 2 is countered in chapter 3, "A Progress," where domesticity provides an end to circulation. The first two chapters are told by an omniscient narrator; chapter 3 is narrated in the first person by Esther Summerson, who offers first an account of her early life as a (presumed) orphan and her eventual move to a school for governesses, where she is sponsored by an anonymous benefactor. Esther learns the lessons of the school so well that she is eventually kept on as a teacher. She becomes a beloved companion of her pupils, and when she is finally called away to work for her anonymous sponsor, her distraught pupils want keepsakes from her. They ask her "only to write their names, 'with Esther's love'" (*BH* 75). This writing, inscribed "with love," seems as replete with meaning as the "law writing" seems empty. If circulation destroys the proper name, domestic affection presumably reseals it.

Noticing this clue in Esther's writing of chapter 3, we might conclude that the ideology of the domestic woman in the novel provides the space of essential value in a world of increasingly chaotic circulation. Esther's story in many ways emphasizes her successful internalization of the rigors of domestic work. She assumes the keys of John Jarndyce's estate, Bleak House, with seeming gratitude, and she provides motherly care for the orphaned wards of Chancery, the neglected Jellyby children, and for Jo.[53] She combines the orderliness of household economizing "with love," compensating for the emptiness of the various systems of work and value in the novel. The opening of Esther's narration in chapter 3 provides the possibility of narrative motion, an escape from the terrible stasis of chapters 1 and 2, and "A Progress" toward narrative closure.

Domestic femininity works in this period as a series of metaphors about nature, value, and virtue. The domestic seems to provide, as Nancy Armstrong has put it, "a magical space," exempt from the dangers of the market: "If the marketplace . . . came to be conceived as the centrifugal force that broke up the vertical chains organizing an earlier notion of society and that scattered individuals willy-nilly across the English landscape, then the household's dynamic was conceived as a centripetal one."[54] What we should notice in regard to *Bleak House* is that domestic ideology serves the same metaphorical functions as the bank, as it was understood in the currency debates of the 1840s: a centripetal force to limit, order, and regulate the wildness of a total interchangeability. As a monopoly bank of issue, the Bank would act as the "home" of circulating currency, repairing old notes and recasting old coins as they return, and guaranteeing their reference to fixed values. If the masculine world of the market represents a circulation without end, then feminine domesticity represents the fantasy of the circuit's closure. Domesticity "finishes" the rough world of circulation, reterritorializing the "homogeneous, empty" landscape of the nation, just as the art of "finance" (Old French *finer*, to finish) is meant to provide an end to the movement of capital's circuit, in the form of a boomerang-like "revenue" (Old French *revenir*, to come back).[55] When industrial development produces an infrastructure without any limit, its infinite movement is controlled by the metaphor of the home and the bank.

HOME OF COIN: DICKENS IN THE BANK OF ENGLAND

The power and similarity of the banking and housekeeping metaphors are strikingly demonstrated in another piece by Dickens, an 1850 article for his magazine *Household Words*, prepared in collaboration with his assistant W. H. Wills.[56] The piece is called "The Old Lady of Threadneedle Street" – the Bank of England's colloquial nickname since the late eighteenth century – and the article describes a behind-the-scenes tour of the Bank as a visit to the "Old Lady's House." The contradictions of finance are displaced here into the language of domesticity, and thus the article reveals a great deal about the ideological work of "household words" in this era.

After commenting briefly on "the honour of visiting the Old Lady," the narrator of the article is shown into the "Hall – the teller's hall," through the "elegant waiting room," and into the "parlour," where can be found "no easy chair, no cat, no parrot," in short "no domestic snugness," but only "a long table for the confidential manager of the Old Lady's affairs."[57] The article continues in this vein, pursuing in an extended way the metaphor proposed in the Bank's nickname, until the narrator arrives at one of the vaults: "The apartment in which the notes are kept *previous* to issue, is the Old Lady's store-room. There is no jam, there are no pickles, no preserves, no gallipots, no stoneware jars, no spices, no anything of that sort, in the Store-room of the Wonderful Old Lady. You might die of hunger in it" (OLT 339, emphasis original). To this point, the metaphor of Bank as house is pursued only ironically: the narrator of the piece finds the stately house strangely unaccommodating. Here especially, among the paper notes, we find nothing that could sustain life. This money is only paper, and though the paper notes are "representatives of weightier value" (i.e. gold) (OLT 340), they do not serve to make the "house" a "home." The powerlessness of paper money, mere representation of value, is described in the same terms as the emptiness of the linguistic sign for the law writer, Nemo: as starvation. So far though, the article rehearses the familiar point made by *Dombey and Son*, exploiting the double meaning of the word "house" to show that the values preserved by the careful management of the commercial house, "Dombey and Son" (money), are inadequate to the values preserved by good management of the domestic house, Dombey and daughter (love).[58] Or more briefly, the article shows that there are things which money cannot buy.

But while "you could die of hunger" among the paper notes, the opposite seems to hold for metal. In the "cellars" (OLT 340) where coins and ingots are stored, Dickens and Wills flip the metaphor and violate the logic of their joke: "One vault is full of what might be barrels of oysters . . . Another is rich here and there with piles of gold bars, set cross-wise, like sandwiches at supper, or rich biscuits in a confectioner's shop . . . A pile of these lying in a dark corner [is] like neglected cheese, or bars of yellow soap" (OLT 340). The housekeeping metaphor began by exploiting the dissimilarities between its two terms, Bank and house: the parlor has *no* furniture; the store-room has *no* food. But the metaphor ends up taking over the depiction of the Bank, as the Bank's solvency is compared with the ability of the prudent housekeeper to keep food in the house. As if to confirm, then, that good banking is good housekeeping, the article goes on to detail some of the Bank's systems of internal regulation, its means of keeping itself "clean" and in good order, focusing on the mechanized system for detecting light coins, the separation of the bank into its two departments (per the 1844 Charter Act), and the complex system of administering the national debt. The narrator then offers several anecdotes concerning acts of extraordinary loyalty on the part of Bank employees, many of them drawn from John Francis's anecdotal *History of the Bank of England* (1848), a copy of which Dickens appears to have owned.[59] The narrator concludes these stories by suggesting that "the kind Old Lady of Threadneedle Street has, in short, managed to attach her dependants to her by the strongest of ties – that of love" (OLT 342). The Bank functions as the "home" of the national economy here, and the principles of good domestic management are shown to be the secret of stabilizing the value – in gold – of the national currency.

As with many articles in *Household Words*, this piece seems focused on explaining the technological mysteries of modern life in comfortingly familiar terms. The national bank, the article suggests, is just a homey sort of place, well-kept and safe. But the housekeeping metaphor that helps accomplish this piece of consumer education has an added significance, for it plays out the gendered catachresis in the word "economy," a catachresis buried as well in the title of Dickens's magazine. Once literally the "law" or "management" (*nomos*) of the "household" (*oikos*), "economy" comes to denote a total exchange of objects and a theory of their relative value.[60] "House rules" becomes the theory of the national/global "house." And literal "household words" – terms for domestic commodities and common tasks – become the metaphor for something like the "talk of the nation" in the line from *Henry V* from which Dickens takes his magazine's title: "familiar in his mouth as household words."[61] Thus the banking/housekeeping metaphor that drives the "Old Lady" piece is the one that governs the magazine as a whole; the title announces that the publication is about national subjects, discussed in familiar, "household" terms. The metaphor is an economic one, or one at least that plays on the two gendered meanings of the word "economy" in modern usage: (feminine) household scrimping, "economizing," preserving; and (masculine) "political economy," market, world of finance.

The metaphorical connection between banking and housekeeping that shows up in the Bank of England's nickname ("the old lady"), the Dickens–Wills article, and the title of Dickens's magazine, seems inevitable within a certain logic of industrial build-up. The metaphysics of circulation, as "an economy of the proper without irreparable damage,"[62] involves a paradoxically simultaneous loss and accumulation. The ideology of industrial progress holds that factories cause accidents but also create "revenue": value that comes back to the investor as a "return," to be circulated once again. They create pollution, but also cheap commodities. They produce dirt but also wealth. In the City, as Dickens remarks in the celebrated opening paragraph of *Bleak House*, "mud . . . accumulate[es] at compound interest" (*BH* 49).

As industrial society is perceived to cause constant decay, the bank and the household appear to be realms of compensation, control, preservation. Coins and notes wear out in their motion through the market, but on their return "home" to the bank they are restored. In this era when masculinity is constructed as the duty to work, the male commuter, like the coin, is described as suffering a great deal of wear in the process of circulation. J. C. Loudon's 1838 handbook for suburban gardeners, for example, opens as follows:

The enjoyments to be derived from a suburban residence depend principally on a knowledge of the resources which a garden, however small, is capable of affording. [Among these are] The benefits experienced by breathing air unconfined by close streets of houses, and uncontaminated by the smoke of chimneys; the cheerful aspect of vegetation; the singing of birds in their season; and the enlivening effect of finding ourselves unpent-up by buildings, and in comparatively unlimited space . . . [63]

Here urban life dirties and chafes at the male commuter. Suburban domesticity represents an end to his daily circuit, a place where, like the bank,

he can expect his security to aggregate. Walter Bagehot writes in his review
of Dickens, "You have no idea of the toil, the patience, and the wearing
anxiety by which men of action provide for the day, and lay up for the
future" (CD 85). The dirtiness of "the City," the wearing away of work,
and the "sweating" of debased coin, are part of the expenditures of circulation. These potential losses are recouped by the logic of "returns." The
household and the bank are shelters from the crashing risks of circulation.
The labor of housekeeping causes value to accumulate at home, as worn
clothes, for example, are mended and household decorations made from
scraps. It is, I think, this sort of accumulation by thrift that is suggested
in the "Threadneedle" part of the Bank's nickname. Threadneedle Street is
the physical address of the building, but its inclusion in the epithet "Old
Lady of . . ." hints at a deeper association. If the Bank is a house, its "work"
is figured as the unpaid needlework of the housewife. The metaphorization
of banking as housework then obscures women as wage laborers. In fact in
this era low-wage piece-paid sewing was a widespread occupation for both
single and married women, but figuring needlework as "housework," that
is, as a "labor of love," obscures needlework as wage labor and appears to
evacuate women from the money economy. As the putative stability of the
land economy wears out, the bank and the middle-class home are propped
up as shelter from the whirling public world of circulation, imaginative
locations that provide an origin and end of value. Just as bank finance is
offered as a limit to the wildness of the economic sign, the middle-class
home is constructed as the limit to the threat of wandering female desire.

The point of all this, in terms of the rhetoric of the Dickens–Wills article,
would be to show that while a financial network capable of linking a world
economy creates certain risk, in the end it is the most stable and just form of
social organization. Or perhaps more simply: while paper money can let you
starve, gold will not. But the ability of gold to provide "nourishment" and
to insure the natural affection of kinship seems also drawn into question
here, given the article's emphasis on the importance of the way value works
only in a system, a network of standardized exchange. The first hint of
this comes at the opening of the article, where the narrator contemplates
"the honor of visiting the Old Lady": "In all parts of the civilized earth
the imaginations of men, women, and children figure this tremendous Old
Lady of Threadneedle Street in some rich shape or other" (OLT 337). From
the start the power of this house comes from its centrality in a global system.
This notion of the Bank as center of a network exerts some tension against
the "house" metaphor. The housekeeping figure construes England's gold –
literally its wealth, and symbolically its "love," its sentimental coherence as

nation – as food; its essential value and its reliability are compared to the use-value of food, its ability to sustain life. The network metaphor, however, treats gold and notes alike as exchange values, celebrating and marveling over the infinite interchangeability of all money, paper and metallic. The principle of interchangeability itself seems to take over the piece at times, producing a bewildering variety of figures for money in circulation: The bank is "the sun ... around which the agriculture, trade, and finance of this country revolves"; it is the heart "through whose arteries and veins flows the entire circulating medium of this great country" (OLT 338); it is a "print-shop" publishing "popular prints and literature"; inasmuch as its print returns as often as it leaves, it is "a huge circulating library" (OLT 339). Its money lives in a multitude of forms:

A sensation of unbounded riches permeated every sense, except, alas! that of touch. The music of golden thousands clattered in the ear, as they jingled on counters until its last echoes were strangled in the puckers of tightened money-bags, or died under the clasps of purses. Wherever the eye turned, it rested on money; money of every possible variety; money in all shapes; money of all colours. There was yellow money, white money, brown money; gold money, silver money, copper money; paper money, pen and ink money. (OLT 337)

The value of this money, stored as it is, untouchable, in the vault of the national bank, only exists in relation to its system. Only when a coin has "currency" can it be personified, as it is here, to live its jingling life, exhausting itself gleefully as it rubs from hand to hand, until it returns to die, rather like a salmon, back at its point of origin. Animating the coin, then, always means contemplating the scope of this circuit of exchange. In these passages money works according to Jean Baudrillard's formula, inspiring not exactly greed, but rather a "passion for the code."[64]

What is fascinating about money is neither its materiality, nor even that it might be the intercepted equivalent of a certain force (e.g., of labor) or of a certain potential power: it is its systematic nature, the potential enclosed in the material for total commutability of all values, thanks to their definitive abstraction. It is the abstraction, the total artificiality of the sign that one "adores" in money.[65]

Money signifies nothing except its unlimited exchangeability, and thus it conjures the systematicity of its own network, a network which was congruent, for Dickens and Wills, with Empire. Their joy at the sight of the home of English money refers to the racialized range of its exchangeability.

The name of Britain's financial network is "civilization," and it is only from within this network that the Bank can be figured as the home of English coin. A metaphorical assertion of natural affiliation arises out of the metonymic boundlessness of a global market.[66] At this ambivalent historical moment when "household words" becomes "political economy," economics becomes a matter of national and imperial housekeeping, that is, a matter of cleaning up the dirt of wearing exchange. When the economy appears as an infinite network, its rough circulation is finished by the Bank. And banking here is the belief that circulating value will "return" as revenue, that circulation is finite, that value in motion will meet itself in some moment of closure.

MORE MARKET METAPHYSICS

Thomas De Quincey

On the first page of *The Logic of Political Economy* (1844), Thomas De Quincey declares that "political economy does not advance."[67] There is a fatal "laxity" with which its proponents treat the "distinctions which are elementary to the science."[68] While "masculine good sense will generally escape in practice from merely logical perplexities . . . yet errors 'in the first intention' come round upon us in subsequent stages, unless they are met by their proper and commensurate solutions."[69] Under normal circumstances, De Quincey argues, a "masculine" rationality will presumably dominate, but the field of economic thought is flawed at its origins, in a way which threatens the triumph of "good sense." To correct the errors of the system, De Quincey argues that the language of political economy must be stabilized so that its terms refer reliably to single concepts and not to several indistinguishable ones. If the terms are stabilized, then the advance of philosophical thought will be insured: "it is indispensable to the *free* movement of thought that we should have names and phrases for expressing our ideas upon which we can rely at all hours as concealing no vestige of error."[70]

The term De Quincey seeks primarily to clarify is "value." Smith's *Wealth of Nations* distinguishes "value in use" from "value in exchange," in order to explain why some articles command a market price while some necessities of life do not. Smith writes: "Nothing is more useful than water: but it will purchase scarce any thing; scarce any thing can be had in exchange for it."[71] But as I argued in chapter 1, Smith's conception of value is somewhat equivocal, taking on different emphasis at different times. In Book 1 he states that "labour . . . is the real measure of the exchangeable value of all commodities," but in his examples he suggests that the forces of market supply and demand are the primary factors that control prices, notwithstanding the amount of labor a commodity might contain or might command in the market.[72] These two poles of Smith's theory of value – as defined by labor, and by supply and demand – are taken up by Ricardo and Malthus respectively, and provoke a series of disagreements the two writers addressed in a lengthy correspondence in the last years of their lives. De Quincey, however, regards all these distinctions, back to Adam Smith, as logically flawed, and he takes the debate back to first principles.

First, he scolds Smith for distinguishing between useful things and merely ornamental things or luxury goods. Diamonds, Smith writes, "are of no use, but as ornaments,"[73] But De Quincey argues that use is the "sole ground upon which, at any price, a man buys anything at all."[74] Thus the fact that diamonds are demanded in the market demonstrates, according to De Quincey, that they provide "utility" of some kind to their buyers. Second, De Quincey argues that in the debates over what "determines" value, no one has distinguished between possible meanings of the word "determine": the "*principium essendi,*" principle of essence; and the "*principium cognoscendi,*" principle of knowledge. When Smith writes, for example, that labor is the *measure* of a commodity's value, he suggests that labor-time is like a yardstick with which one can figure out or gain *knowledge* of value. This effort to *know* value, De Quincey argues, is bound to fail. Value cannot be measured against any standard commodity, like gold, because such a "standard – a value that will '*stand*' still when all other objects are moving" – is impossible to find, since "none can be privileged from change affecting itself."[75] As to what determines the *essence* of value, what value is in itself, De Quincey suggests political economists have been silent.

In this critique, De Quincey pinpoints the instability that fuels all the texts I am discussing here: Because of the market's principle of endless substitutions, the concrete or absolute knowledge of things is impossible, since their values mirror each other. However, De Quincey goes on to draft a crucial leap of faith with which this instability in the market is symbolically resolved. He looks for the essence of value, arguing that without such a firm foundation of truth the language of political economy will revolve as restlessly and as statically as commodities in the market itself. "To seek for the cause or ground of value," he writes, "is not only no visionary quest, speculatively impossible and practically offering little use, but is a *sine qua non* condition for the advancing by a single step in political economy."[76]

De Quincey proposes "the cause or ground" as follows. Though he offers his remarks as a defense of the Ricardian system, and though in at least two earlier essays he attacks Malthus for his late concession to Ricardo that labor is a measure of value,[77] he follows the tradition of Malthus in approaching the problem of value not through labor but through market demand. The "ground" of value De Quincey finds in the "strong affirmative attraction of the article concerned; in a positive adaptation of this article to each individual buyer's individual purposes."[78] This "adaptation" he calls the object's "intrinsic serviceability," or its "teleologic use," a usefulness that inheres in its make-up, which it is destined to provide to its consumer regardless of the artificial and temporary fluctuations of the market.[79] Endowed with this essential and immutable quality of utility, each object in the market will inspire a greater or lesser degree of "affirmative attraction" in the heart of the consumer. Each consumer will pay in accordance with this feeling of "attraction," and thus De Quincey concludes – in a final dizzying step – that the value of any commodity is truly represented in the average sum purchasers are willing to offer for it, that is, in its market price. Value is a degree of subjective consumer desire, and this desire, according to De Quincey's careful reasoning, is the only stable point in an endless circulation of differences. De Quincey sets out to firm up the value concealed beneath the shifting appearances of objects. But he argues finally that the force determining the true and final cost of a commodity – that is, the internal quality of usefulness which governs the price the object may fetch – is discernable only in its price. Costs are determined by prices.[80]

In this logically treacherous argument, De Quincey asserts the founding principle of neoclassical economics as it is practiced today: commodities have value only if they command a market price.[81] Neoclassical economics considers it irrelevant *why* any particular economic agent may desire a commodity, or which desires might be more socially beneficial.[82] The desire of the consumer is primary: untheorized and untheorizable.

The consumer, as De Quincey conceives her or him in this essay, is equipped with a defining interior principle which exists prior to the encounter with the market, and which cannot be in any meaningful way altered by the social world of language or objects. This essential character finds its own authentic expression in the desire for market goods. Desire for commodities here is not the corrupting influence of wealth as in Adam Smith, nor a symptom of social vanity as in Rousseau, nor a disavowed expression of envy as in Marx. It is the purest essence of the human, and it is this metaphysical essence that drives and orders the total system of the market.

I suggested in chapter 1 that the subjective or marginalist theory of value amounts to a kind of romantic economics. The consumer from De Quincey onward is a version of the romantic artist: the one who can access the heart's truest and purest feeling and give it objective expression, here not in the work of art, but in each new purchase. In De Quincey's philosophy of value we should also recognize a historical shift in the symbolic vocabulary of gender. In eighteenth-century economic discourse, the fickleness of the consumer, the unpredictability of consumer demand and confidence, is perceived as a symbolically feminine form of irrationality, one that threatens a stable order of masculine reason and power. De Quincey reverses the symbolic poles of earlier political economy, claiming what had once been the "feminine" and inconstant affect of the individual as the rock on which the modern market system is built.

What we have seen in *Bleak House* and "The Old Lady of Threadneedle Street" is a portrait of a chaotic and groundless marketplace, which can only be ordered and centered by the principles of private, symbolically feminine experience. This is the pattern presented in De Quincey's *Logic of Political Economy*, a text that constructs a private realm of inner life to order the disorderly theory of production and exchange. This similarity does not simply demonstrate a sympathy between Dickens and De Quincey as analysts of modern life. It serves to place Dickens at the center of nineteenth-century economic discourse, in touch with the fundamental problems of industrial capitalist markets and the symbolic vocabulary political economists drew on to confront these problems.

Walter Bagehot

Bagehot made his name, to a great extent, in the debates over the 1844 Bank Charter Act. His first published work was an 1848 review of three commentaries on it by prominent supporters and critics. From this early article to his most famous work, *Lombard Street*, Bagehot is a theorist of the money market, that is, the market for business capital, which centered on the commercial banks in London's Lombard Street. According to Bagehot, financial crises were caused by a glut of loanable money available at temptingly low rates of interest. "John Bull can stand a great deal," Bagehot wrote in a number of places "but he cannot stand two percent."[83] That is, when interest rates go down to two percent, investors get restless and entrepreneurs get greedy. With money available so cheaply, an entrepreneur is more likely to borrow to start a risky project, like a railroad to a destination which no one yet wishes to reach (a scheme frequently embarked upon in the 1840s boom). Private small investors making only two percent may take their money and buy high-risk stocks. With more risky and often fraudulent projects getting financed, more eventually fail, triggering a panicked sell-off. Stock prices drop, as all investments begin to appear less reliable, and very rapidly all exchanges can be affected.

Bagehot may be best known today for his sexual politics, publicized through the agency of Virginia Woolf, who preserved in *Three Guineas* his notorious pronouncement on women's education. In response apparently to a request from Emily Davies that he lend his support to the foundation of a women's university, he replied:

I assure you I am not an enemy of women. I am very favourable to their employment as labourers or in other menial capacity. I have, however, doubts as to the likelihood of their succeeding in business as capitalists. I am sure the nerves of most women would break down under the anxiety, and that most of them are utterly destitute of the disciplined reticence necessary to every sort of co-operation.[84]

The passage might be easily dismissed as an example of the casual misogyny of the business world, but in fact it offers a quite precise demonstration of the sexual metaphors which define and lend support to Bagehot's economics. Bagehot's key concepts seem to take their shape from metaphors of masculine self-restraint and feminine indulgence, and his defense of the market as a mode of social organization rests on this same opposition. In his article "Investments" he writes, "we hope that the people will be wise – that capitalists will exercise discretion – that merchants will not overtrade – that shopkeepers will not overstock – that the non-mercantile public will bear the reduction in income – that they will efface superfluities, and endure adversity, and abolish champagne."[85] He advocates "self-denial" over "a feverish and irrational excitement," and he warns "that railways should not be promoted by maiden ladies, or canals by beneficed clergymen."[86] He refers in another place to "country clergymen, squires, and ladies who, from ignorance of the business world, are not commonly able to employ [their savings] commercially."[87] It is this feminized and irrational lot, inclined to throw their savings after attractive but doomed railway schemes, who are the greatest enemies of England's commercial stability, in Bagehot's account. In these examples, the world of business is a world of fearful risk and alluring temptation. Ranged against the forces of panic and luxuriance and the risk of irrecoverable loss are the forces of a "masculine" self-denial, wisdom, and endurance of hardship. These are the traits of a good business man, and these are the traits which must be cultivated throughout the English public, for the English and Irish working classes are also represented by Bagehot through this particular trope of femininity: "The most important matters for the labouring classes, as for all others, are restraining discipline over their passions and an effectual culture of their consciences. In recent times these wants are more pressing than ever. Great towns are depots of temptation, and unless care be taken, corrupters of all deep moral feeling."[88]

In this context the full significance of Bagehot's objection to Dickens becomes more clear. Bagehot's complaint is that Dickens lacks the masculine qualities necessary for the regulation of social and economic systems. Dickens's work is characterized by "an overflow of a copious mind, though not the chastened expression of an harmonious one" (CD 83). His imagination has "an endless fertility of laughter-causing detail" (CD 91), but it lacks what Bagehot calls the "practical sagacity" (CD 80) or "broad sagacity by which the great painters of human affairs have unintentionally stamped the mark of unity on their productions" (CD 84). The feminized excesses of Dickens's imaginative overproduction do, in Bagehot's view, lead to a kind of glut of Dickens's products on the literary market. (Bagehot suggests that Dickens can hardly be blamed for this, given the unrestrained demand for his writing from an equally feminized English reading public: "No other Englishman has attained such a hold on the vast populace; it is little, therefore, to say that no other has surmounted its attendant temptations" [CD 107].) But the sexual and economic metaphors governing the piece do not take up this supply–demand argument in any extended way. Rather, Dickens's lack of reticence is used to diagnose the particular haphazard qualities of Dickens's representation of English life. An indiscriminate imagination produces the discontinuous vision of London as newspaper, in the passage I began with: "everything is there, and everything is disconnected." His works then, while evocative in their "microscopic detail," are simply "graphic scraps" (CD 83) that do not reveal the "binding elements" of society (CD 81).

Bagehot argues that the world of social and economic values, far from being discontinuous and chaotic, is unified, governed by subtle and quirky but ultimately perceivable cycles which a mind of sufficiently masculine "sagacity" could understand and describe. In *Bleak House* the focus on the legal system qua system threatens to abolish the metaphysical "unity" Bagehot insists upon. In one way, as we have seen, *Bleak House*'s critique of value under representation seems to be resolved by the metaphor of sexual difference it deploys, a rhetorical formula quite close to Bagehot's. But finally it seems that there is good reason for Bagehot to be uncomfortable with the novel's treatment of the market, for in the end it fails to calm the fears it incited.[89]

THE MERITS OF THE SYSTEM

> This old lady had a grandson who was a sailor; and I wrote a letter to him for her, and drew at the top of it the chimney-corner in which she had brought him up, and where his old stool yet occupied its old place. This was considered by the whole village the most wonderful achievement in the world; but when an answer came back all the way from Plymouth, in which he mentioned that he was going to take the picture all the way to America, and from America would write again, I got all the credit that ought to have been given to the Post-office, and was invested with the merit of the whole system. (*BH* 561)

Esther's narrative is designed to compensate the reader for the terrors of Chancery. Early on Esther is given a number of nicknames by her guardian and eventual suitor John Jarndyce – Dame Durden, Mother Hubbard, Mrs. Shipton, etc. – all of which refer to single women in folk-tales or nursery rhymes (*BH* 956n). At the opening of the novel she is an orphan, unmarried and of unknown parentage; the multiplicity of these nicknames emphasizes the instability of Esther's ties to the patronymic system and raises the question both of her origin and of her eventual marriage. Esther is occasionally called "old woman" (*BH* 148), and this phrase along with the others that refer to Esther as single home-maker subtly recall the Bank of England's nickname, The Old Lady of Threadneedle Street. The Old Lady in Dickens and Wills's article provides a center for a frighteningly complex network; *Bleak House* nominates Esther to promote "the merits of the system."

There is one other character whose nickname also seems to link her tangentially to the Bank. Early in the novel Esther encounters a woman named Miss Flite, who cheerfully claims that she has been driven insane by the long delay of a Chancery suit, and now attends the court sessions every day. Esther calls this character "the old lady" (*BH* 81,107), and the Phiz illustration that introduces her is captioned "The Little Old Lady" (*BH* 80). The nickname "The Old Lady of Threadneedle Street" first appeared in print in a 1797 cartoon by James Gillray, but at least one source, W. M. Acres's *The Bank of England from Within*, mistakenly attributes the name to the story of Sarah Whitehead. Whitehead's brother worked as a teller at the Bank but was convicted of forgery and hanged in 1812. After the hanging she began to visit the Bank regularly in mourning clothes asking to see her brother, and because of her costume she was called "The Bank Nun." Whether she lost touch with reality or acted with clever reason seems to be an open question: the Bank granted her a pension in 1818 on the condition that she stop loitering around the building.[90] Miss Flite's polite derangement, and her constant presence in Chancery Lane seem to connect her with this particular old lady of Threadneedle Street. It would be a mistake to place too much weight on these rather slight connections, however suggestive they may be. Still, the larger correspondence between banking and domesticity – the point these smaller clues would lead to – seems clear. The lesson that good banking is like good housekeeping is one that the *Household Words* article affirms outright, and the link between economic and domestic values is one that *Bleak House* seeks to establish through its story of Esther's "progress."

The danger posed by the systematized world of Chancery and the Bank can be described in Barthes's terms as the "metonymic confusion" of the bourgeois sign. "Metonymic confusion" is Chancery's problem, in that the sideways-shifting network of writing threatens to bury the meaning of any of its documents. The detective, Mr. Bucket, charged with solving all of the novel's "connexions," declares that he has so much knowledge about so many different people that "a piece of information more or less, don't signify a straw" (*BH* 782). That this might be true of all signs – that their true value might be rendered indistinguishable in their systematization – is the novel's central worry.

But while value is shown in every corner of the novel to be indeterminable, the novel's closure is not achieved through any sorting or ordering of failed metonymy. Dickens's Bank article explains the bank system not strictly by showing how it moves and orders things, but by claiming that running a bank is like running a house. The question of connections is solved, then, not by metonymic restructuring, but by metaphor, for domestic femininity is a dead metaphor for the industrial era's construction of the extra-economic sphere: nature, affect, home. Proving Esther to be the perfect domestic care-giver – "the best wife a man could have" (*BH* 915), as Jarndyce puts it in his sales pitch to Alan Woodcourt – the novel seeks to recenter social value. Domestic ideology resolves the metonymic blurring of signs by asserting the metaphorical transcendence of a naturalized feminine virtue.

In her lapse between (nameless) father and husband, Esther circulates through many circles of professional and social life, like the novel's other anonymous narrator. But, much more prominently in the end, she is also exchanged between men, and the reliability of the (marriage) market system is tested through the problem of establishing Esther's "value." Esther's representation of herself in retrospective narration is always characterized by undervaluation. Why, she is always asking herself, does everyone make the mistake of valuing me so highly? The main danger of the novel, then,

is that Esther's intensely overdetermined goodness – figured by Dickens
in the language of natural affection – might not "signify a straw." This
is the same threat of the obliteration of natural value figured elsewhere:
Richard Carstone's affection for his guardian, John Jarndyce, for example,
is "warped" and "perverted" by a Chancery system which, "if two angels
could be concerned in it . . . would change their nature" (*BH* 547). Essential, transcendental, natural value is eroded by the industrial systematicity
of modern life. Mr. Bucket asks, "What is public life without private ties?"
(*BH* 732). That private life can in fact pin down public circulation – that
it can preserve the patrilineal logic of the name – is what the novel seeks to
demonstrate.

Thus while the novel begins by protesting the way that male plaintiffs
are treated like objects in the Chancery system, it concludes by trying to
show that the system that organizes objects – the market – is successful in its
distribution of women. The marriage plot's climactic scene stresses Esther's
status as a restless commodity, judged, evaluated, and finally exchanged.
John Jarndyce explains his decision to give Esther to Woodcourt saying that
he "determined not to throw away one atom of my Esther's worth" (*BH*
914). Woodcourt's discriminating mother is allowed to receive Esther on
approval, as it were, when she is invited to Bleak House for an extended visit,
to be persuaded of Esther's "true legitimacy" (*BH* 914). Because her goodness
and utility as domestic care-giver have been evaluated in her circulation
through the various levels of society in the novel, her narrative argues for
the market-system's ability to create stable representations of value. The
persistently economic language in the scene of Esther's exchange suggests,
as D. A. Miller has demonstrated in detail, that the putative consolation of
the domestic sphere is itself shown to be a commodity: once Woodcourt has
received Esther from Jarndyce, the private protection once offered by Bleak
House is transported to a new location – according to market demand –
and set up in a novel but equivalent form. But, as I have tried to suggest
here, the exchange of Esther does more than deconstruct the discourse of
privacy (this is the direction of D. A. Miller's essay), for if this is a message
we can draw from the metaphor of marriage as market, the novel's closing
transaction also seems to invite us to read the metaphor in the other sense:
to see the market as marriage. The force of the former reading is to disrupt
the construction of the domestic as locus of uncoerced "natural affection."
In the latter reading, the metaphor serves to invest the free market with the
sanction of nature.

De Quincey's argument in *The Logic of Political Economy* is that the
essence of a thing, the substance that determines its value, is the "strong

affirmative attraction" it exerts on a purchaser. The attraction is gauged by a price and fulfilled through a purchase; each transaction is thus a union of desire, in effect a good marriage. Esther, in a kind of parody of this formula, begins the novel resolved to "win some love" for herself (*BH* 65); by the end she is desired by two men, Jarndyce and Woodcourt, and the measure of their desire has been negotiated and standardized in their exchange of Esther between them. Woodcourt accepts Esther on Jarndyce's terms, as indicated by the way he picks up Jarndyce's nicknames and calls her "Dame Durden" (*BH* 935). The measure of Esther's value is triangulated "between men"; thus standardized, Esther's name links the two men in the particular form of commodity fetishism that Eve Sedgewick calls "homosociality."[91]

However, there are a number of elements of Esther's narrative that trouble the text's attempt to naturalize the market. Any question of a natural or essential value is blocked by Esther's exclusion from the structure of her "evaluation," and by her final non-identity with herself. Esther's struggle for identity in the novel is related through the story of her search for her parents. Just as Esther's competent and affectionate management of the household system is offered as the solution to the bad economics of the court, so her keys finally open the secret of Lady "Dedlock" – that she is Esther's mother. When the mother's secret is truly "unlocked," however, when it threatens to become public knowledge in the world of "Fashion," she takes flight suicidally into a snowstorm. Esther goes abroad with the detective, Bucket, to find her. The snow, however, comes down in "icy blots" (*BH* 894), "so thick with the darkness of the day, and the density of the fall, that we could see but a very little way in any direction" (*BH* 837). The inky "blots," like the storm of ink on Nemo's desk, obscure Lady Dedlock's path and recall the snow-like whirl of the Chancery papers. She returns eventually to Nemo's grave, and Esther finds her there, dead, the next morning. When Esther identifies her mother's body, the whirling snow has become the hair that obscures her mother's face: "I lifted the heavy head, put the long dank hair aside, and turned the face" (*BH* 869). This trope of the hair obscuring the face – the final mark of Lady Dedlock's identity – recalls the focus throughout the novel on Esther's face, the face that was changed during her illness, by a disease contracted from Jo and spread first from the pauper's grave where Nemo is buried. When Esther looks in the mirror for the first time after she has recovered, she describes the scene as follows:

There was a little muslin curtain drawn across it. I drew it back: and stood for a moment looking through such a veil of my own hair, that I could see nothing else.

Then I put my hair aside, and looked at the reflection in the mirror, encouraged
by seeing how placidly it looked at me. I was very much changed – O very, very
much. (*BH* 559)

The obscured face, the veiled mirror, refer to the failure of the body as a
seemingly indexical sign of family connections.[92] Lady Dedlock early on
recognizes Nemo's handwriting on a legal document, and she decides to
try to find him. The signature, the flair of the body that makes it its own,
promises here as well an indexical representation of identity. But by the
time Lady Dedlock traces Nemo he is dead, buried at the yard which is the
source of Esther's illness, and where Lady Dedlock herself will die.

Esther's determination to "win some love" is announced in chapter 3, as
she describes her lonely childhood, overhung with the cloud of illegitimate
birth, and explains her desire to be good: "I would strive as I grew up to
be industrious, contented, and kind-hearted . . . and win some love to
myself if I could" (*BH* 65). Although Esther finds her parents and recovers
her family, she is not granted their love. As her story shows, she must
create or "win some love" as she did at school, systematically, by outwardly
demonstrating her goodness and usefulness. Thus in important ways Esther
always lacks the principle that the novel has offered as the metaphysical
ground to the mechanical system: "natural affection," "the strongest of
ties," the uncoerced sentiments of kinship. While Esther's name – signed
"with love" – is the one that can seal system and sentiment for other
characters, she herself takes on the "namelessness" of her father. Although
her name would be Woodcourt after her marriage, the novel's final chapter,
"The Close of Esther's Narrative," never mentions this name. She refers to
Woodcourt here as "my husband," "him," or "the doctor" (*BH* 934–35); she
continues to be called by her "old lady" nicknames, "Dame Trot, Dame
Durden, Little Woman! – all just the same as ever" (*BH* 934). The family
name, the logic that unites the economic and the domestic, is still absent.

Bleak House attempts to settle the unsettled question of value that pervades the economic discourse of the 1840s and 1850s. All the texts I have
treated here work in some way to "domesticate" the market, to give it a
"home," to provide a metaphysical center, to invest it "with love." The
banking legislation of the 1840s sought to provide the market with a central node, a place of return; Bagehot suggests the world of exchange can
be ordered by masculine restraint. While no single metaphor controls each
text, they all argue in some way that the problem of value in the market is a
problem of subjective perception, of individual judgment, of private desire.
The problems of the free market are projected back into the subject. And

while the rhetoric that attempts this inner projection of a political construct may seem to us littered with gaps and aporias, it becomes by the end of the century the accepted foundation of economic analysis. The uncomfortable awareness in these texts that value is produced in a collective social matrix of signification will yield to the illusion that value is indistinguishable from the desire to consume.

CHAPTER 4

Esoteric solutions: Ireland and the colonial critique of political economy

In the manuscript collection of the National Library of Ireland, there is a diary recording the impressions of an anonymous English traveler who toured Ireland in 1837. In a digression on the "manners" of the Irish people, the writer comments on the frequent, idiosyncratic use of the English word "elegant":

> The word *Elegant* is applied by them to almost every thing: two kennel makers with their faces like the mud they grope in will accost one another with, "we[ll] Pat and how are ye, by the powers you look elegant this cold morning." [I]f by a fire side "let the fire alone ye spallpeen it will be an Elegant one by and bye["] – A dead pig at a butcher shop will also have the appelation of being elegant.[1]

The anecdote illustrates a broad perception in the era preceding the Irish Famine that the Irish are completely outside the system of market value that encompassed English society. The story seems to point out that a person living in utter poverty can have no power to discern what is "elegant" from what is not. But reference to the "faces like mud" invokes the question of national and racial difference, which will grow increasingly important within the analysis of Irish economic life. In this discourse, once the disastrous scope of starvation in Ireland becomes clear, the representation of the problem will begin to change. The scorn of the above observer seems linked to his judgment that the Irish are outside British economic systems, with no ability to discern filth from finery, or the human body from dirt.[2] Real elegance is lost on "kennel makers." In the period of the Famine, however, commentators begin to claim that Ireland simply has a different economy from England's, one that cannot be understood in English terms.

In their book *Political Economy and Colonial Ireland*, Thomas Boylan and Timothy Foley have documented this gradual shift in economic theory and popular ideology in Ireland over the course of the nineteenth century. The Famine, they show, was a watershed in this process, providing clear evidence for cultural nationalists to argue that Ireland could not be ruled through the abstract or universal principles of classical political economy. This cultural critique of political economy emergent during the Famine gave rise to inductive and historicist approaches by later Irish economists, most notably J. E. Cairnes and T. E. Cliffe Leslie.³ What I have tried to suggest, however, is that an emphasis on national particularity will become one of the important conditions of possibility for the neoclassical defense of the market, in the work of Jevons and the marginalists. As I argued in chapter 1, the presumption of an absolute national difference (whether conceived in explicitly racial terms or not) strengthens the claim to a priori desire, central to the marginalist conception of subjectivity. It also offers an unacknowledged alibi for the persistence of poverty, and indeed famine, in a global market.

But while by the end of the century the categories and assumptions of neoclassical analysis were beginning to take on the appearance of human nature, this was by no means the case in 1850. In this chapter I examine representations of Ireland during the Famine, all of which are fractured in some way by the crisis of economic analysis that characterized this period. These texts are decidedly non-canonical, often obscure, but I focus on them not simply to provide background for their literary big brothers. I am interested rather in demonstrating the literary quality of these views of Ireland, noticing the way that the same terms and strategies used by Dickens, De Quincey, Bagehot, and others are employed in the Irish debate to argue specific points of economic policy and theory.

Ireland's economy had been shaped by direct English control since the seventeenth century, when large areas of rural land were confiscated from a native aristocracy and awarded to a Protestant settler class. Though the Navigation Acts of 1671 forced all British overseas trade to pass through London, thus making Irish ports completely dependent on English, an exception was made for outbound British ships to provision in Irish ports. Salt beef for West Indian traders became a staple Irish product.⁴ As demand from English urban populations rose, over the course of the eighteenth century, Irish production of food for export increased, and live cattle, butter, and bacon began to supplant salted provisions. As the social geographer Kevin Whelan puts it, Ireland became "the larder of the First Industrial Revolution," and the Catholic Irish "a permanent, proliferating and potato-dependent underclass."⁵

Rising grain prices, particularly during the Napoleonic Wars, led to increased tillage farming, while the unusual productivity of the potato in the damp Irish climate, and the potato's exceptional nutritive value, made it possible to squeeze tenant farmers and agricultural laborers onto very small parcels of land. With competition for land leases quite high, given the excellent subsistence that even small plots could provide, larger farmers were willing to pay an extremely high proportion of cash earned from grain and livestock in rent, and to live on the produce of small potato gardens. Labor on these larger holdings was provided by a class called cottiers, who sublet patches of potato ground, and sometimes received a small cash wage, in return for a specified number of days of work. This system of subletting was called conacre, and it encouraged uniform dependence on potatoes as subsistence food, while enabling the maximum cash value of land to be paid out to rent.[6] The unusual success of the banking industry in Ireland in the half-century preceding the Famine – a time when commercial and manufacturing development was stagnating – provides some indication of the need felt by Irish landowners for the handling and transfer of rent monies.[7] By 1845, the ratio of bank branches to people in Ireland was greater than that in England by a factor of three.[8]

The productivity and profitability of Irish land made it central to the economic history of Britain in the first half of the nineteenth century. The agitation of Irish landlords was significant in the passage of the 1815 Corn Laws, the protectionist measures designed to keep British grain prices relatively high.[9] The ongoing fight between supporters of the Corn Laws and advocates of free trade defined English economic discourse in this period, but the Corn Laws were repealed only in 1846, when the failure of Irish potatoes prompted the import of American corn meal by the British government. But if Ireland is at the center of this era's economic history, it is also central to the history of British economic thought, both because Ireland served as a nearby testing ground for experiments in political economy, and because Irish economists made significant contributions to the nineteenth-century debate on value.

The popularity of simplified and novelized versions of political economy in England during the 1820s – with the works of Jane Marcet and Harriet Martineau – may have been the impetus for Richard Whately's *Easy Lessons on Money Matters* (1832). But it was Whately's book that became the most widely used school text in the empire.[10] With the publication of this book, and its use through the 1830s, political economy became a standard academic subject in Irish schools. Whately was appointed Archbishop of Dublin in 1831 and the next year endowed a chair in political economy at Trinity College.[11] In 1832 Whately became commissioner of the national education system, and he used this post to institute the teaching of political economy across the curriculum, generally with his textbook. By 1848 all teachers in the national system were required to pass standardized exams certifying their competence in central subjects, political economy among them.

The first occupant of the Whately Chair at Trinity was Mountifort Longfield, who applied the demand theory of value to the problem of wages. In Longfield's work, as we saw in chapter 1, labor functions for the first time as a commodity in the strictest sense. Longfield was considered the founder of a "Dublin School" of political economy, all of whose members followed Whately and Longfield in their mistrust of any theory of value based on labor or on the cost of production. And it is their theory of value as a function of desire which would win out in later neoclassical economic thought. Just as with the teaching of political economy in the schools, it seems that in the realm of pure theory, strategies developed in colonial Ireland took on a leading role in metropolitan Britain.

There is no mystery, however, in this case of reverse colonization, where technologies of modern statehood seem to have migrated from colony to metropole. In the first half of the nineteenth century, Ireland served as a test case for a number of experiments in governance. In response to an increasingly effective movement under Daniel O'Connell for the repeal of the 1801 Act of Union, the 1830s witnessed a series of measures to monitor and control the Irish population. Along with the national schools program, the most striking of these is the 1836 Police Act, which consolidated diverse local agencies into a professional civilian constabulary and instituted a series of reforms of municipal courts. Emphasis was on the neutral enforcement of the rule of law, and in pursuit of this goal a standard of ethical detachment was cultivated among recruits at the national training depot in Dublin.[12] "Thus Ireland," as Oliver MacDonagh writes, "came to possess a coherent, stratified, paramilitary police at a time when the lonely, untrained village constable was still the instrument of law enforcement over most of rural England."[13] By 1850 there were 14,000 members of this police force; in 1870 the same number were still in place, despite regular population decline. In Ireland by this point there was 1 policeman for every 425 citizens, twice the ratio found in England.[14]

The Ordinance Survey of Ireland, begun in 1824 and published 1833–46, offers a similar example. Partly to provide military maps, and partly to aid in the accurate assessment of land values, this project eventually set the entire island down in a scale of six inches to one mile, long before such scientific surveys were available for England, Wales, or Scotland.[15] The process of standardizing the values of comparable areas of land was continued in a national assessment project begun in 1830.[16] With these two schemes, every corner of the once mysterious Irish landscape was evenly overlaid with the

grid of the modern state. The concentric circles of direct military rule –
where English power would not extend beyond the thin "pale" line – was
gradually replaced by the even authority of the nation, where power perfuses
every tissue of the society.[17] It is this impulse toward standardization and
regulation, toward a "homogeneous, empty" landscape, that we saw in
Dickens's depiction of Chancery. In *Bleak House* the court runs like a
factory, a "slow mill," grinding away in an exquisitely refined orderliness
which takes no account of the needs of the truly deserving.

The development of modern transportation systems in Ireland seems
to have been understood within the same rhetoric of standardization. On
March 14, 1848, a man named Locke from County Limerick watched a new
steamship on its first landing near Dublin and made the following note in
his diary:

Witnessed the arrival at Kingstown of the first of the steamers intended for the
Dublin & Holyhead line – *The Banshee*. She finished the distance from Liverpool
in 17 hours 35*m*[inutes] beating her consort by one hour. The unrivalled scenery of
Dublin Bay, and the fine vessel, novel in her mechanical adaptations, and a perfect
model of naval symmetry, gliding with great velocity through the calm waters of
the basin, huge columns of black smoke pouring from her funnels, and mimic
fountains jetting from her prow – filled me with a delight – and I forgot all care.

I observed to a gentleman . . . on the pier – where is the repeal of the Union
now? and he replied, pointing to the steamer – There is the true link between the
countries.[18]

Rapid transport and modern machinery inspire Mr. Locke's carefree optimism here. And both he and his interlocutor interpret this technology
of efficient circulation in explicitly political terms, as providing the "true
link" in the Union.

It is precisely such a mechanical kind of standardization which the
name "political economy" came to signify in the 1840s – a theory that
treats people like objects, concerned not with their humanity but only their
efficient movement. But while it is crucial to notice the colonial origins of
these modern techniques of statehood, lest we mistake methods of social
control for genuinely democratic reforms, we need to see one other aspect
of British political economy in order to understand its application during
the Irish Famine. This other element was religion. In this era which Boyd
Hilton has called "the age of atonement," the idea of Divine retribution for
earthly improvidence that ran through Malthus's population theory was
reinforced by the evangelical movement within the Church of England.
This blending of calculation and belief resulted in what Hilton calls a

"soteriological economics," a theory oriented toward the goal of individual salvation, stressing personal responsibility for poverty and hard work as atonement for sin.[19] In this view, to interfere in labor or trade contracts was seen as a follied attempt to perfect an irrevocably sinful life on earth. Prudence and economy were seen as spiritual duty, and good investments were valued not as a means of increasing collective national wealth, but as evidence of moral rectitude. The social and philosophical foundations of Smith and Ricardo's work are largely discarded here, and political economy becomes a patchwork of religious and moral precepts.

This evangelical brand of political economy was by no means universal among British political elites, but it formed a common ground of opinion on economic policy among factions that agreed on little else. According to Peter Gray's typology of political opinion in *Famine, Land, and Politics*, "soteriological economics" informed the liberal Tory position of Peel and his followers and was also a core belief of one important Whig faction, a group of fervent evangelicals Gray calls "moralists."[20] Whig moralists never held perfect sway over party or government, but they had sufficient power to influence both Peel's government of 1841–46 and Russell's administration that followed it. The central figures here were Charles Wood, Chancellor of the Exchequer, 1846–52, and Charles Trevelyan, Assistant Secretary to the Treasury, 1840–59. Trevelyan in particular made his position at the Treasury a central one during the debate on Irish relief and land reform. His 1848 report on this work, which I examine below, remains a central statement of the period. While after the middle of the century the "moralist" position on poverty would become untenable, in the 1840s it united evangelical Whigs and non-extremist Tories and formed a center of English political opinion.

Within this complex framework, British policy in Ireland attempted to render an errant Irish population fit for the systematicity of modern life, and fit for the stern judgement of a Protestant God. Schools taught children the English language and forbade Irish, in order to produce a mobile labor force, unencumbered by the regional character of their speech. English maps regulated the rights of property ownership and rent, translating all place-names into English and standardizing boundary lines, so that any British subject could understand the terms of a lease, and not just someone who grew up learning the traditional organization of a particular estate or *clachan*.[21] Lessons for Irish children taught the skills of rational calculation, in order that the Irish might be drawn into the Protestant economic universe – where poverty was punishment for sinful waste and irrational habits, and where wealth was the sign of a contrite soul.

One indicator of the power of these views is the debate leading to an Irish Poor Law. The English Poor Law of 1834 had instituted the notorious regime of workhouses as the only means of government assistance to the poor, and a Royal Commission headed by Whately was formed to determine whether the English system would work in Ireland. The Commission surveyed conditions among the poor in different regions and made its report in 1836. But despite Whately's clear philosophical predisposition in favor of any measure that would encourage the transition to wage labor, his report recommended strongly against the workhouse system in Ireland. Because of Ireland's high population and its crowded agricultural economy, the report argued, many of the unemployed were legitimately unable to find work, and thus the government could not assume, as it did in England, that only the disabled and aged were in need of assistance. The report urged government to establish a Board of Improvement to stimulate agricultural production, fund public works projects, and encourage emigration. Critics of the report objected that, by eliminating the threat of incarceration in the workhouse, it lacked means to force individuals to compete in a wage labor market. This position won the support of Lord Russell, at the time Home Secretary, and he forced through a plan of workhouses in the Irish Poor Law of 1838.²² Whately and his critics did agree that the solution to Irish poverty lay in forcing the Irish into wage labor. They disagreed on whether Irish conditions and Irish culture were unique. The original report's insistence on Irish specificities and exceptions was countered by a universalist belief in personal redemption through regularized labor.

The most general assumption of English policy toward Ireland on the eve of the Famine was that natural laws of the marketplace – seen by many as Divine laws – had been blocked and perverted by a series of historical accidents, and that it was the responsibility of good government to remove these obstructions, and to convert the Irish into rational wage laborers. The subject as conceived in this imperial model is still roughly the subject of the eighteenth-century context of Adam Smith. Market circulation is still conceived as it was by Smith and Condillac, as a process of progressive "abstraction." The division of Irish territory into standard grids, the enforcement of a neutral rule of law by a professional police force, all facilitate what Smith would broadly have called the division of labor – the generalization of a mass of idiosyncratic operations into common component parts. British political economy in the 1840s assumes, just as Smith did in his history of economic civilization, that human consciousness will be produced anew, out of the new technological conditions of the division of labor. Within this paradigm, anything that increases the smoother flow of value, the refinement of equivalences, is to be praised. The social costs of any measure are, quite explicitly, irrelevant in this model, for the institution of such new systems will itself create new social conditions around it.

TREVELYAN'S MACHINE OF HISTORY

The clearest and most famous illustration of this economics of atonement as applied to the Irish Famine is an 1848 *Edinburgh Review* article by Charles Trevelyan, who served as Assistant Secretary to the Treasury and oversaw Famine relief works after the summer of 1846. In this essay, republished as a volume entitled "The Irish Crisis," we see the main currents of English political economy since Adam Smith. Trevelyan presents a triumphalist version of Condillac's world history, a radical vision of the abstraction of social labor, justified by an evangelical belief in an angry God.

Trevelyan was appointed to the Treasury in the new Whig administration of Lord Russell, Peel's majority having crumbled after he revealed his position on the Corn Laws. Potato blight – a fungal infestation – had become evident in Ireland during the harvest of 1845. Peel's administration developed two programs of relief to deal with the crisis: importation of American corn meal, which would be sold by the Government to wholesalers at a minimum cost to prevent food prices from becoming inflated; and a series of public works to provide temporary wage labor. While this system was designed around a wage-labor model, it did represent an effort to insure adequate food supplies. But Peel's position became untenable in July 1846, when his effort to repeal the Corn Laws cost him Tory support. The Whig administration of Russell followed, and Trevelyan continued at the Treasury, in charge of Irish relief. Within a year Trevelyan completely overthrew Peel's system, calling it a "monstrous centralization."[23] "A large proportion of the people of Ireland," he writes, "had been accustomed to grow the food they required, each for himself, on his own little plot of ground; and the social machinery by which, in other countries, the necessary supplies of food are collected, stored, and distributed, had no existence there" (IC 253). What defines Trevelyan's repulsion at Peel's program is the metaphor of nature and its "monstrous" other, a trope which demonstrates that we are still at this point solidly within the universe of Condillac. "The monstrous" signifies the violation of nature, and nature here is a process of social abstraction, the spontaneous progress of circulation, standardization, and rationalization. At each stage in this process the regular "machinery" of circulation, which constitutes society in Trevelyan's view, will adapt and develop new capacities: this is the natural course of history in Condillac's terms. Peel's error, for Trevelyan, was to artificially supply a mechanism of circulation, geared to the people of Ireland at their present stage of economic development – i.e. as savages. By supplying this artificial support, Peel's program will fix the Irish at this savage stage and arrest the process of abstraction. This amounts to a "monstrous" inhibition of the natural "machine."[24]

Trevelyan's rhetoric can be set in stark relief by contrasting it with that of Dickens. Writing to his publisher from Switzerland that same summer on the change of governments, Dickens held "no sympathy with the course taken by the Whigs in regard to Ireland after they had defeated Peel."[25] Dickens roundly condemns

the gentle politico-economic principle that a surplus of population must and ought to starve ... I am convinced that its philosophers would sink any government, any cause, any doctrine, even the most righteous. There is a sense and humanity in the mass, in the long run, that will not bear them; and they will wreck their friends always, as they wrecked them in the working of the Poor Law Bill. Not all the figures that Babbage's calculating machine could turn up in twenty generations, would stand in the long run against the general heart.[26]

Here the "machine" is a monstrous and artificial creation, which human beings must struggle against. Whereas "the mass," in Trevelyan's view, needs to be cleaned up and rationalized, for Dickens it possesses a fixed core of human characteristics, a "heart," which must dictate social good.

Trevelyan's view of the Irish economy and his vision of the Famine seem entirely prescribed by the version of Enlightenment rhetoric he employs. This is most plainly apparent in his tirade against what he perceives to be the cause of the entire system of land use in Ireland: the potato. He opens his report by asking, "what hope is there for a nation which lives on potatoes?" (IC 230), and he refers to the potato as "the deep and inveterate root of social evil" (IC 320). Trevelyan seems to base his analysis on a misunderstanding of the Irish term "lazy bed," which described the common method of growing potatoes in elongated hillocks – in fact an extremely labor-intensive and highly productive method of cultivation.[27] He declares however that Irish agriculture was "slovenly" (IC 231) and proceeded only "at the smallest expense of labor" (IC 232). Because he assumes that the potato yielded great amounts of food in Ireland without requiring any strenuous work, Trevelyan concludes that "the people had no incitement to be industrious" (IC 233), and as a result "agriculture of every description was carried out in a negligent, imperfect manner," while "domestic habits" were "of the lowest and most degrading kind" (IC 232). The easy living, which Trevelyan thought was available on potato conacre, had led to a damaging self-sufficiency among the peasantry:

The relations of employer and employed, which knit together the framework of society, and establish a mutual dependence and good-will, have no existence in the potato system. The Irish small holder lives in a state of isolation, the type of which is to be sought for in the islands of the South Sea, rather than in the great civilised communities of the ancient world. (IC 231)

Trevelyan's ill-informed grudge against the potato seems to be that it arrests the natural process of the social "machine," unraveling the fabric of social relations, the "market" of desire and self-perception that Adam Smith described, and obviating any need for a further division of labor. The "deep and inveterate root" seems itself to have a monstrous agency in this account, combating nature's Divine law of development and locking the Irish out of the process of modernization. Even the high level of rural crime – commonly used to intimidate recalcitrant landlords or leasing agents – Trevelyan blames not on a history of colonization, but on the potato: "That agrarian code [of retribution] which is at perpetual war with the laws of God and man, is more especially the offspring of this state of society, the primary object being to secure the possession of the plots of land, which, in the absence of wages, are the sole means of subsistence" (IC 232).

Trevelyan draws abundantly on Adam Smith's rhetoric in describing the results of "the potato system." Where he discusses the practice of subleasing that Irish agriculture had produced, one of his sources describes entailed estates as "clogged with . . . restriction"; he describes bankrupt landlords as "embarrassed" (IC 241). In Book I of *The Wealth of Nations*, Smith describes the division of labor in "savage" societies as being "very much clogged and embarrassed."[28] Trevelyan calls the practice of long-term leasing and subleasing "an endless chain," and he writes of Irish landlords: "we have it in our power to strike off the fetters which at present impede every step of their progress in the performance of the duty they owe to themselves and those dependent on them" (IC 240).

These now clichéd figures of free trade produce for Trevelyan an illusion of Ireland as retrograde in global history. His plan to "stimulate the industry of the people" and "augment the productive powers of the soil" involved the gradual suspension of Peel's programs and the cessation of all special government aid after November 1, 1847. After the extremely high mortality of the winter of that year, the late summer seemed to promise an end to the fungal infestation. Writing apparently in October of 1847, Trevelyan declares that "the famine was stayed" (IC 269) by the government efforts and that no aid would be given beyond the system of Poor Law workhouses. He concludes:

there are sure grounds of hope for the future. The best sign of all is that the case of Ireland is at last understood. Irish affairs are no longer a craft and mystery. The abyss has been fathomed. The famine has acted with a force which nothing could resist, and has exposed to view the real state of the country, so that he who runs may read. (IC 214)

Penetrated now by enlightenment, the occult complexity of Ireland has become mundane. The Famine has made Ireland "legible," speeding up the process of history with a "force which nothing could resist." Having destroyed the unnatural dependence on the potato, the Famine has restarted the engine of industry and abstraction, and "reason is now able to make herself heard" (IC 315). The scouring away of unreason and illegibility seems to Trevelyan to have been an instance of Divine will:

The deep and inveterate root of social evil remained, and this has been laid bare by a direct stroke of an all-wise and all-merciful Providence, as if this part of the case were beyond the unassisted power of man. Innumerable had been the specifics which the wit of man had devised; but even the idea of the sharp but effectual remedy by which the cure is likely to be effected, had never occurred to any one. (IC 320)

But the cost of all this cleanness and light was grave indeed, and for all but the most hard-headed Whig "moralists," Trevelyan's pronouncement of Divine victory must have appeared glib and self-serving. Regular London news reports and daguerreotype prints of Irish suffering would have rendered Trevelyan's account suspect. Even by the fall of 1846, official correspondence from Treasury officers in Ireland had begun to question what Peter Gray calls Trevelyan's "optimistic theodicy."[29] But by the time Trevelyan's essay appeared in January 1848, the London markets had just suffered their devastating crash. His pronouncement of health for Ireland and success for the English administration were premature, with numerous English firms in bankruptcy and the potato blight carrying on for the next three years.

ESOTERIC SOLUTIONS

Critics of Trevelyan's extremism in general favored a continuation of direct government intervention into the food market and the agricultural economy in Ireland. While these critics often justified their proposals by arguing that this was simply the most efficient way to encourage the growth of wage-labor capitalism, they did calculate more realistically what was required to keep people from starving in the short term. Irish economist Isaac Butt argued eloquently, for example, that famine was an exception to the normal rules of circulation:

The folly of relying on private enterprise to supply the deficiency, is proved incontestably by the result. Private enterprise has not saved us from the quarters of the famine . . . All the ordinary demands of civilized life are, doubtless, best met by those spontaneous processes in which the self-interest of man directs his activity and energy in the channels best adapted to supply these demands; but sudden and extraordinary emergencies must be met by other means.[30]

Butt's proposal still conceives of the Famine, however, as an exceptional circumstance, essentially alien to the capitalist market, and not produced or encouraged by it. Another advocate of government intervention was the radical MP George Poulet Scrope, who argued that the Irish Poor Law should be extended to offer relief to any destitute person, and a plan to reclaim and improve waste lands should be established to create agricultural jobs.[31] A proposal similar to Scrope's in general terms can be found in *The Winter of 1846–7 in Antrim*, by Shafto Adair. Adair agrees with Scrope and Butt in supporting government aid to hasten the development of a rationalized labor market. However, his justification for this proposal represents a clearer departure from the terms and assumptions of Trevelyan's school. While Adair advocates free movement of labor, he develops this position only through a complex theory of character, nation, and empire. While he argues that the "mighty principles of civil society" are universal, he claims at the same time that because of its particular mystery, Ireland must be governed by "esoteric" knowledge.[32]

In many ways Adair himself follows the improving path that Trevelyan would recommend for the owners of Irish estates. Set to inherit extensive family lands in County Antrim, Adair spent most of his life in England, making "many and prolonged visits" to the family holdings only after 1840 (*W* 7). From these visits he had become "well satisfied that [he] had a very clear understanding of the general social condition of the country" (*W* 7). But when in the fall of 1846 a large group of men entered Ballymena, a market town on the estate, demanding employment, Adair "felt at once it was [his] duty to be present, as the representative of the proprietor, my father" (*W* 8). What he found in the winter of 1847 persuaded him that he still had very much to learn: "I awoke as from a deep slumber, to behold

the measureless spread of the awful calamity which still devastates Ireland –
and many better informed than myself awoke like me to wonder at and
deplore the depth of our ignorance" (*W* 7). A year later Trevelyan would
write: "the people in some parts of the West of Ireland neglected to a
great extent to lay in their usual winter stock of turf in 1847, owing to
the prevalence of a popular impression that the Queen would supply them
with coals. *Ireland has awakened from this dream* by the occurrence of the
most frightful calamities" (IC 315, my emphasis). By educating himself
about conditions on his father's estates, Adair has ended the sleep of reason
and brought Ireland into the light of knowledge; the Famine has, "made
Ireland known," just as Trevelyan put it. The airing of its occult secrets
will now permit their exposure to rational evaluation and modernization.
However, in Adair's rhetoric, the hidden truths of Ireland become known
not only to the Whitehall administrators, but to Ireland "herself": "Not
in England alone, has knowledge of this Irish condition been a mystery.
Ireland has been a mystery to herself" (*W* 8). And thus the theory of
history as a civilizing machine verges, in Adair's text, on a very different
narrative of development, one where self-knowledge will lead to natural
progress.

The mystery that revealed itself to Adair in Ballymena was "a class whose
numbers, almost whose existence, would never have been known but for
the famine, which drove them into the labour market" (*W* 10). They were
"members of that almost mendicant, but not migratory, class so numerous
throughout Ireland, to whom the Potato afforded a cheap means of subsistence, and who hung upon the skirts of society, in town or country, doing
little or no work and now for the first time compelled to undertake systematic labour" (*W* 9). Trevelyan's equations are apparent here: the potato
indicates idleness, isolation, and ignorance. The "calamity" has thrust these
people into view, and Adair proposes in the rest of his pages, that if they
can be kept from starving they can contribute eventually to the labor of
the nation and the empire. They will, he writes, be "insensibly transformed
from spasmodic exertion to continuous industry" (*W* 68), forced out of
their "foul dens" (*W* 35) and "unclean nests" (*W* 36) which only the densely
cultivated potato had made possible. "The mighty principles of civil society
which have formed the greatness of England, the habits of local administration, the equality before the laws, the accountability of delegated power
to the delegating body, are truths irrespective of race, or clime, and will one
day be recognized in their extension throughout the whole family of man"
(*W* 27–28). For Adair the Famine presents an opportunity to implant these

"principles of civil society," establishing an open circulation of goods and people through the once-occult townlands of Ireland.

And yet, in striking contrast to Trevelyan, Adair insists that in order to develop its civil and economic institutions, Ireland must first understand and change its "character." "Mere regulation," he writes, "will not suffice, a new spirit must be breathed into the quivering limbs of the social body. All present arrangements must be considered as merely temporary palliations; and none can be effectual which do not aim at an elevation of the industrial character" (*W* 29). In the old political economy the machinery of the market produced "character," industrial or otherwise; Adair argues, in language that reflects the New Testament sensibilities of the coming era, that "spirit" and character must exist first.[33] Against Trevelyan's benevolent machine, here "mere regulation" suggests the cold and mechanical inhumanity of *Bleak House's* systems, and "the gentle politico-economic principle that a surplus of population must and ought to starve." Adair insists on providing this "regulating" machinery with a "heart" and a "spirit."

But if character must precede institution or "abstraction," whence can it be derived? Adair proposes his answer when he claims that "the regeneration of Ireland must be esoteric" (*W* 6). That is, it must come from within the circle of Ireland's self-knowledge, accounting for the obscure or occult sensibilities of the hidden interior.[34]

Adair argues this point from several angles. He first suggests that the institutions of feudalism are still latent within Irish agrarian society and that they should be made explicit and revived in order to cultivate mutual dependence between landowner and tenant. "In Ireland where feudalism of tradition is still so rife, and tradition one great means of social control, a power waits upon the steps of the descendant of an old family, unknown probably in the oldest properties in England" (*W* 31). Feudal allegiance is an "esoteric" solution, since it will be recovered from Irish history, not imposed by English theory. English administrators were attempting simply to require by law that all funds for Poor Law workhouses should be raised from local property taxes. For Adair this is forcing a desirable end where it should be rather coaxed out of the native character in which it already inheres: "That property may eventually be as able as it is bound, to support the infirm and destitute of the community I hold to be incontrovertible, – but this innovation must be engrafted on the *unwritten customs* of the community by no superficial or hasty progress" (*W* 38, emphasis original). Under the present English policy, Adair indicates here, the evil "writing" of the law has waylaid the prior, natural "speech" of the nation ("the unwritten customs"). This writing must be introduced organically, made to emerge from within the purity of the voice, "engrafted" into Ireland's own character.

Because he advocates local, native control of relief and agricultural development, Adair favors increased power to the local Poor Law Unions, the governing bodies established to administer the workhouses. As centers of local knowledge and paternal concern, these boards will be "the only body which can combine the pliability of individual action, with the firmness of official administration" (*W* 52). The local union would be constituted "as an executive body, for all, against none" (*W* 54), and it would thus "arbitrat[e] between the poverty and the property of the Union district" (*W* 55). Intimate knowledge of "character" would thus be administered mechanically, by disinterested professionals. Adair laces the rhetoric of the human deep into the heart of the machine.

Adair's splitting off from the tradition of the old political economy is perhaps clearest in his plan for assisted emigration. Able workers, he argues, should be allowed to relocate in the settler colonies of the empire without cost to them. This would encourage a "systematic distribution of labor" (*W* 62), both by bringing workers to labor-starved markets in settler colonies, and by increasing land available in Ireland for the remaining population. These are standard arguments, employed in both England and Ireland. However, Adair explicitly indicates that the psychic or characterological injuries caused by leaving the native village should be compensated by encouraging a sense of nationality, in this case a British one. As opposed to "emigration," which Adair defines as "the thrusting forth of unwelcome inmates from the parent home, as young ravens are driven forth into the wilderness," Adair proposes "colonization, by which systematic facility is afforded to industrious men to found, under other skies, British homes within the circumference of the British Empire" (*W* 60). This striking formulation illustrates Homi Bhabha's notion of national identity as metaphor. "The nation," Bhabha writes, "fills the void left in the uprooting of communities and kin, and turns that loss into the language of metaphor."[35] The vital character of the emigrant, bred in Irish isolation, will be stripped as he is turned in the great wheel of circulation. In order for colonization to succeed, "character" has to be replaced by a new "circumference," a metaphorical notion of commonality with a great circle of invisible allies. The significance of place is taken over by an idea of domestic belonging; rather than being ejected from their "home," the colonists will carry with them the abstract qualities of "British homes," wherever the labor market might take them. The mechanical system must be provided with a metaphysical center, a home, a heart. Perhaps Adair's colonists would take their cue from Dickens: "In all parts of the civilized earth the imaginations of men, women, and children figure this tremendous Old Lady of Threadneedle Street in some rich shape or other."[36]

POTATO MONEY

Fungus and fungibility: Jonathan Pim and Jasper Rogers

With the increasing focus on the specificity of Irish economic conditions during the years of the Famine comes a keen interest in interpreting the potato. Debate over the virtues of the crop was not new in the period, but the Famine marks a watershed in long-standing arguments, shifting their basic terms and assumptions. Perhaps the most famous assessment of the potato's role in Irish culture is Trevelyan's dark pun, the "root of social evil." For Trevelyan it is a plant which produces freakishly large amounts of food from almost no land and even less labor, enabling an unnatural regime of idleness and overbreeding. But Trevelyan's damning of the potato as the "root" of earthly evil points toward an important feature of the Famine debate, and that is a certain connection between potatoes and money. The link Trevelyan hints at is taken up directly by at least two commentators on political economy in Ireland, Jonathan Pim and Jasper Rogers, both of whom argue that for the Irish potatoes functioned as a medium of circulation, as cash.

In one of a series of pamphlets of 1847, Rogers writes "the potato has become the labour coin of the agricultural community. It is, in fact, as much the currency which pays for that description of labour in Ireland, as gold in England... It is... the *bona fide* representative of gold, unjustly permitted to usurp its place."[37] Rogers argues that "the principle is radically wrong which permits labour to be paid for by aught but money, and monstrously absurd that allows the coin of the realm to be represented by a perishable vegetable."[38] Stocks of harvested potatoes function as what he calls a "*Phantom Bank*,"[39] an insubstantial and occult store of value, which – when it fails – will threaten the security of gold reserves in English banks. In this analysis the potato is the dark prince, subverting the true order of light and power that gold signifies, and corrupting its otherwise legitimate reign. Unlike most observers, Rogers acknowledges the potato's extraordinary nutritive power, but he concludes, like Trevelyan, that the "phantom" potato saps the economic life of the country: "the Irish Labourer is not that active and energetic workman at home that he is abroad"; "the system holds him bound by its chains, almost at the lowest depth of human endurance."[40] The dead metaphor in the concept of the free market is revived here, as the tyrant potato binds the Irish worker and prevents the upward course of civilization.

Jonathan Pim's *Conditions and Prospects of Ireland* likewise argues:

> Potatoes were not merely the food of the people of Ireland, but in many places they supplied the place of capital and of a circulating medium. They were the capital which enabled the poor cottier to exert his industry, and the coin in which his labour was paid . . . The loss of potatoes depriving the poor man of his capital, paralysed his industry.[41]

Rogers and Pim derive from these potato-thoughts very different policy conclusions from Trevelyan. While Trevelyan urges non-intervention, to obliterate the class addicted to the evil root, Pim and Rogers argue for government-sponsored work programs, to promote the growth of money wages and the "social machinery" that, for them, money always entails.

In different ways all three of these interpreters of the potato, however, seem to invest it with the imaginative powers of what Marx calls "the fetish form of capital."[42] Neither Rogers nor Pim truly sees the potato working as commercial or interest-bearing capital in Marx's sense. They treat the potato as serving in a variety of monetary functions – as store of value, means of payment, and medium of circulation – and thus they exhibit the same confusion over different forms of money which Marx finds typical in bourgeois political economy. But these analyses of the potato depend on and follow from the fetishized view of capital which Marx diagnoses. With the institutionalization of interest-bearing investments, "capital appears as a mysterious and self-creating source of interest, of its own increase."[43] This idea of money as a self-expanding thing is "the misrepresentation and objectification of the relations of production, in its highest power: the interest-bearing form, the simple form of capital, in which it is taken as logically anterior to its own reproduction process."[44] "Fetish capital" is not an object, but a way of seeing that constructs an object in a blur of social processes. It is, in this way, the ancestor of that crucial twentieth-century object, "the economy": a concept of total money, its shape and its movement, which takes on the appearance of guiding or producing the total social organization of life on the planet.

The gradual rise of the potato as an almost exclusive food source in Ireland developed in response to the colonial seizure of Irish land and the demands of capitalist market farming. This was a system of cultivation that had grown up only in the last couple of hundred years, alongside increasing pressure to maximize agricultural profits. However, these accounts by Pim and Rogers proceed as if the processes of history were inherent properties of the potato itself. During the Famine, when things begin to go wrong, the fetishized potato takes on a dangerous agency of its own, creating a distopian social world, in the same way that fetish capital, supposedly self-producing and self-sustaining, is thought to create utopian progress. In these texts, the potato stands on its own and evolves grotesque ideas out of its starchy brain.[45]

While it seems wrong to equate the potato with coin or money per se – since the circulation of heavy and voluminous potato supplies never arose as a uniform standard of value for other goods – we can see in Pim's and Rogers's idea of potato-money an important divergence from the classical liberal analysis of Irish economic life. Saying that potatoes worked as a form of money suggests a kind of functionalist or at least comparative analysis, in which both England and Ireland, though different, are recognized to have systems of circulation that each operate within the logic of their particular climate, culture, and history. The point of this argument, for Pim and Rogers, is to demote the status of the potato and restore the rule of gold. And still there is an impulse in these texts to consider English and Irish economic life as distinct things, and to compare the way each has been formed through unique adaptations.

The importance of this potato money theory can be highlighted if we contrast it with the representation of the potato most common in earlier debates in politics and political ecnonomy. This status of the potato is clarified in an argument advanced by Catherine Gallagher and Stephen Greenblatt. In the works these two examine, from Arthur Young's celebration of potato productivity in the 1790s to Cobbett's condemnation of it in the 1830s, the potato is understood as a dangerous social and economic anomaly. Because it could be cultivated and consumed by individual families (without the capital-intensive operations of milling and baking that wheat entailed), it stood for an asocial existence, a completely anomic isolation.[46] For Malthus and other political economists, the potato's productivity spoiled the equilibrium of wage rates, removed the fear of unemployment, and promised a terrifying expansion of working-class population.[47] From this point of view, potato subsistence placed the Irish outside the circuit of British custom and capital, and thus hopelessly retarded the progress of world history.

In the era of the Famine, however, potato commentators move toward the idea of a distinctly Irish situation, requiring its own "esoteric" solution. Even in Trevelyan's otherwise classical account, the subtle link he suggests between potatoes and money, as "root" causes, suggests that in Ireland one finds not the absence of a social system, nor the vacant exterior of Britain's economic atmosphere, but rather a system unique unto itself, one that operated without English money, but with a money-system all its own.

While these accounts suggested that for the Irish poor potatoes functioned as money, it seems clear after some recent historical debate that the Irish economy, even in the rural western regions of the country, was rather uniformly monetized on the eve of the Famine. While Lynch and Vaisey in their 1960 history of the Guinness Brewery argued that western Ireland functioned generally outside the monetary system of Great Britain, other research has persuasively disputed their claim.[48] The evidence provided by the Devon Commission on Irish land use, to cite just one mid-nineteenth century example, indicates that even in very isolated regions usurers often provided rent extensions by discounting rent bills, i.e. by loaning cash at interest.[49]

Potato money in Foster's Letters

One could almost argue that this idea of Irish potato money was taken literally in the English popular imagination, for several stories in the London press depict the Irish in a state of confusion over the use and significance of money. In one of a long series of columns in the London *Times*, describing a tour of Ireland in 1845 and 1846, Thomas Campbell Foster recounts a visit to a Galway pawnshop where several large denomination bank notes and a gold guinea had been pawned, and were sitting in a special drawer with their tickets, waiting to be redeemed. Foster's visit to Ireland had been engineered by *The Times* as a way of contesting the evidence presented by the Devon Commission reports. That document, with its emphasis on landlord irresponsibility and the need for legal reforms to manage relations between landlord and tenant, carried a whiff of government interventionism. By contrast, Foster's letters adopted a "populist moralism" that emphasized moral regeneration of the Irish people.[50]

After describing the pawned money in the Galway shop, he suggests these cases confirm his observation that the Irish people are "unused to consider the relative value of money and how it can best be laid out," and have no understanding of "the commercial use of money."[51] Apparently after this account appeared in *The Times*, local newspapers in Galway and Tralee suggested that the credulous Foster had been conned in this encounter and "served in a manner most laughable, and well worthy of an Irish wag."[52] Foster responds sarcastically in a later column by retelling the story of the pawnshop, adding the following meeting with its owner:

In going out we met Mr. Murray, the shopkeeper, who seemed anxious to account for the pawning by various surmises, such as the 10£ note being a daughter's fortune that the poor people did not like to break into, and the guinea being a heir-loom or a pocket-piece. In answer to my question, – "Was a guinea ever left unredeemed and sold as a forfeited pledge?" he replied that this had frequently occurred.[53]

Even if we put to one side the question of whether the pawning was real, Foster's interpretation of what he sees is a little hard to gather. He may be ready to accept that the money was pawned rather than spent because it had some special significance or "sentimental value," as the modern phrase would have it. The suggestion here would be that the Irish are bound to the fixed ties of kinship – the dowry, the keepsake – and that these notes or coins are tenaciously associated with their family connections, such that their money-value cannot be abstracted from its specific form. Even when the whole value of the coin or bill would be lost, if the loan could not be repaid, the Irish (Foster suggests) would prefer to sacrifice its whole value, rather than change it to repay the pawnbroker. Or alternatively, with his question about whether coins and notes had been abandoned at the pawnshop, Foster may believe the owners were ignorant of the money's transferable quality. In either case, Foster's Irish characters mistake abstract signs of value for objects of concrete utility.

Potato money in Dickens's Household Words

In 1850 Charles Dickens published an article in his magazine *Household Words* that makes similar reference to the Irish and their supposed unfamiliarity with money. Dickens tells the story of an Irish man who put some bank notes in a stocking and buried them in his garden. When he retrieves the stocking several months later, he finds it "full of the fragments of mildewed and broken mushrooms."[54] The story is placed in an article on the history of forgery, and, like his "The Old Lady of Threadneedle Street," this piece celebrates the talents of the bank staff, here in their ability to detect authentic bank notes even when partially destroyed. When the bank manager asks the Irish character what he put in the stocking exactly, the man responds as follows: "'There was a twenty as was paid to me by Mr. Phalim O'Dowd, Sir, and a ten as was changed by Pat Reilly, and a five as was owen by Tim; and Ted Connor, ses he to ould Phillips – '."[55] The manager cuts short this explanation, and, after getting a list of the bills the man had stored there, sends the man away. Overnight the bank staff separates and partially reconstructs the fragments of the bills, verifying the man's claim. The next day the man comes back and has his money returned in new bank notes. Dickens describes his reaction in this way: "the man, occasionally murmuring an exclamation of surprise, or a protestation of gratitude, but gradually becoming vague and remote in the latter as the notes re-appeared, looked on, staring, evidently inclined to believe that they were the real lost notes, reproduced in that state by some chemical process."[56]

In this story of 1850, all the complex dimensions of earlier reporting on Irish potatoes seems to be symbolically crystallized. Potato supplies for winter and spring months were often stored in pits and covered with earth. This method effectively preserved the fall harvest for several months, and it was part of the evidence supporting the observations of writers like Pim and Rogers, that in rural Irish society the potato functioned as money or capital: a store of value that could be put away against future need. Diseased potatoes, however, would not keep in this manner, even though they may have looked healthy when dug in the fall, and when the storage pits were opened the potatoes would have completely rotted. The character in this story treats his capital, this time made up of paper, in the traditional manner, and it suffers the same fate as the vulnerable fungus-infested potato. The story recreates in parable form the grim scene that was lived out thousands of times in rural Ireland, where potatoes were found rotten, and people confronted the possibility of outright starvation. Given this allusiveness, the story seems to show that money is better than potatoes, or that wage-labor agriculture is better than subsistence farming, because the transferable value of money can be effectively saved, invulnerable to rust and contamination. As in Foster's account of pawned notes, the man here treats money as if it were an object of use, like a potato, rather than a sign of abstract value. Again this misuse of money is connected with the character's allegiances in a system of kinship and traditional obligation ("Ted Connor . . . ould Phillips," etc.). In Irish society as it is represented in these stories, the abstract qualities or "commercial uses" of money are indistinguishable from specific objects of value.

Stories of this nature, where Irish characters are "fish out of water" in modern urban surroundings, were a part of the literature of the "stage Irishman," long a staple of the British theatre. The diarist's anecdote with which I opened this chapter bears one of these characteristics: the misunderstanding what constitutes elegance. Samuel Lover's novel *Handy Andy* contains a similar episode, in which Andy, the bungling servant, is sent to pick up a letter in town. He believes the largest letters and those with the greatest amount of postage due are the most valuable and so purloins one of these, instead of bringing the one addressed to his employer.[57] Another post office scene appears in an 1852 *Household Words* piece, where an Irish migrant laborer in England believes he can send a £5 money order for the cost of postage fees alone.[58]

But the stories about pawned and buried money seem to take on a different significance in the time of the Famine. Beyond demonstrating the illiterate bumbling of Irish characters – though this does not seem entirely beyond the aims of Foster and Dickens – these stories portray Irish people with relatively large sums of money, which they handle according to the rules of a non-monetary economy. In Foster, the story is offered as explicit evidence that, even when they possess commercial capital, the Irish will not make "commercial use" of it. That is, they will not invest it in improving their farms, but hoard it superstitiously until it moulders or is lost. The characters here do not confuse the "elegant" with the "filthy"; they know the value of money perfectly well, and understand the issuing function of the bank. However, they refuse to treat money as a circulating medium. In these representations, Irish money gets stuck. Thus it seems that these stories function as popular cultural refutations of the "old political economy" that Trevelyan applies to the Irish situation. Where Trevelyan argues that the Famine has rationalized Irish economic life, so that capital may circulate, these stories show the opposite: even when possessed of capital, the Irish will treat it in the old "slovenly" way, preventing its productive movement. Trevelyan argues that "unclogging" the paths of free circulation will set the natural machine of history into motion in Ireland, and Ireland will advance into a capitalist future. These stories see the Irish as somehow fundamentally unfit for such a future, incapable of relinquishing older social ties in order to act within the system of abstract value.

As such then, the stories assert that the principles of character have a determining influence over economic behavior. The forces of Irish identity, or prior "being," cannot be engineered away here by the imposition of "artificial" social systems. This is clearly the philosophical position underlying Dickens's rhetoric: "machines" cannot change "hearts." Foster as well indicates that this is the direction of his analysis in the introduction of his collected *Letters* to *The Times*. Here he draws on the Romantic understanding of racial character, which would dominate later English policy in Ireland and structure Matthew Arnold's famous assessment of Celtic literature. He quotes with approval from J. G. Kohl's 1844 *Travels in Ireland*:

It is the English who constitute the soul and pith of the British power, and it is to them that the Irish owe it if they are able to participate in the wide spread commerce of Great Britain and to share in all the opportunities and advantages that stand open to a British subject. The vigorous, speculative, and persevering Anglo-Saxons, force the indolent and unenergetic Celts along with them on the road of glory and national greatness; they pull them forward somewhat rudely perhaps, but they do pull them forward.[59]

Add Renan's notion of Celtic "effeminacy" – which, it should be pointed out, is nowhere to be found in Trevelyan's assessment of Irish culture – and we have the eventual formula of Arnold's analysis here complete. However, where this German account foresees the Irish pulled into history by the "vigorous" English, later accounts will stress, like Dickens's story of potato money, the total recalcitrance of the Irish racial character, and its final inability to participate in abstract capitalism.

ASENATH NICHOLSON'S NEW DOMESTIC ECONOMY

Perhaps the most striking negotiation between the Enlightenment and romantic paradigms of economic thought in Famine discourse can be found in the unusual work of Asenath Nicholson. An American Protestant evangelist and abolitionist, Nicholson traveled from New York to Dublin in the spring of 1844, "for the purpose," as she put it, "of personally investigating the poor" (see note 61). She stayed for four and a half years and published two books on her visit. The first, *Ireland's Welcome to the Stranger*, describes travels around Ireland in 1844 and was published in 1847. The second, *Lights and Shades of Ireland*, offers an account of the relief work she took up in the gathering crisis of 1845–47 and documents conditions among the poor in these years.

Born Asenath Hatch in rural Vermont, to a family of strict Congregationalists, Nicholson passed her early life as a school teacher before moving to New York sometime around 1830. There she married a business man, William Nicholson, and with him ran a number of temperance boarding houses in the city, which themselves became meeting places for a variety of abolitionists and political reformers.[60] "It was in the garrets and cellars of New York," she writes in her first volume, "that I first became acquainted with the Irish peasantry, and it was there I saw they were a suffering people."[61] Nicholson committed herself to the redress of the massive social inequalities she saw in New York's immigrant slums, and after the death of her husband in 1843 she decided to travel, alone, to Ireland. She writes:

I came to gather no legends of fairies or banshees, to pull down no monarchies, or set up any democracies; but I came to glean after the reapers, to gather up the fragments, to see the poor peasant by wayside and in bog, in the field and by his peat fire, and to read to him the story of Calvary.[62]

She aims in part to bring the Bible to Catholic Ireland, to "read . . . the story of Calvary" to anyone prepared to listen. But what becomes more evident in her writing is her determination "to see the poor peasant," to see the "fragments" of Irish life more or less obscured by previous tourists, Celticists, and surveyors. Her books develop a keenly observed critique of Irish social and economic conditions, one that resonates in profound ways with a larger critique of British political economy that was gaining currency in the 1840s.

The phrase "new domestic economy" I have used in my title is a gesture toward economist Pedro Schwartz's book *The New Political Economy of John Stuart Mill*. In this work, Schwartz presents Mill as an influential critic of the rational principles associated with what he once called the "old political economy" of Smith, Malthus, and Ricardo,[63] and an advocate of a more humane science of wealth and progress. Mill's works on economics are exactly contemporary with Nicholson's two volumes, spanning the middle years of the 1840s, and if we read for the economic perspective developed in Nicholson's texts, we find that the two writers have a great deal in common. Her critique of the "old political economy," however, invokes the domestic household as a model of economic efficiency, tempered and motivated by sentimental feeling. Thus she proposes a new political economy through the vision of a transformative domestic economy. Nicholson deploys the values associated with domestic femininity in this period to develop a scathing critique both of British government policy during the Famine and of laissez-faire political economy in general. While valuing the industry and efficiency stressed in classical political economy, she excoriates its "mechanical" disregard for individual humanity, and compromises its "machine" of circulation with the disciplined tenderness of family relations. Like Dickens's Esther Summerson, she attempts to order the chaos of circulation, "with love."

Nicholson lands at Kingstown in the early summer of 1844. As she grows familiar with the hungry street people of Dublin and the attitudes of the elite Protestant classes, she proposes the solution to poverty in Ireland that will carry through all her work, describing travels over the whole of Ireland from 1844 to 1848. She writes:

Suppose fifty ladies in the city, who have leisure, should go out at ten in the morning, and mingle promiscuously with the poor upon the street, ascertaining who is worthy, and who unworthy . . . who are idle from necessity, and who from choice . . . By four o'clock in the afternoon each could ascertain the true condition of twenty persons at least, making in all a thousand, who might be truly deserving, and who, with a little assistance of work and necessaries, would soon be placed beyond want. But be careful that the payment be a full equivalent.[64]

Middle-class women here spread to the poor the principles of thrift and economy. They discern the diligent and assist them in setting up independent households, where they can support themselves by the careful, rational management of their market-rate wages. These middle-class women "mingle promiscuously with the poor," like both the government inspectors and reporters on poverty in this era, and the prostitutes who were frequently objects of their official interest. Here, and throughout her work, Nicholson frankly asserts the responsibility of women to go out alone, risking, as she did, the scandal of being seen as a streetwalker, to spread the cure of economic efficiency.

In her second book she praises the women of the Belfast Ladies' Association on this account. This group set up a series of "Industrial Schools" for poor children. These schools are so effective, Nicholson argues, because they are organized and supported not by paid administrators, presumably male, but by volunteers, that is, by women. Professional relief workers, she argues, sequester themselves in offices and when touring among the poor "take the highest seat in a public conveyance . . . the most comfortable inns [and] . . . the best dinner and wines." Volunteers, however, work out of a "kindly spirit" and are "found mingling with the poorest, often taking the lowest seat, curtailing all unnecessary expense." They "loo[k] into the causes of distress, that [they] might better know how to remove them."[65] In other words, volunteers apply the principles of domestic economy to the task of helping the poor, mingling the techniques of efficient administration with feelings of affection and care.

Through the public work of these women, Nicholson writes, "the highways and hedges were faithfully visited, the poor sought out, their condition cared for, and the children of the most degraded class were taken and placed in a school, which continues to flourish on an extensive scale."[66] Like Trevelyan, Nicholson here sees poor relief as a means to bring a "hidden," pre-modern Ireland into the light of industrial modernity. In the description that follows this passage, the "industry" taught in the Industrial schools becomes a consuming metaphor for self-improvement, in language reminiscent of Charles Babbage or Andrew Ure, proponents of the supposedly healthful qualities of repetitive machinery labor:

The happy effects of industry on the minds of the children were striking. That passive indifference to all but how a morsel of bread should be obtained, was exchanged for a becoming manner and animated countenance, lighted up by the happy consciousness, that industry was a stepping-stone which would justly and honourably give them a place among the comfortable and respectable of the earth . . . While these benevolent women were teaching the practice of industry to the poor, they found the benefit react upon themselves, for they too must be industrious.[67]

However, for Trevelyan, Babbage or Ure, machines and money reshape private desires and domestic habits. For Nicholson the process is exactly the reverse: In her hands "industry" is first of all a quality of human behavior, a value best taught at home, which will itself radiate through the public arena of the market and transform it.

The power of domestic economy is most fiercely defended in Nicholson's description of the first moments of crisis, in the winter of 1845–46, when starving people began to multiply on the streets of Dublin, and when the first shipments of American corn meal were released by the English government into Irish wholesale markets. She opens this chapter not by enumerating the conditions of suffering among the poor – though she does go on to specify these in compelling detail – but by excoriating the domestic habits of rich mothers. While the Irish poor had been widely accused of laziness, she argues that it is "the rich" who "are idle from a silly pride and long habits of indulgence . . . Their late hours of rising and of meals," she writes, "necessarily unhinge all that is good in housekeeping, and where all is left to servants, economy must come in by-the-by."[68] The typical daughter of this class, Nicholson also complains, is frivolously educated: "She is sent to school, and goes the routine of a genteel education. She can work Berlin wool, perhaps read French, and possibly German, play the piano, and write a common-place letter, in *angular* writing, made *on purpose* for the ladies; but with all this her mind is not *cultivated*, her heart is not disciplined."[69] This indiscipline at the heart and hearth of what should be, in Nicholson's view, Ireland's leadership class, results in disaster at a time of crisis:

When the famine had actually come, and all the country was aghast, when supplies from all parts were poured in, what was done with these supplies: Why the best that these inefficient housekeepers *could* do. The rice and Indian meal, both of which are excellent articles of food, were cooked in such a manner that, in most cases, they were actually unhealthy, and in all cases unpalatable.[70]

After describing the rejection of the corn by the Irish poor she concludes, "Had the women of the higher classes known how to prepare these articles in a proper manner, much money might have been saved, and many lives rescued, which are now lost."[71] The suffering results here from a misunderstanding of what it means to be a good woman. The crisis of the Famine is a crisis of motherhood.

In one way it might seem that Nicholson's emphasis on good housekeeping here is simply an extension of the principles of market efficiency and economic rationality that were proposed by the classical economists. Nicholson was certainly a free-trader of sorts. Her discussion of Irish history focuses on the English inhibition of Irish trade as a perennial cause of poverty.[72] Like Trevelyan, she prefers private voluntary relief, organized by concerned women, over government-organized efforts by male professionals. But in Nicholson's account there is no dire logic of atonement for sin. For Trevelyan the Famine is a Divine hand, sweeping clean the cluttered corners of the Irish landscape. Nicholson's economics differ from this providentialist view in clear ways. First, she espouses a kind of Smithian optimism about the improvements that domestic economy will bring. For Adam Smith, economic efficiency – in the form of the division of labor – would yield public good; in Nicholson, *domestic* efficiency – organized by what she calls "the rational mother" – increases public good. Secondly, economic efficiency is characterized not merely by rational discipline, but by, in the phrase I quoted above, a "disciplined heart." This concept of a rationally ordered love, a classic union of what were considered masculine and feminine principles, appears also in Nicholson's metaphor of domestic efficiency as a kind of industrial machine. In her discussion of the Belfast Ladies' Association, she comments on the "mutual confidence" these women feel in each other. She argues that to "those moving in the machinery" – that is, the metaphorical machinery of the industrial school system – this mutual confidence was "like a heavenly influence distilling unperceived into the hearts of all."[73] The sentimental heart of the industrial machine here is like the loving domestic home, the center of an industrial economy whose free movement and efficiency is only heightened by its love.

Nicholson's particular politics of domesticity draws from a number of popular movements in this period. It exemplifies a growing American emphasis on domestic femininity, as proposed for example in Catherine Beecher's 1841 *Treatise on Domestic Economy*, a volume reprinted many times through the 1840s and 1850s.[74] Students of the English novel will also recognize what Catherine Gallagher has called the metonymic discourse of domesticity, where the maternal power of the feminine household is shown to benefit every person that comes in contact with it, transforming national morality and economy slowly as its example spreads.[75] The politics of domesticity in these movements formed one important cultural wing of the critique of the old political economy. Against the cold logic of the market, they pose the warm affections of the heart. Nicholson's insistence on the political and broadly social power of domestic feeling echoes with the critique of industrialization in the 1840s. Her metaphor of the machine with the feeling heart anticipates the cruder pronouncements of Dickens's *Hard Times* in 1854.

But a different intellectual touchstone for Nicholson's texts is a new evolving understanding of the concept of nationality and its true meanings. Nicholson's first book presents documentary evidence of Irish poverty on the eve of the Famine. The second presents a stronger call for action to stem the mortality of the Famine and prevent its recurrence. Perhaps to further her claims to the authority of these arguments, Nicholson opens this second volume with a two-hundred page summary of Irish history. Throughout this section of the book, she favors the view which was held out to her by the Irish poor: Ireland was a great nation in ancient times, a land of saints, whose history had been rewritten by its conquerors into a string of defeats. She writes,

When searching for truth concerning a nation 'scattered and peeled,' as the Irish have been, the true ore can better be found in the unpolished rubbish, in the traditions of a rude nation, retained from age to age, than among the polished gems of polite literature, written to please rather than instruct, and pull down rather than to build up.[76]

In describing her travels, she stresses the spontaneous speech of unlettered peasants and the potentially corrupting and damaging influence of education. She celebrates one Connemara girl she encounters who speaks only Irish, and whose "broadly spread feet . . . had never been cramped by cloth or leather . . . She had another qualification," Nicholson continues, "viz. that of singing: this was always performed in Irish, and with tones and gestures which made every auditor feel to the bottom of his soul."[77] The portrait follows a logic that Seamus Deane has clarified in another context: the necessary link in the cultural nationalism of this period between speech and land.[78] The influence of Irish speech and soil, uncontaminated by the principles of English language or capital, have revealed a superior, because aboriginal, character. Among Irish-speakers from remote regions, the "ruling passions" of hospitality, politeness, and generosity remain pure and are even intensified in the crisis.[79] In the towns, however, where they are presumably exposed to the "polished gems of polite literature," the poor lose their instinctive politeness: "The Irish, whether unlike all others I do not pretend in this particular . . . do not become less savage and impetuous by a superficial, and what may be termed common, education. The labouring classes in towns and villages are less courteous, less humane, and more impetuous, than in remote mountains."[80]

Thus while the remote Irish-speakers are "savage," they possess an innate civility. Though they believe in a variety of superstitions, which Nicholson occasionally enumerates, these "are more poetical than frightful, and they generally turn all supernatural appearances to a favourable account."[81] Nicholson's seeming praise of orality here aligns her decisively with Rousseau. She characterizes Irish speech as a primitive poetry, encoding literal superstitions and erroneous perceptions into metaphorical or "poetic" signs. The celebration of these expressive qualities, however, carries the assumption that the Irish are "younger," or less advanced than their industrialized brother nations: Her travels among the Irish poor convince her "that man, fresh from the hand of the maker, needs no missionary societies to teach him benevolence, nor schools of the polished to teach him gentility; and it is because these have been so defaced by man's education that they must be rubbed up and put on by artificial training."[82]

Nicholson suggests then that only by understanding the spontaneous poetry and generosity of the rural Irish can one gain access to the nation's true character, and shatter the stereotypes of indolence and improvidence. And only by accessing this true character can one provide the sort of education that would develop industry, public and private. Her characterization of the Irish as coming "fresh from the hand of the maker" in fact fits neatly with Thomas Davis's "Young Ireland,"[83] a group which despite its potentially militant character embraced the idea, as David Lloyd has argued, that Ireland was one of the "minor" or relatively primitive members of the family of nations.[84] Davis's economics followed from this view; he argued the case for peasant ownership of land in Ireland, rather than the wage-labor system urged by free-traders in England.[85] Nicholson argues in effect for the "political ethology" which John Stuart Mill proposed, where the fixed laws of production must be accommodated to the particular "desire to accumulate" within a given nation.

The value of what Mill called "ethology" had become widely recognized by 1881, when Gladstone spoke out in the House of Commons against those who would apply the "principles of *abstract* political economy to the people and circumstances of Ireland" as if "proposing to legislate for the inhabitants of Saturn and Jupiter."[86] The "old political economy" that had motivated a sluggish policy of Famine relief was dying, and a new interest in national culture was taking its place. Nicholson's vision of the poetic and polite Irish, marred by being funneled in to the British cash nexus of the towns, contributed to this shift in economic discourse in Ireland during this period. It is in this context that we should place Nicholson's economic thought, though of course she works the flip side of the model from her male counterparts. For her, trade or land legislation could never have the transformative power of the maternal force in the household.

Seeing the work of Adair, Foster, Dickens, and Nicholson as part of the broad shift in nineteenth-century economic thought allows us to trace the common assumptions that informed this Irish reaction, as well as the marginal revolution of the century's close. While the Irish discourse of the 1840s and 1850s centers on the idea of the nation, and the marginalist theory of value on the individual consumer, both rely on the idea of prior character, of an identity endowed by Divine force, exterior to and sheltered from human history. The insistence on the uniqueness of the Irish national character made for an effective critique of England's devastating course of action during the Famine. But while the providentialist political economy of the 1840s was finally discredited, capitalist market expansion certainly was not. One of the opportunities presented then by an analysis of the economic rhetoric of this period is its dialectical dimension: the Irish critique derides classical political economy as a hypocritical justification of free trade, and yet the central category of this critique – the romantic emphasis on natural character – will reemerge as a fundamental assumption within the neoclassical justification of the market.

Because of these similarities, I think, we need to understand the era of the Famine as the beginning of an extended period of transition from European colonialism to what is commonly referred to today as neo-colonialism. The decline of European empires built on the direct institutional control of subject states accommodated a new regime, where global power relations could be represented simply in economic terms, and policy toward newly sovereign states of the Third World could be understood in terms of free trade or fair investment. In the texts by Nicholson and Adair here, the terms of protest against the cruelties of colonial capitalism are the same ones which today enable the hegemonic status of economic globalization.

Nationalism – the emerging platform of all these Famine-era protests – became for Ireland the central term of social analysis by the second half of the nineteenth century, informing the legislative movements for land reform and home rule, the war of independence and civil war, and the shape of political discourse in the Irish Republic after partition. Only recently has the foundational status of nationality been questioned or critiqued, though often, at present, from positions equally amenable to the ideologies of global capitalism. If we place the mid-nineteenth century emergence of cultural nationalism within the broader history of neo-colonial relations, we can begin to see beyond the restricted terms of the debate at the time of the Famine.

The rhetoric of the texts I have examined makes two positions possible: the universal laws of the market, or the timeless specificities of race. Recent scholarship has begun to make it clear, however, that the experience of the subaltern Irish in the century leading up to the Famine escapes the representations generated by both of these positions. The work of geographer Kevin Whelan in particular is crucial in this regard. Drawing on a variety of evidence, Whelan argues that the style of clustered settlement on marginal, rented land – the *clachan* or rundale village – was a recent and highly rational response to particular socio-economic conditions in the eighteenth and early nineteenth centuries: "Rundale villages were not the degraded relics of an archaic, aboriginal settlement form, practicing primitive agriculture in 'refuge' areas. They were instead a sophisticated solution to specific ecological, demographic and social problems, which maximised the carrying capacity of a meagre environment in an expanding demographic regime."[87] The communal use of leased land, in shared pastures and rotated fields for potato garden, may have developed gradually out of older practices of land use in Celtic Ireland.[88] But the specific technologies of the *clachan* originated much more recently, in response to rent pressure, competition for good land, and the characteristics of the potato. This relatively modern style of village settlement spread with unusual speed during the eighteenth century over the once-sparsely populated West of Ireland.

Cormac Ó Gráda's recent work in economic history also confirms that the lifeways of pre-Famine Ireland escaped the analytical frames of both classical political economists and cultural nationalists. His survey of average heights among Irish men, though drawn from scanty sources, indicates that Irish laboring classes had a significant height advantage over English in the same periods.[89] Ó Gráda interprets this, along with other non-traditional indicators, as an indication that standards of living in pre-Famine Ireland were high in comparison with the rest of Europe. The apparent height advantage, he writes, "was not due to higher living standards in the conventional sense of greater purchasing power; nevertheless these results indicated that Irish poverty was mitigated by a nutritious diet."[90] Such recent accounts suggest that the "hidden" corners of the Irish landscape were not the backwaters of filth and poverty that middle-class observers frequently imagined, but rather bustling, modern, and comfortable settlements. These settlements did not conform to the Smithian historiography of the old political economy, since they increased production efficiency through a communal division of labor, not one driven by an increasingly individualized sense of self-interest. The *clachan* exceeded the brief of cultural nationalism as well: its communal technologies violated the boundaries of the family, and were in many ways quite well attuned to the forces of market capitalism, in the particular colonial form it took on in Ireland. What is certainly the case, however, is that these communal lifeways produced a rich cultural heritage, one which was destroyed by the depopulation which Famine-era policies orchestrated, and paved over by the regulated landscape of the family farm. The loss of this communalist heritage, which can only be imaginatively reconstructed today by careful research, is one of the most enduring losses brought about by the Famine.

CHAPTER 5

Toward a social theory of wealth: three novels by Elizabeth Gaskell

The debate over the Irish Famine makes clear the two basic positions in economic thought around 1850. The first is Trevelyan's: the faith in the market as an infallible machine of enlightenment. As I argued above in chapter 2, this is not in fact the view of capitalist markets that the early classical political economists produced, but it was the one Victorian thinkers assigned to them. The other position is the kind of romantic humanism visible in Adair and Nicholson, one that works through theories of human nature, national character, and sexual difference and leads often to a neo-feudal theory of class interdependence. This is the terrain Elizabeth Gaskell enters when she publishes her first novel in 1848.

The problem with the romantic critique of political economy, as I argued in the first section of this book, is that it was in the end very easily absorbed back into mainstream economics, turned toward a new justification of market capitalism. It protested against the kinds of ill-treatment that political economy viewed as inevitable and beneficial, but it failed to show that these abuses were the result of capitalism itself. As a result, its plea for the humane treatment of all people could be assimilated into later nineteenth-century economic theory, which was then able to arm itself against all objections launched on humanitarian grounds. It was classical political economy that claimed that the market could change and actually improve people, though this improvement might come at the cost of their lives. Neoclassical economics claimed only that the market gave people, as individuals, exactly what they wanted.

In *Mary Barton* (1848) Gaskell begins solidly within the romantic tradition, drawing explicitly on a philological theory of national character. With later work in *Cranford* (serialized 1851–53) and in *North and South* (1854–55), Gaskell begins to move out of this position, working toward a broader critique of the philosophies and forces of the capitalist market. She does this by reopening the question of economic history which was so central to the work of Adam Smith.

HOUSEHOLD WORDS: "HOMELY AND NATURAL LANGUAGE"
IN *MARY BARTON*

Mary Barton follows two Manchester working-class families, the Bartons and the Wilsons, through several lean years at the Manchester textile mills. It comments on the economics of the factory production system, but as many readers have noted, it attempts this primarily by depicting the private lives and domestic expenditures of workers and managers. While *Mary Barton* is among a class of socially engaged works that Raymond Williams described as "industrial novels,"[1] we see almost nothing of industrial work, since the novel never takes us beyond the factory door. The work depicted most frequently in the novel is in fact sewing, which we see both as unpaid labor in the household, and, through the title character's apprenticeship to a dressmaker, as paid manufacturing employment. As the novel opens, wages are declining and factory workers are being laid off, as orders for English textiles decrease in the early 1840s. With no provision for their survival, workers and their families begin to starve. Gaskell depicts with stark indignation the suffering workers experience as they try to negotiate with owners and, when they are only ridiculed, eventually strike.

While Raymond Williams's discussion of *Mary Barton* and other "industrial novels" in *Culture and Society* did a great deal to focus critical attention upon these texts, his dismissal of the private and domestic strand of the novel as "the familiar and Orthodox plot of the Victorian novel of sentiment" has become mildly notorious.[2] At least since Rosemarie Bodenheimer's 1981 essay "Private Grief and Public Acts," most readers have assumed some "essential consistency of the novel's internal conflicts."[3] As will be clear from the work of preceding chapters, one premise of my argument here is that the understanding of private life and private desire is crucial to an emerging theory of capitalist markets. However, the conception of the domestic in *Mary Barton* is more radical and far-reaching than that we have seen so far in the English or Irish context. Both Dickens and Wills's "The Old Lady of Threadneedle Street" and the work of Asenath Nicholson posit middle-class femininity as a norm, and then use it as a metaphor to critique the masculinist assumptions of economic theory. *Bleak House* complicates this formula somewhat in its depiction of Esther, by indicating the status of women's domestic labor as a commodity, a hard-earned set of skills that will be bought and sold. *Mary Barton* tries to escape the formula completely. It focuses, like *Bleak House*, on the boundaries of the class system, but instead of looking at the ragged lower fringes of the middle class, it is concerned with the dividing line between working-class survival and starvation. This class setting, and the novel's depiction of women's wage labor, seem to leave behind any attempt to "domesticate" the wildness of the market.

However, while the image of home as middle-class refuge is shattered, the novel bases its critique of political economy on a different and much broader notion of home, one that still rests ultimately upon an idea of domestic womanhood. But to see this conception of home and the debate about economics that it enables in the novel, we need to take several steps backwards, for the novel's most substantial contributions to this debate emerge through its interest in the question of language. As Hilary Schor has pointed out, what unites the novel's two plots most clearly is "a sense that power is linguistically motivated and enabled."[4] Considering the issue of language in the novel, many readers have remarked especially on the novel's interest in speech – as cross-class communication, legal testimony, self-expression.[5] I argued in the first section of this book that political economy in the nineteenth century gradually adopts a philological model of the speaking subject, with all its attendant metaphysics. With this observation in mind, I look here at how *Mary Barton's* representation of language shapes its understanding of the economic problems it depicts.

Dialect speech and professional writing

At first glance, the most prominent clue to the novel's interest in language is its careful use of the Lancashire dialect spoken by its working-class characters. Gaskell not only provides annotation for words and phrases unfamiliar to middle-class ears, she offers etymologies for particular Anglo-Saxon derivations, comparing current Lancashire usage to the language of Chaucer and Wyclif. The word "dree," as in the phrase "dree work," or "dry work," she traces to the Anglo-Saxon "dreogan," to suffer or endure for a long period.[6] When one character declares, "I'll not speak of it no more," using a double negative, she comments in a note that "a similar use of the double negative is not unfrequent in Chaucer" (*MB* 145), and she provides an example from the *Miller's Tale*. As much, then, as providing translations for the middle-class reader, Gaskell seems to be addressing the question of linguistic history. Dialect words, she suggests, are not a crude and random slang but simply terms from a more ancient English, still in local usage. Likewise grammatical idiosyncrasies, she demonstrates, are part of the English literary heritage, only latterly frowned upon.

The importance of dialect can be seen most clearly if we connect it with the novel's broader interest in the particular custom and character of regions.[7] In several scenes local or traditional foods are shown to have great significance. In chapter 2 the Bartons bring their friends, the Wilsons, home to tea, and Mary is sent to the shops to purchase ham and eggs for the meal. "And get it Cumberland ham," her mother instructs, "for Wilson comes from there-away, and it will have a sort of relish of home with it he'll like" (*MB* 50–51). The "relish of home" is also tasted in the sweet clap bread Alice Wilson makes, in a recipe common to her childhood home farther north. But these local peculiarities exist primarily now as nostalgic memories of countryside practices among a new class of urban workers. "The agricultural laborer," we are told, "generally has strong local attachments; but they are far less common, almost obliterated, among the inhabitants of a town" (*MB* 158).

As England urbanizes, Gaskell suggests, local customs and flavors are "almost obliterated," but not completely forgotten. For if a local practice – like a particular saying, or a special way of smoking a ham – is no longer a continuing strategy of everyday life, it can still be retrieved and used on special occasions as a *reminder* of home. This point is made most forcefully in the story of Margaret Legh. Margaret supports herself and her grandfather, Job, by taking in sewing. "Plain work pays so bad," she explains, "and mourning has been so plentiful this winter, I were tempted to take in any black work I could, and now I'm suffering from it" (*MB* 86). The black fabric of mourning dress is a greater strain on the eyes, and the low wages require Margaret often to work into the night with only a single candle. As a result, when the novel opens, she is nearly blind and faced with the prospect of losing her entire income. Rather than suturing up the voids in the masculine world of business, as in "The Old Lady of Threadneedle Street," sewing here is bound to the chaotic and mechanical forces of the market, which sets its own value regardless of human cost.

The solution to Margaret's situation draws, however, on the metaphor of home in a different way. Margaret has an excellent voice and is discovered by a man who delivers scholarly lectures on English folksong at the Mechanics Institute in Manchester, and in similar halls around the country. Margaret is hired by him to sing old-fashioned songs and working-class ballads, like "The Oldham Weaver," which is transcribed in the text. In this lecture-hall setting, the tunes are transplanted from their local context – the conditions of their performance and significance – and staged, partly as musical productions, but also partly as objects of scholarly observation and analysis. Margaret, however, is well rewarded for her work, and in fact most of the money we see in the text comes from her. She loans a sovereign to Mary when times are very bad in the strike, and another to sponsor Mary's emergency trip to Liverpool in the novel's central episode. The novel depicts a generation for the first time displaced from localities of birth, clustered in heterogeneous communities around the giant factories. In this new atmosphere of upheaval, local identity, "almost obliterated" by economic change, reemerges, no longer as a way of life, but primarily as a commodity. The patterns of activity that had once produced a lifetime of home-like tastes and sounds are gone, but these tastes and sounds can be fleetingly recaptured, to be consumed in an evening meal or a concert, and then remembered sadly.

One effect of all this local detail is to emphasize the exotic peculiarity of the Lancashire working class, much in the tradition of Edgeworth and Scott's marketing of Irish and Scottish locations, and Dickens's presentation of poor street culture for fascinated middle-class readers in *Oliver Twist*. But alongside this regional exoticism, the text makes an argument that the poor remain closer to an original English linguistic heritage, while a more mobile middle class becomes increasingly distant from it. This idea emerges in the contrast drawn between the dialect of the main characters and the language of various professionals in the novel. During the strike, a London union organizer addresses the Manchester strikers, we are told, "with a forced theatrical voice" in a speech sprinkled with erroneous classical allusions (*MB* 237). This is set off from the "more homely and natural language" of the workers (*MB* 237). It is after listening to this inflated speech that John Barton conspires to murder the mill owner's son, Harry Carson. The poisonous and artificial language of the middle-class professions is responsible not only for this crime, it seems, but also for the initial failure of the police to solve it. The police investigating this crime work according to formalized procedure, focusing on orderly professional process and cultivating a cool emotional detachment. They report the murder to Carson, the father, as follows:

The policemen looked at each other. Then one began, and stated that having heard the report of a gun in Turner Street, he had turned down that way . . . that as he (the policeman) came nearer, he had heard footsteps as of a man running away . . . That he had even been startled when close to the body, by seeing it lying across the path at his feet. (*MB* 261)

The police proceed in just the routinized and repetitive fashion the language here indicates (that . . . that . . . that), and they perceive only the surface of a string of occurrences, without insight into their cause or connection. In their mechanistic approach, they grope blindly into the case, stumbling over the victim in the dark. They refer to each other likewise by number, as in "officer No. B. 72" (*MB* 276) and operate with a machine-like regularity, no matter what particulars they are dealing with. Contrast this with the evaluation of the murder scene later that night, by Mary's aunt, Esther:

She crossed into the field where she guessed the murderer to have stood; it was easy of access, for the worn, stunted hawthorn-hedge had many gaps in it. The night-smell of bruised grass came up from under her feet . . . She hushed her breath with involuntary awe, but nothing else told of the violent deed by which a fellow-creature had passed away . . . Suddenly . . . she became aware of something white in the hedge. (*MB* 288–89)

The feelingless language of the police blinds them to the key features of the crime scene, but Esther's view of the scene is depicted as one of enormous emotional and psychological depth, and this allows her to find a piece of evidence the police missed. Esther is on the street at night because, now estranged from the Barton family, she works as a prostitute.[8] This becomes crucial in the novel's understanding of women's labor, a theme I will return to below.

As a result of their errors, the police accuse the wrong man, and his trial takes up much of the novel's third volume. Here again Gaskell satirizes the heavily conventionalized and elaborate language of lawyers and celebrates the clear expressions of the working-class witnesses brought to testify. The lawyers speak, we are told, in a "garb of unaccustomed words" (*MB* 397). When a key witness who can provide an alibi for the accused man is finally located, the barrister for the defense

took heart when he was put in possession of these striking points to be adduced, not so much out of earnestness to save the prisoner, of whose innocence he was still doubtful, as because he saw the opportunities for the display of forensic eloquence which were presented by the facts; 'a gallant tar brought back from the pathless ocean by a girl's noble daring,' etc. (*MB* 395)

The novel portrays the speech of the middle class and the professional world as undergoing a pitiless standardization. While their English becomes artificial and homogenized, the working class still retains some closeness to a supposedly truer character of Englishness. This is still preserved in what the novel describes as "rough Lancashire eloquence" (*MB* 220) or, in a crucial reference, "racy Lancashire dialect" (*MB* 440). "Racy" in the early nineteenth century referred to that quality of things that identifies them with a certain place. It was used in particular to describe wines: a "racy vintage" was one redolent of the sun and soil of its region.[9] In Gaskell's metaphor, the dialect of the working class, like the Cumberland ham, still contains some of the tang of home; it is "racy" in that it displays the character of the race. This depiction of the working class places them

closer to an imagined core of essential English traits. The novel thus frames
its political-economic questions with the idea of a national, or what the
twentieth century will call – in a concretization of Gaskell's metaphor –
racial, character.

The artificiality of professional language is associated in the novel with
writing, as the police read from their notes, the union organizer displays
his knowledge of classical letters, and the lawyer for the defense is seen
persistently scribbling: "scratch, scratch, scratch" (*MB* 365). Writing betrays
Mary in a key scene, when she travels alone to Liverpool in search of the
sailor who can provide an alibi for the innocent man. She does not write
down the name of his ship, preferring to trust to memory, but she does carry
with her the defense lawyer's business card, on the back of which she writes
an address where she is to rendezvous with her friends that evening. This
card, however, is lost, and Mary is stranded on her own in an unfamiliar
city. The gruff sailor who gives Mary shelter tries to bring her out of a faint
by burning a quill pen. His wife comments that "burnt feathers is always
good for a faint" (*MB* 377), indicating the need to destroy the artificial
influence of the pen before Mary can be revived.

This Liverpool episode takes place under an "Indian ink sky" (*MB* 356),
recalling a similar description of a grim Manchester winter earlier in the
novel: "Houses, sky, people, and everything looked as if a gigantic brush
had washed them all over with a dark shade of Indian ink" (*MB* 81). The
threatening aspect of the landscape in these scenes is written in ink. An impending storm of writing appears also in the representation of Margaret's
grandfather, Job Legh. Job is an amateur biologist; his interest in plants
and animals, however, is entirely absorbed in the Linnean classification of a
collection of specimens. Rather than searching for underlying principles of
morphology and adaptation among disparate species, as in the comparative
biology of Cuvier, Legh follows the eighteenth-century practice of extensive cataloguing and labeling. When Mary asks him to explain part of his
collection, he offers only a list of Latin terms: "[Mary] was not prepared for
the technical names which Job Legh pattered down on her ear, on which
they fell like hail on a skylight; and the strange language only bewildered
her more than ever" (*MB* 77). Familiar with Latin, Job functions also as
liaison to the lawyers during the trial episode and is thus tainted with their
professional detachment from the truth of the case. This is indicated in his
persistent assumption of Jem's guilt in the murder (*MB* 305). Moreover,
Job's commitment to technical systems of written information conditions
his views on political economy. He is anti-union, staunchly liberal, arguing
that the solution to the loom-weavers' poverty is simply "to set trade free,

so as workmen can earn a decent wage, and buy their two, ay and three, shirts a-year; that would make weaving brisk" (*MB* 130).

The most treacherous bit of writing in the novel turns out to be the bit of evidence Esther finds at the murder scene. The white flash in the hedge "prove[d] to be a little piece of stiff writing paper compressed into a round shape. She understood it instantly; it was the paper that had served as wadding for the murderer's gun" (*MB* 289). Written on this scrap of paper is the name "Mary Barton," along with her address. The paper, Mary herself is able to deduce, is from a valentine sent to her by Jem Wilson; her father tore off a piece of it to serve as packing for the gun.[10] A valentine here would represent the novel's vision of the best use of writing – a blend of technical skill or convention, in shaping letters and spelling words, carefully executed to express an inner truth – a truth, as we say on Valentine's Day, of the heart. This is the arrangement provided in *Bleak House*, where Esther's name, signed "with love," seals the gap between the forced routinization of work and the spontaneity of natural affection. But here the power of writing, as an enduring way to record spontaneous truth, has failed. In this use of Mary's written name, the element of spirit, feeling, or love, has been discarded, and the pure material technology of writing, the mass of the paper itself, is turned to violence.[11]

Carlyle and Trench

The references above depict writing as a mechanical or artificial system of communication, one which, like any machine created by human art, is prone to breakdown, as in the card gone astray, or misuse, as in the cynical ambition of professional politicians and lawyers. A further clue to this interest in writing and speech can be found in Gaskell's epigraph, which she takes from Carlyle's 1832 essay "Biography."[12] In this piece, a sort of grown-up version of the free-wheeling *Sartor Resartus*, Carlyle argues that biography is the true subject of all science and art. "Of [the] millions of living men," he writes, "each individual is a mirror to us . . . from which [we] would gladly draw aside the gauze veil; and, peering therein, discern the image of his own natural face, and the supernatural secrets that prophetically lie under the same."[13] But the difficulty, as this entangled metaphor suggests, is that once the "veil" is drawn, we must still discover the mystery of human behavior beneath the surface reflection. "Deep as we dive in the profound," he continues "there is ever a new depth opens: where the ultimate bottom may lie . . . is altogether a mystery to us."[14] And yet impossible as they are to discover, the real motives of human behavior

remain the only truth human beings have it in their power to even begin
to discern: "Other hope in studying books," he argues, "we have none:
and that it is a deceitful hope, who that has tried knows not?"[15] Thus, he
reasons, any sort of book, even a work of fiction, a "fictitious biography,"
may contain some shred of human truth. "Of no given book, not even
of a Fashionable Novel, can you predicate with certainty that its vacuity is
absolute."[16] Here, having reluctantly embraced the world of popular fiction,
he apostrophizes the humble novelist, and it is this passage Gaskell quotes
on her title page:

How knowest thou, may the distressed Novelwright exclaim, that I, here where
I sit, am the Foolishest of existing mortals; that this my Long-ear of a Fictitious
Biography shall not find one and the other, into whose still longer ears it may be
the means, under Providence, of instilling somewhat? We answer, None knows,
none can certainly know: therefore, write on, worthy Brother, even as thou canst,
even as it has been given thee.[17]

It would be easy to read the passage as an elaborate apology by the female
novelist for the book that follows, reminding us that even the worst of
novels may be worth something. But concealed in what could be read as a
gesture of modesty, we have a concise indication of just the difficulty the
novel will explore: How do you find human truth in a world of technical
exteriors? How to locate the "heart" of human existence beneath the fleeting
reflection?

Gaskell's interest in these issues can be further clarified if we position her
depiction of the operation of language, in history and in the mind, alongside that of other early Victorian philosophers of language. By the 1830s the
materialist approach to language, derived through Condillac but associated
in England with Horne Tooke, was declining, as English students began to
study under continental philologists. Rejecting Condillac's concern with
the development of the mind as a perceptual apparatus, the philological
school assumed the mind to be an a priori coherent entity, a stable point of
observation. Where Condillac argues that the mind develops its capacity
for thought only through the use of signs, philologists assumed that the
unity of the mind preceded the acquisition of language, or any other social process. Borrowing from Auguste Comte's philosophy of positivism,
the philologists looked to study language as actually spoken, ignoring the
broader philosophical question of the observing subject.

These philosophical positions are important in understanding the new
theory of language that emerged in Gaskell's lifetime, but they do not give
any sense of the new movement's extraordinarily widespread public appeal
and cultural impact. The writer most successful in bringing philology to

non-scholarly audiences was perhaps Richard Chevenix Trench, the man who would succeed Whately in 1863 as Archbishop of Dublin. Beginning in 1845, Trench gave a series of lectures on language study which were published in 1851 as *On the Study of Words;* a further series of lectures produced another volume, *English Past and Present,* which appeared in 1855. By the time of Trench's death in 1886, *On the Study of Words* had gone through nineteen editions, *Past and Present* thirteen.[18] As late as 1927 they were still in print, bound together in an *Everyman Library* edition.

The two central themes of Trench's work correspond to the presentation of language in Gaskell's novel. The first is his understanding of character. Where Enlightenment writers had searched for underlying principles of psycho-linguistic formation, nineteenth-century thinkers adopted a comparative approach. The differences in linguistic history uncovered in these comparisons were understood as indicators of differences of character between linguistic groups. As Trench puts it, the "thought, feelings, and experience" of a people are "arrayed . . . in the garment and vesture of words."[19]

It is of course our English tongue, out of which mainly we should seek to draw some of the hid treasures which it contains, from which we should endeavour to remove the veil which custom and familiarity have thrown over it . . . There is nothing that will more help to form an English heart in ourselves and in others than will this. We could scarcely have a single lesson on the growth of our English tongue . . . without not merely falling on some curious fact illustrative of our national life, but learning also how the great heart which is beating at the centre of that life was gradually shaped and moulded.[20]

For Trench this exploration of national character is the natural object of language study, and its greatest moral lesson. His second series of lectures was delivered during the Crimean War, and he suggests that

it is one of the compensations, indeed the greatest of all, for the wastefulness, the woe, the cruel losses of war, that it causes and indeed compels a people to know itself a people; leading each one to esteem and prize most that which he has in common with his fellow-countrymen, and not now any longer those things which separate and divide him from them."[21]

We can see here somewhat more crudely the point Gaskell seems to propose in her annotations of Lancashire dialect. While the principles of locality that once gave the "relish of home" to English agrarian lifeways are gone, there yet remains a more powerful underlying unity among all of the English nation – linking region, class, and gender – one demonstrated in the history of its language.

This is the great paradox of language study in the Victorian era: While the philologists rejected the Enlightenment theories of the mind and the construction of its representations as airy exercises in metaphysics, they end up basing their methods on a metaphysical proposition of their own. The avowed positivist method for scientific observation of spoken languages produces, in the hands of writers like Trench, a belief in the a priori collective identity of a nation, a more or less coherent national character which distinguishes it from all others.

This conception of national character flows from a more fundamental model of the speaking subject that all three of these texts share. The metaphors both Gaskell and Carlyle use to describe the interiors of thought and the exterior surfaces of representation are offered in a virtual catalogue in Trench. Language, he suggests, is the "garment" of thought, as it is the "garb" for Gaskell in the trial scene. This "garb" can be used either to conceal true thoughts and feelings, just as for Trench modern language has cast a "veil" of custom and familiarity over the deep truths it can, in the correct hands, display. But even if the covering, the veil or garment, conceals more than it reveals in some cases, there remains, as Carlyle argued through the same metaphor, a deep kernel of truth. Studying the national language will reveal, according to this theory, a national heart. For the tub-thumping Trench, character is something that can be affirmatively grasped, while for the more cautious Gaskell and Carlyle, this truth of character may be finally a mystery. And yet even their more pessimistic accounts are based on the idea of an autonomous character which exists in the mind independent of its representation. It cannot be measured in any direct way, but it can be felt and approximated. This is affirmed again in the debate Gaskell stages between Carson, the mill owner, and Job Legh. Frustrated at his fumbling for words, Job says "I can't rightly explain the meaning that is in me. I'm like a tap as won't run, but keeps letting it out drop by drop, so that you've no notion of the force of what's within" (*MB* 457). The mechanical representation of thought, the faucet that forms the words, may be sticky and untrained, or it may be slick and silvery, but the force of individual thought is nonetheless a constant. It is a force that exists in an ideal sense, independent of and ultimately controlling its final casting into language.

Economic outcomes

Mary Barton's representation of Manchester life is proposed through this controlling metaphor of writing and speech. The written language of the law, journalism, and the professions distorts the speech of witnesses and workers. Writing stands for mechanism and artifice, speech for spontaneous truth. The economic problems in the novel – the starvation following from the layoffs, and the workers' resulting strike – are shown likewise to be problems of an obfuscated speech, in the broadest sense, that is, problems both of failed communication and of obscured individual feeling. The strike is set in motion when the mill owners bid aggressively for a foreign order of textiles. If they cannot outbid the continental mills, they will lose the order and risk bankruptcy. They try to rehire laid-off power-loom weavers at a reduced wage, and the weavers strike. The text tries to present the interests of labor and capital as fundamentally united in this moment: "Distrust each other as they may," the narrator offers, "the employers and the employed must rise or fall together" (*MB* 221). However, we are told, "the masters did not choose to make all these facts known. They stood upon being the masters, and that they had a right to order work at their own prices" (*MB* 221). The deep truth, the narrator suggests here, is that the workers and owners are "bound to each other," as Gaskell's preface puts it, "in common interests" (*MB* 37). But this truth, which is the "heart" of the matter, is obscured by a false surface. The owners do not think "of treating the workmen as brethren and friends, and openly, clearly, as appealing to reasonable men, stating the exact and full circumstances" (*MB* 232). They instead view the workers as secondary to the mechanical system of the market, which must push and pull according to its own logic. Carson indicates this when he argues, "we cannot regulate the demand for labour" (*MB* 456). For him, the market is beyond human control, and workers need to live by its harsh rules.

None of the owners recognizes workers as subjects of authentic and autonomous perception and inheritors of English character, as the novel insists they should do. All the tragedy resulting from the strike, the privation, the violence, and the depression of business, are caused by the failure to speak the truth, in the labor negotiations, and to acknowledge the truth of common character. The final position of the novel seems to be that both workers and capitalists are at fault in the crisis: the owners for relying on the rigid and coldly logical view of the market as machine, and the workers for being swayed toward violence by the artificial language of the union organizer. "Combination is an awful power," the text concludes. "It is like the equally mighty agency of steam; capable of almost unlimited good or evil. But to obtain a blessing on its labours, it must work under the direction of a high and intelligent will" (*MB* 223). Factory machines and machine-like institutions possess here a dangerous "agency" of their own, one that threatens to destroy the people they are meant to serve. What the novel argues for is a return of human agency to these potentially wild and chaotic systems, to regulate the power of the machine with the touch of the human.

Mary Barton does seem, however, to sidestep the middle-class view of sexual difference that fuels so many of the other critiques of political economy we have seen. There is no woman in the novel whose work expresses only her love. In the long days of Mary's dressmaking apprenticeship, and in Margaret's homework sewing, there is a close continuity between wage labor and household labor, as work necessary to sustain life, as economic activity. However, the novel's conception of homely character and natural speech still relies on the metaphor of sexual difference, and thus in the end it cannot make good on the escape from middle-class sentimentalism which its focus on women's labor might have enabled.

The Victorian ideology of the domestic we have seen elsewhere is a version of the romantic union of supposed masculine and feminine principles, as in Wordsworth's famous notion of "the discerning intellect of Man/ ... wedded to this goodly universe," or the ideal of "a feeling intellect."[22] The novel proposes this sort of symbolic marriage in several places. When John Barton and his friend George Wilson discover a family in their neighborhood starving, they care for the family's children as "rough, tender nurses," and provide what the text calls "heart-service and love-works" (*MB* 99). In another scene the care of children is similarly described as "a work of love" (*MB* 153). This linking of work and love, that is, rational and orderly labor with spontaneous feeling, resolves the conflict represented throughout the novel between the mechanical and the human, between writing and speech. The affection of Mary's father is unbalanced because he applies all his rational powers to the public sphere: to his work as a union activist and a socialist.[23] The Barton home is thus endangered by the lack of a mother's love.

This danger is set up at the start of the novel, with the death of Mary's mother in chapter 2, leaving thirteen-year-old Mary – the only surviving child – to be raised by her father. John Barton's love on its own proves ineffective, for, the narrator explains, "while he was harsh and silent to others, he humoured Mary with tender love," giving her "more of her own way than is common in any rank with girls of her age" (*MB* 58–59). Mary is put in charge of keeping the household, but while she proves competent at managing the money and cooking for her father, she is also left, because of "her father's indulgence ... to choose her own associates" (*MB* 59). This "tender" love of the father Gaskell later contrasts to "the mighty power of a Mother's love" (*MB* 64). Absent this fiercer spirit, Mary takes up an illicit liaison with Harry Carson, the roguish son of the mill owner. Mary's feelings are diverted to the dashing Carson because she "had been dazzled and lured by gold," that is, because she fantasizes about becoming a middle-class lady. Her affection for Harry is referred to as "a bubble, blown out of vanity" (*MB* 160). "Bubble" is the term used most often to describe irrationally inflated stock prices and recalls a long tradition of metaphors for stocks and paper money as "airy" and insubstantial. The danger impending should this bubble "crash" is shown in the figure of the prostitute, Esther. While Mary expects Carson to marry her, Carson intends to abandon her; this was likewise Esther's situation. Left with a child after an affair with an army officer, Esther turned to prostitution as her only means of survival. In the middle of the novel, however, at the height of the strike, Mary suddenly realizes her true feelings for the Wilsons' son, Jem. Obscured by the empty, inflated "bubble" of the market, Mary's "natural language," the voice of her true character, cannot be heard. Jem's sincerity finally "unveils her heart to her" (*MB* 176), but this revelation of truth comes nearly too late. Harry Carson turns up dead, murdered by Mary's father, in revenge for what he sees as the cruelty of the capitalists. But because the whole town knows of Jem's feelings for Mary, and Mary's secret relationship with young Carson, Jem is accused of the crime.

As Mary Poovey writes, the circumstances of Jem's trial, the journey to Liverpool, and Mary's resulting illness, all work to "effectively block Mary's speech."[24] For Poovey the interior origin of speech, which the novel outlines in this way, results in a kind of "(Proto) psychology," a pre-Freudian notion of an unconscious part of the mind. In this way, for Poovey, *Mary Barton* helped delineate the psychological in a way that facilitated its disaggregation as an autonomous domain."[25] What Poovey calls the "disaggregation" of the psychological, the splitting off of an a priori, pre-social realm of character, is precisely what was required for neoclassical economics to take shape. In the accounts of later economists, consumer desire is seemingly produced out of this mysterious inner realm. This desire is a kind of pure speech, often obscured, generally hidden and unavailable to public view, but measurable in the overall movement of consumers in the marketplace.

The force of homely speech and true character – the solution the novel proposes to the cruelties of capitalism – seems to rely on a concept of maternal power, for it is the absence of the mother that leads to the problem of Mary's obscured speech and unrecognized desire. However, it is the figure of the prostitute that finally scrambles this triumph of speech over writing. For while Mary's true feelings were nearly distorted by the artificial longing for wealth and status, Esther is shown to have acted on her truest desires, in going away with the soldier. Mary's feelings for Carson are diagnosed as simple "vanity," as Esther is likewise described as having been vain, but her love for the soldier and their child is presented as quite real. Together they had, Esther says, "three years of happiness. I suppose I ought not to have been happy, but I was" (*MB* 209). The pure access Esther possesses to natural feeling and intuition is confirmed by her role in the murder case. On the street at the time of the murder, she has natural insight into the facts of the case. She is led to diagnose the problem that caused the murder – the problem of "writing" (the valentine) gone astray. In the end the novel's formula of a priori character and sexual identity produce this paradox. The novel's theory of "natural language" forces it to embrace an expressive theory of female desire, one which is finally inconsistent with the vision of a just society it attempts to work out.

"COLD LION": HISTORY AND RATIONALITY IN *CRANFORD*

In reading *Mary Barton* I have tried to show that the novel draws on the emergent terms of neoclassical economics – character and authentic desire – in order to critique popular conceptions of classical political economy. The critique of political economy is arranged in the novel as a battle of speech versus writing, the human versus the machine. While successful in its own sentimental terms then, the novel's critique is one that political economy is already beginning to assimilate. *Cranford* begins a more complex project that moves beyond the romantic attack on the machine and toward a broader analysis of market capitalism itself. This is a project that is most fully realized in *North and South*, one that works not through the evocation of character or region, but through an examination of history.

Written between 1851 and 1853, and published serially in *Household Words*, *Cranford* looks back at a fragment of the rural gentry; its mode is the comedic and gently satiric depiction of manners, not the realistic depiction of hardship. Its focus on "The Last Generation in England" – an early title – sets up its interest, however, in the question of history. In the opening of that original story, Gaskell mentions Southey's idea of writing "a history of English domestic life."[26] "The phases of society are rapidly changing;" Gaskell writes, "and much will appear strange, which yet occurred only in the generation immediately preceding ours."[27]

The question of how things change is most consistently addressed in *Cranford* as a question of style. The outmoded women's fashions of the Cranford women, the pattens on their shoes and the great folding calashes that cover their heads, are, like their sense of social hierarchy, based on an eighteenth-century notion of class. Wealth in Cranford matters less than title and reputation; protective elements of dress to prevent muddy hems or to preserve elaborate hair styles indicate an overriding concern for the codes of aristocratic femininity – leisure, display, the absence of work. To a rising middle-class readership, with its emphasis on charitable visiting, good works, and modesty, such pretensions (particularly among women who can barely afford them) are both comical and admonitory. The novel calls to its reader in just this way, soliciting, creating, and confirming a sense of the reader's own modernity – in a world of sincerity and rationality, in contrast with the absurd dissembling and class paranoia of the Cranford gentry.

The history of style the novel presents is not limited to dress but extends also to language. In its contrast between older modes of ornament and rhetoric with modern sincerity and directness, *Cranford* turns *Mary Barton's* theme of authentic speech into a meditation on style. This is an aspect of the text explored by Hilary Schor, in her chapter "Affairs of the Alphabet," which emphasizes the elaborate Johnsonian style of letter-writing Deborah Jenkyns was taught while working as her father's amanuensis. Deborah is confined by the rule of her father and by the writing of Johnson. This relationship of stylistic control, for Schor, reflects Gaskell's own struggle for editorial control with her some-time publisher Dickens, where by contrast the novel's narrator, the young visitor Mary Smith, is able to make stylistic choices of her own and to escape from the role of "letter-writing daughter."[28] But as in *Mary Barton*, the debate about representation – the relation between style, writer, and meaning – is linked in *Cranford* to a debate about value and the nature of economic history.

The clearest view of these questions comes in the novel's discussion of old letters, a discussion that looks ahead, I argue, to the episode of the bank failure in chapter 13. After the death of Deborah Jenkyns, her younger sister Matty proposes, with the help of Mary Smith, to read through all the old family letters the two sisters had kept. The main purpose of this reading is of "destroying such as ought not to be allowed to fall into the hands of strangers."[29] The necessity of culling out these documents is not, as we might suppose from other Victorian novels, to do with material losses or damage to family reputations. There are no contested deeds or wills here, no dark family secrets. Rather the letters must be burned, Matty says, because "no one will care for them when I am gone" (*C* 44). They "had been only interesting to those who loved the writers; and . . . it seemed as if it would have hurt her to allow them to fall into the hands of strangers, who had not known her dear mother, and how good she was, although she did not always spell quite in the modern fashion" (*C* 46). The danger here is that anyone who had no feeling for the writers of these letters might make fun of their errors or old-fashioned attitudes. That is, a stranger would take the writing at its face value, would see the words and not the feelings they evoked, however haphazardly, and would not look upon them with love.

The love felt by the writers, in most cases Matty and Deborah's parents – is clearly interpreted by Matty and Mary as they read through. The Rector, Matty's father, wrote to his fiancé with "eager, passionate ardour; short homely sentences, right fresh from the heart (very different from the grand Latinised, Johnsonian style of the printed sermon preached before some judge at assize time)" (*C* 43). The future Mrs. Jenkyns's letters from this time were passionate only about "her longing for a white 'Paduasoy,' – whatever that might be," and for other items of her trousseau (*C* 43). In later writing however, Mary notes, "it was pretty to see . . . how the girlish vanity was being weeded out of her heart by love for her baby. The white 'Paduasoy' figured again in the letters, with almost as much vigour as before. In one, it was being made into a christening cloak for the baby" (*C* 44). The best letters are valued for their "fresh" sentiments, spontaneous feelings that are uncluttered either by the ornaments of Johnsonian style, or of wealth. Their presumably fertile sentiments are cleared finally of the "weeds" of ambition and fashion. When all trace of these underlying feelings is gone, however, when anyone who recalls or feels them is dead, the letters are reduced to words on paper, meaningless in essence, and must be burned.

This understanding of the old letters parallels the treatment of bank notes in a later scene in the Cranford shop. When a working-class customer tries to pay with a note from Matty's bank (a joint-stock bank Deborah had invested in), the shop clerk explains that "from information he had received, the notes issued by the bank were little better than waste paper" (*C* 123). Seeing that the man would not be able to make the special purchases he had in mind with the £5 note he had brought, Matty exchanges his note for gold, gold she had set aside for special purchases of her own. When Mary and the shopkeepers object that she will likely never be reimbursed for the note she says, "'I can't explain myself' . . . suddenly becoming aware that she had got into a long sentence with four people for audience . . .'I am quite clear about it in my own mind; but, you know, I can never speak quite as comprehensibly as others can'" (*C* 124). If the bank indeed fails, she says, she will have only acted in "common honesty" (*C* 124). Later at home, when questioned again by Mary, she responds,

I was very thankful, that I saw my duty this morning, with the poor man standing by me; but it's rather a strain upon me to keep thinking and thinking what I should do if such and such a thing happened; and, I believe, I had rather wait and see what really does come; and I don't doubt I shall be helped then, if I don't fidget myself, and get too anxious beforehand. (*C* 126)

What makes a bank note work is just what makes the old letters significant to Matty: their combination of writing and feeling. Printed bills circulate on "confidence"; love letters on "love." Matty insures the note by acting in accordance with this formula. She rejects the abstract arguments that tell her to let the shop customer lose the value of the note. Their arguments for her exist in a world of "long sentences," of "anxiety," and endless "thinking and thinking" – in other words, the world of financial modernity as Walter Bagehot imagines it. She acts with a spontaneous awareness of "duty" and "common sense," and so insures that the note lives through at least one final exchange before it becomes worthless. Just as letters devoid of the love that produced them are fit only to be burned, money without the element of feeling is reduced to "waste paper."

Paper and ink only circulate when propelled by a force of character, confidence, love. Like *Bleak House, Cranford* argues that when these human forces are drained from the market, paper and ink cease to signify reliably. At the same time, however, while *Cranford* presents this now familiar critique of the mechanism of writing, the more substantial weight of its satire falls on the sort of spontaneous and uncalculated acts on which Matty places a premium. For while Matty's payment of the gold, as Andrew Miller points out, looks toward the honor and responsibility presumed in an earlier time,[30] the irrationality of this act is part of a long catalogue of economic irrationalities, and the satirical portrayal of these is also one of the novel's central comedic devices.

I have often noticed that almost every one has his own individual small economies – careful habits of saving fractions of pennies in some one particular direction – any disturbance of which annoys him more than spending shillings or pounds on some real extravagance. An old gentleman of my acquaintance, who took the intelligence of the failure of a Joint-Stock Bank, in which some of his money was invested, with stoic mildness, worried his family all through a long summer's day, because one of them had torn (instead of cutting) out the written leaves of his now useless bank-book . . . this little unnecessary waste of paper (his private economy) chafed him more than all the loss of his money. (*C* 40)

This passage on private schemes of thrift opens the chapter "old letters," in which Matty sifts through the family correspondence, and it launches a theme that continues throughout the novel. Paper, envelopes, string, butter are all objects of "private economy." Miss Matty's particular interest is candles (*C* 40). This indeed seems a most rational commodity to safeguard. But this small bit of scrimping is wiped out by Matty's determination to leave all her money in a firm that everyone advised her was unsafe.

The list of private economies in this early chapter establishes a continuing focus on irrational behavior in general, behavior that appears justified by practicality or efficiency, but in fact results in a loss. Matty, for example, wears her second-best cap in the morning, before the agreed-upon hours of visiting, in order to preserve her best. But the desire to look one's best leads Matty to become confused one day and to answer the door "with one cap on top of another" (*C* 60). The cap is itself a center of economic life: "the expenditure in dress in Cranford was principally in that one article referred to. If heads were buried in smart new caps, the ladies were like ostriches, and cared not what became of their bodies" (*C* 73–74). Again, the pleasure in saving or spending with regard to one special item overwhelms any awareness of loss or gain elsewhere. The power of these privileged objects is further indicated in a related passage, where Miss Pole, after being snubbed by the self-styled leader of Cranford's social world, Mrs. Jamieson, argues to Matty that they should accept her rudely belated invitation: "Miss Pole, in addition to her delicacies of feeling, possessed a very smart cap, which she was anxious to show to an admiring world; and so she seemed to forget all her angry words uttered not a fortnight before, and to be ready to act on what she called the great Christian principle of 'Forgive and forget'" (*C* 73). The commodity here possesses the power of agency and carries its owner where it will. Miss Pole follows the compulsion of the cap, which longs to compete with its sisters, and she bends her powers of reason in order to accommodate it.

This satire of economic irrationalities becomes unmistakably clear in the novel's brief fish-out-of-water episode, when, after the loss of her bank shares, and under the guidance of Mary and her father, Matty opens a small shop. Here we see the economic practices of the Cranford gentry transplanted into the world of commerce. Mary reports "the only alteration I could have desired in Miss Matty's way of doing business was, that she should not have so plaintively entreated some of her customers not to buy green tea – running it down as slow poison, sure to destroy the nerves, and produce all manner of evil" (*C* 46). Fond of children, Matty also adds an extra candy to every measure she sells them, effectively losing money in every transaction (*C* 148).

These features of the novel satirize the irrationality of old economic habits, pointing out the follies of a swiftly retreating past. However, it is crucial to notice also that the new world of abstract calculation which seems to be intruding into Cranford life is revealed in the end to be equally irrational. In its satire of "small individual economies" and Matty's commercial practices, the novel portrays behaviors that are superstitious, mistakenly considered, or based on outmoded and absurd social codes. Each instance of irrational or "magical" thinking is, in the progress of the novel, demystified, brought under the light of scientific analysis, and rationally understood. However, in all these demystifications some element of magic inevitably returns.

Matty is gradually taught, for example, that it is best for her to allow customers to buy what they like, and for her to give them only what they have bought. But she takes in these lessons only through further deception.[31] Mary persuades her to sell green tea by making "a happy reference . . . to the train oil and tallow candles which the Esquimaux not only enjoy but digest" (*C* 146). She pursues a similar strategy on the candies: "I remembered the green tea, and winged my shaft with a feather out of her own plumage. I told her how unwholesome almond-comfits were; and how ill excess in them might make the little children" (*C* 148). What Matty learns here is the theory of "exogeny of tastes," a theory that follows from De Quincey's argument that the desire of the purchaser is the final indication of the value of the commodity. Since the assessment of utility is absolutely individual, no one can judge – ethically or aesthetically or medically – what might please another consumer. Matty comes to believe, as Jevons puts it, that "every mind is inscrutable to every other mind."[32] But this theory is presented to Matty here not in the name of rational calculation or self-interest but of interpersonal kindness. The deregulation of buying and selling works not as a self-perpetuating force but as an incidental effect of an older social code of paternalism and obligation.

This pattern, where things are "rationalized," or standardized into abstract components, only to be invested once again with irrational belief, extends beyond the little experiment in shopkeeping, and can be seen to underlie one of the major episodes of the novel's middle chapters: the arrival of a magic show in Cranford. The magician bills himself as Signor Brunoni and affects a "foreign" accent, and from his first arrival in Cranford he provokes much thought and discussion of things foreign. Miss Matty orders a turban, "having heard that turbans were worn" (*C* 81). Moreover, Mary relates, "I think a series of circumstances dated from Signor Brunoni's visit to Cranford, which seemed at the time connected in our minds with him, though I don't know that he had anything really to do with them" (*C* 89). There are rumors of robbers afoot and "carts that went about in the dead of night, and guarded by men in dark clothes" (*C* 89). These rumors "occasioned as many precautions as if we were living among the Red Indians or the French," and Mrs. Forester "inclined to the idea that, in some way, the French were connected with the small thefts" (*C* 90). Speculation abounds on the nationality of Signor Brunoni, most guesses falling for French or Turkish (*C* 90). Miss Pole reports: "an Irish beggar-woman came not half an hour ago, and all but forced herself in past Betty, saying her children were starving" (*C* 90). Provoked by the association of conjuring and foreignness, the town invests its every dark corner with a gallicized, or gaelicized, oriental mystery.

The panic subsides only when the magician himself takes sick and it becomes known that Signor Brunoni is really an English man named Brown (*C* 102). The reports of robberies turn out to have been fantastic exaggerations, and the magic tricks themselves are the object of a careful scientific analysis on the part of Miss Pole, who reads an article from the encyclopedia which explains common magic tricks through a series of lettered diagrams: "Ah, I see . . . conjuring and witchcraft is a mere affair of the alphabet" (*C* 84). All the elements of magical thinking are carefully brought into the light of scientific explanation. Metaphysical forces are demonstrated to have been ordinary constructions of signs after all, "affairs of the alphabet."

However, this flowering of enlightenment seems not to take away from the power of magical or metaphysical belief – whether belief in the transmutation of matter or in the "matter" of race. Miss Pole's circle shows no interest in her secrets of slight-of-hand. Mary describes the show as follows:

We *were* astonished. How he did his tricks I could not imagine; no, not even when Miss Pole pulled out her pieces of paper and began reading aloud – or at least in a very audible whisper – the separate 'receipts' for the most common of his tricks. If ever I saw a man frown, and look enraged, I saw the Grand Turk frown at Miss Pole; but, as she said, what could be expected but unchristian looks from a Mussulman? (*C* 87)

Mr. Brown's anxiety lest his magic be exposed appears to Miss Pole as another sort of magic: the compulsion of race. Much as in the philological studies of R. C. Trench, racial character serves as a founding metaphysical – or magical – assumption.

An even more thoroughgoing demystification of metaphysical investments under the sign of race takes place with the return from imperial India of Peter Jenkyns, Miss Matty's brother, who had run away as a young man and was presumed dead. Matty has by this point opened her shop and is herself a licensed agent of the English crown, selling tea and sweets – the addictive consumer goods of the European colonial system. This provisional solution to her financial crisis is obviated when Peter arrives with extravagant gifts of muslin and pearls, as well as the proceeds from the sale of his Indian land. The magic and danger of Signor Brunoni's orient seems then to be dispelled by Peter's return. Just as Signor Brunoni was in the end Sam Brown, any magical power attributed to the orient turns out simply to be a matter of imperial occupation, a matter of money.

However, the atmosphere of magic continues to pervade the rationalized and modern world which, by all accounting, we should end up with at the novel's close, just as the "mystery" of the orient (even though we know it is all make-believe!) seems to have brushed off on Peter, whose skill as a story-teller is considered "so very oriental" (*C* 154). In a passage just preceding Peter's arrival, Mary Smith considers the idea that Matty might take in pupils for hire, but she laments that Matty has few skills that she might usefully pass on.

As for the use of globes, I had never been able to find it out myself, so perhaps I was not a good judge of Miss Matty's capability of instructing in this branch of education; but it struck me that equators and tropics, and such mystical circles, were very imaginary lines indeed to her, and that she looked upon the signs of the Zodiac as so many remnants of the Black Art. (*C* 131)

Matty perceives geography as just so much conjuring. The genius of the passage, however, is that of course tropics and equators *are* imaginary lines, spun across the sensible universe in a projection of uniform space. Science looks like magic to the untutored women of Cranford, but science, Mary's line subtly points out, rests on acts of the imagination, creating things that did not exist, to invest the sensible world with the order of reason. The more rational things become, the more magic they seem to retain.

It is Martha, Miss Matty's maid, who commits the novel's most egregious act of economic irrationality and provides its most succinct statement of this theme. When Matty's bank fails, Martha is let go but refuses to be dismissed. She explains, "I knew when I'd got a good Missus, if she didn't know when she'd got a good servant" (*C* 129). When Mary begs her to "listen to reason," she answers summarily, "Reason always means what some one else has got to say" (*C* 129). What the novel suggests finally about economic arrangements is that no matter how carefully they are reduced to "reason" and to rational principles – that is, no matter how completely they are translated into a language of numbers – the foundation of reason itself will always be invested with the subjectivity of the perceiver, with the unreason of metaphysical concepts.

The elements of magic can be reduced to their primary "alphabetic" principles, but in the novel these letters of the alphabet themselves wander like Mr. Holbrook's herd of "six-and-twenty cows, named after different letters of the alphabet" (*C* 32). These and other magic animals animate the district of Cranford, like the legendary circus lions that visited the town in Matty's childhood, and the lion-shaped pudding Martha prepares on the day that news of the bank crash arrives. The following afternoon, when Mr. Smith comes to help sort out Matty's finances, they all sit down to a lunch that concludes with "a little of the cold lion, sliced and fried" (*C* 141). The proliferation of these Asiatic fantasy creatures within the orientalized world of the English gentry transforms the cold circulation of financial numbers into a hot-blooded circus. Just as it is being dragged into modernity, as its archaic class structure is being dissolved by the modern financial market, Cranford becomes an exotic location, where, the day following the hunt, the meat of the fierce beast is taken cold.[33]

As Derrida has recently pointed out, the word "conjure" has an ambiguous double meaning; to "conjure" can mean both to banish magical spirits, and to call them forth.[34] Magic in *Cranford* serves a similar double purpose. Finance capitalism seems to exert a rationalizing force in history, standardizing and monetizing social relations, and exorcising the ancient ghosts of bigotry and superstition. At the same time, the novel indicates the way irrational beliefs persist within modern market society, the way capitalism calls into being metaphysical spirits of its own. On one hand the novel gently mocks the styles and habits of the previous generation, suggesting that they lead to "panics" and "crashes." Like John Francis's *History of the Bank of England, Cranford* ridicules the selfish irrationality of the old joint-stock bank managers. But it stops short of endorsing the "scientific principles" of modern banking,[35] recognizing the unscientific foundation of an emerging capitalist modernity. In one way it seems to teach the lessons of modern economics – that value and price are identical. But it also points out the fantastic foundations of this theory, in particular the hypostasized notion of racial character it presumes.

TOLERATION AND FREEDOM IN *NORTH AND SOUTH*

In her second and final industrial novel, Gaskell continues to focus on the cultural and psychic dimensions of economic history. The somewhat limited critique of political economy that *Mary Barton* produces, through its interest in philology, and its founding theories of character and national identity, develop in *Cranford* into a more complex examination of economic development and cultural change. This trend is, I will argue, completed in *North and South. Mary Barton* develops its critique as a battle between speech and writing, a motif we saw in the Irish journals of Asenath Nicholson. *North and South* transforms this battle into a more nuanced series of debates about the nature of industrial production, which are carried on by Margaret Hale and John Thornton. Here the English authenticity of the working class is not a factor; the issue is discussed in middle-class drawing rooms which, given the ineffectuality of the official universities as *North and South* portrays them, function as a sort of vanguard college of public policy. And while the underlying issue of authentic character does play a role in the novel's economics, the theory of political economy it produces emerges from a more sophisticated and far-ranging critique of capitalism. The novel approaches these questions by presenting its reader with a complex discussion of the political-economic background of religious disestablishment.

The clue to the novel's interest in the separation of church and state comes with one of its opening gambits: the Reverend Hale's crisis, a crisis not of faith, but of doctrine. He declines the long-awaited offer of a lucrative position in a town church and resigns his modest vicarage in the rural parish of Helstone. To his daughter Margaret, he explains that he has no "doubts as to religion" but rather "smouldering doubts by the authority of the church."[36] He finds himself unable "to make a fresh declaration of conformity to the Liturgy" (*NS* 68). His split with the Church of England causes him to forfeit income and social status and precipitates the family's move from the bucolic "south" to the "northern" industrial city of Milton. It launches moreover the novel's dialectical examination of the clash between the quasi-feudal society of Helstone and the rationalized world of the industrial city, where social relations derive only from "testing everything by the standard of wealth" (*NS* 129), as Margaret puts it soon after the move. The question I begin with then is why does an "industrial" novel, a novel explicitly concerned with trade, markets, wages, and the social relations they imply, open with a principled refusal of the privileges of the state church?

There is in the novel a general concern with secularization, and Hale's renunciation of his living might be placed within this theme. The narrative's dialectical form, as well, demands some opening device to propel the southerners into their new northern digs, and set the clash of cultures with which Gaskell is concerned into motion. However, these answers do not go far enough. To see the broadest consequences of the church and state question in *North and South*, it will be helpful to look at Marx's exploration of this issue a couple of decades earlier in his review essay "On the Jewish Question." Here Marx takes on one of his Young Hegelian colleagues, Bruno Bauer, critiquing a series of Bauer's articles on the debate over the extension of political rights in Germany to Jews. Bauer, in good critical

fashion, rejects the debate in its popular form and seeks its underlying assumptions. He argues that the question of granting or withholding citizen
status to Jews ignores the privileged status of Christianity within the state,
and he asserts that "any religious privilege at all . . . must be abolished."[37]
"Religion no longer exists," he reasons, "when there is no longer a privileged religion. Take from religion its power of exclusion and it ceases to
exist."[38]

Bauer's solution to religious intolerance and persecution is the disestablishment of state religion. He argues, as Marx puts it, that we should learn
to see all religions merely as "different snake skins that history has cast off,
and recognize man as the snake that used the skins for covering."[39] That
is, Bauer suggests that citizenship should be based not on the particularity
of creed or ethnicity, but on a universal idea of "man."

Marx picks up his response at this point. He notes rapidly that a state
without an established church in fact exists in North America, and that,
far from withering away, religion flourishes there "full of freshness and
strength."[40] This contradiction between the seeming logic of Bauer's argument and the persistence of religious thinking in the secular democracy is
what Marx sets out to explain.

The creation of a state distinct from a religious authority grows, he
suggests, from a conception of universal human rights, of the "snake that
used the skins for covering." Rather than granting privileges to particular
contingents, the secular state grants universal rights, among these the right
to worship. Marx argues however that disestablishment of state religion in
fact presumes the continued existence of belief: "The incompatibility of
religion with the rights of man is so far from being evident in the concept
of the rights of man, that the right to be religious, to be religious in one's
own chosen way, to practice one's chosen religion is expressly counted
as one of the rights of man."[41] Marx proceeds to critique the other "rights
of man" with the same process of negation, beginning with the right to
liberty:

The practical application of the right of man to freedom is the right of man to
private property.
    What does the right of man to property consist in?
    Article 16 (Constitution of 1793): "The right of property is the right which
belongs to all citizens to enjoy and dispose at will of their goods and revenues, the
fruit of their work and industry."
    Thus the right of man to property is the right to enjoy his possessions and
dispose of the same arbitrarily, without regard for other men, independently from
society, the right of selfishness.[42]

While it proclaims the end of privileges that accompany the inheritance of property, the capitalist/democratic state presupposes the continued existence of property, and the special pleasures and powers that accompany it. While it proclaims religious freedom, it presupposes religion and therefore presumably the continued social exclusion of certain creeds and races. "The state still allows private property, education, and profession to have an effect in their own manner . . . Far from abolishing these factual differences, its existence rests on them as a presupposition."[43] While the state is constructed as an arena of equality, it presumes the persistence of inequality, discrimination, in short of oppression. The universal human, the "man" on which the notion of rights is founded, is the abstract individual, delinked from social processes which create or distribute social power or material resources. "None of the so-called rights of man," Marx concludes, "goes beyond egoistic man, man as he is in civil society, namely an individual withdrawn behind his private interests and whims and separated from the community."[44]

This connection detailed by Marx between the abolition of the state church and the subjectivity of the market helps us see why *North and South* opens with Reverend Hale's resignation. The novel protests, mildly, against the social and political privilege of the established church. It portrays Hale's decision as a principled and moral one, and it enlists our sympathy in the loss of social standing and wealth that must accompany his transition from conforming vicar to "dissenter." Very little is made of the particular doubts Hale feels, and we learn nothing of his interest in any other church. It is not the doctrinal dispute the novel stresses, but its socio-political significance. This interpretation is the one made by Mrs. Hale, née Beresford, as she recalls her own family's aristocratic connections: "Poor dear Sir John! It is well he is not alive to see what your father has come to! Every day after dinner, when I was a girl, living with your Aunt Shaw, at Beresford Court, Sir John used to give for the first toast – 'Church and King, and down with the Rump'" (*NS* 80). Mrs. Hale's awareness of her drop in status reminds us of the social and political power that has flowed from established religion in English history.

Recognizing the question of disestablishment at the starting point of *North and South*, we can see that the novel, in its portraits both of London and Milton, depicts English society in the gradual process of separating church and state. The most serious legislative barriers to religious freedom had fallen in the 1820s and 1830s, with the repeal of the Test and Corporation Acts and the so-called Catholic Emancipation of 1829. It was only the 1891 Religious Disabilities Removals Act that abolished the last religious requirement for Parliamentary election, by which point, as one historian puts it, the government acted "as a sort of neutral arbiter between various Christian denominations and non-Christian belief." This, however, was only a "concluding stage in the century-long process of piecemeal and practical dismantling of the old confessional state."[45] Gaskell portrays this transition in terms very close to Marx's. She makes clear that the link between religion and political power per se has almost dissolved, and details the system of universal equality that replaces the earlier requirements for citizenship status. This leads the novel toward its radical critique of political economy, but also toward a fundamental contradiction. It insists on a repoliticization of the private fields carved out by the secular democratic state – faith, conscience, and character – but it must acknowledge that, given its confinement to these "private" sectors, the critique will have little purchase.

The atmosphere of Milton that Gaskell depicts is not so much one of secularization as one of increasing religious toleration. Nicholas Higgins, the mill worker who Margaret meets in her first days at Milton, is an avowed atheist, at least at the novel's start, declaring "I believe what I see, and no more" (*NS* 133). His lack of belief, however, brings him no disadvantages in the earthly life of the factory town, as we can assume such openly stated views might have done in the southern parish of Helstone, where the lives of the poor and the working class, both spiritual and practical, were so carefully monitored by the Vicar, Hale. Rather it is Higgins's political views only which have any impact on his position within Milton society. At the same time, however, Higgins is perfectly willing to permit his daughter Bessie's religious convictions. He forbids Margaret from "preaching" to her, saying "she's bad enough as it is, with her dreams and her methodee fancies, and her visions of cities with goulden gates and precious stones. But if it amuses her I let it abe, but I'm none going to have more stuff poured into her" (*NS* 133). Higgins's attitude toward religion here is a wholly individualistic one, recognizing the right of any person to entertain beliefs as she or he might choose. For him faith can provide "amusement" or comfort of a sort, but it is judged solely on these grounds of psychological utility.

This is not, of course, the attitude toward religion we find within the Hale family; however, Margaret and her father, like Nicholas and Bessie, have also agreed to disagree on the question of faith. Margaret's sense of faith goes far beyond the provision of psychic consolation, and yet her father's defection from the Church of England causes no concern on Margaret's part for either his ethical integrity or the fate of his soul. The text seems to argue then for the existence of an underlying humanity that unites differences of doctrine, and indeed belief. This becomes clear at the end of one of the novel's several seminars on faith and economics, where Higgins has visited the Hales for tea. After debating with Mr. Hale about the union, the strike, and the church, Higgins prepares to leave the house. But, in spite of his declared views, he stays while Mr. Hale leads a prayer: "Higgins looked at Margaret doubtfully. Her grave sweet eyes met his; there was no compulsion, only deep interest in them. He did not speak, but he kept his place. Margaret the churchwoman, her father a Dissenter, Higgins the infidel, knelt down together. It did them no harm" (*NS* 296–97). Religious practice here is not a matter of "compelled" adherence to particular doctrine, but rather a forum for common human "interest." This underlying human concern unites these three in spite of their differences. It does Margaret "no harm" to hear a prayer from her dissenting father. Neither Margaret nor Higgins is influenced in their views; neither is tempted to change allegiance because of exposure to a different faith. The passage thus speaks against an earlier establishment view which would locate in dissenting or Catholic churches a threat against the moral integrity of the nation, one which would lure congregations out of established churches and into a variety of subversive or corrupt religious practices.

The same point, though specifically directed at the Protestant/Catholic split, gets worked out in the novel's Spanish plot. While Margaret's brother Frederick appears, on his return to England from Spain, both "dark" (*NS* 310) and "effeminate" (*NS* 313), the text's paranoia about the contamination of racial characteristics from the south does not seem to extend to its treatment of Roman Catholicism. Frederick does convert to Catholicism upon his engagement to Dolores, the daughter of his new employer, but he is afraid to announce the engagement to his family because of the religious question. "That's the only objection I anticipated. But my father's change of opinion – nay, Margaret, don't sigh" (*NS* 325). The conversion Frederick undertakes does not split the family, as he fears. He forgets his concern that this might be the case when he learns that his father has already left the church, and the ties of family persist in spite of the rapid fragmentation of its religious practice. And again there is little concern that the individual views of Frederick or his father will undermine the allegiance of Margaret to her own church. In fact the only character to express this sort of concern – the traditional "terror" of revolution associated with the Catholic horde – is Dixon, the Hales' housekeeper, and her views are roundly satirized. "She had, with all her terror, a lurking curiosity about Spain, the Inquisition, and Popish mysteries . . . she asked Miss Hale, whether she thought if she took

care never to see a priest, or enter into one of their churches, there would
be so very much danger of her being converted?" (*NS* 494). Margaret, for
her part, dismisses these fears and sees in the trip to Spain the prospect of
reunion with her brother, not the danger of magic or Papal authority.

Henry Lennox, Margaret's early, red-herring suitor, takes a similar view
of the insignificance of doctrinal differences. However, his readiness to
dismiss the importance of particular articles of faith seems to stem less from
an awareness of an underlying humanist ethic than from a keen sensitivity
to worldly goods. "I have been told," he remarks, ". . . that there was no call
upon Mr. Hale to do what he did, relinquish the living, and throw himself
and his family on the tender mercies of private teaching in a manufacturing
town . . . if he had come to entertain certain doubts, he could have remained
where he was, and so had no occasion to resign" (*NS* 466). Mr. Lennox
freely admits the individual right to choose one's religious convictions and
practices; however, his attitude toward this choice is a hedonistic one. If it
pleases the individual to make decisions based on conscience, he suggests,
then it is the right of the individual to indulge in these pleasures. However,
he sees no reason to sacrifice material comforts or money on the basis of
these convictions. That is to say, Lennox also sees religion as a set of surfaces
to human life. Underlying the array of religious choices, he also finds an
arena of universal humanity, where individuals of all conviction are as one.
But while for Margaret, her father, and perhaps Higgins, this underlying
stratum is a forum for ethical thinking, for an effort toward the broadest
notion of a good society, the common bond Lennox understands is one of
utter self-interest.

Lennox's entire London set, in fact, displays this utilitarian understanding of religion, what we might call a hedonics of religious conviction.
This becomes clear at the endless dinner parties which Edith and the
Captain throw after their return to London, and in which they include
Margaret, as poorish relation and object of match-making. The parties are
carefully composed, with guest lists designed to produce the most amusing
conversations:

Mr. Henry Lennox and the sprinkling of rising men who were received as his
friends brought the wit, the cleverness, the keen and extensive knowledge of which
they knew well enough how to avail themselves without seeming pedantic, or
burdening the rapid flow of conversation.

These dinners were delightful; but even here Margaret's dissatisfaction found
her out. Every talent, every feeling, every acquirement; nay, even every tendency
towards virtue, was used up as materials for fireworks; the hidden, sacred fire,
exhausted itself in sparkle and crackle. They talked about art in a merely sensuous

way, dwelling on outside effects, instead of allowing themselves to learn what it has to teach. They lashed themselves up into an enthusiasm about high subjects in company, and never thought about them when they were alone; they squandered their capabilities of appreciation into a mere flow of appropriate words. (*NS* 497)

Like Higgins, Lennox's friends view religious freedom as an opportunity for diversion. The light of "sacred fire" here is used up for mere entertainment. Again, this circle concedes absolutely the right of the individual to believe or not to believe just as she chooses. However, this abstract individual, who underlies all religious convictions, and selects among them, is simply a machine of self-interest. Religious choices are here drained of any ethical content, any vision of the good or the social. Such ponderous content of religious discussion, the passage indicates, might weigh down or "burden" the conversation here which, in two crucial references, is understood by the dinner-party participants as a game of "rapid flow." This "mere flow" of words, used for their formal pleasures, their sensuous possibilities, rather than their social reference, parallels and leads us toward the economic understanding of industrial society as the "mere flow" of manufactured commodities, which are valuable not in their contribution toward any social good, but only in their capacity to please the abstract individual.

In all these different situations, we see a critique of established religion which conforms to the liberal position set out by Marx's rival Bauer. For all of these characters, doctrinal practices or questions of faith and doubt are simply "snake skins" which cover the exteriors of human life. The novel makes clear that the increasing freedom of religion it argues for requires an abstract conception of the human being, the subject who can choose among the possibilities of faith and doubt. And while it seems on the one hand to offer this subject of universal rights as a subject of heightened ethical consciousness, unconcerned with the niceties of doctrine, on the other hand, particularly in its indictment of London society, the novel shows that the subject of universal rights is necessarily a subject of self-interest, responsible only in the end for its own pleasures and pains.

The structure of religious freedom is thus shown to tend toward a fatal egoism. The novel makes the same point in its portrayal of the rights of property and wealth, that is to say its discussion of political economy. In the Hales' migration from south to north, the novel depicts the wholesale dismantling of an earlier class system, based on the distinction between "gentlemen" and common folk. This point is made thanks to Margaret's observation of the lifeways of the industrial city. While Mr. Hale is impressed with the "energy" (*NS* 108) of Milton, Margaret keenly feels the loss of social status that accompanies their move. In searching for a house servant to assist Dixon, she finds that "Mr. Hale was no longer looked upon as the Vicar of Helstone, but as a man who only spent at a certain rate" (*NS* 109). Milton society functions on a principle of male abstract equality. There are no a priori differences between men, only their ranks as measured by money. As we see in the character of Thornton, this abstract liberty produces an ideology of individualism. It considers all men as possessed of the same rights but functions to obscure the continuing power differences created by money, or indeed by creed, race, or gender. Margaret, both because of her status as a woman, and because of her anachronistic habit of visiting the poor, sees that despite the presumption of universal independence, Milton society keeps some of its members *dependent* on others, as Margaret and her mother find their fate dependent on the Reverend's crisis of conscience. Her insight produces the novel's critique of democratic capitalism, a critique which finally makes a convert of John Thornton.

However, with advantages of power generally removed from the language of politics, wealth and influence or poverty and helplessness can only be construed as consequences of individual free choice. This is the philosophy Thornton expounds, particularly at the first of two seminars over tea with the Hales. Here he argues that the suffering of the poor "is but the natural punishment of dishonestly-enjoyed pleasure, at some former period of their lives. I do not look on self-indulgent, sensual people as worthy of my hatred; I simply look upon them with contempt for their poorness of character" (*NS* 126). Thornton begins his theorizing with the concept of the subject of universal rights. Because he starts from this foundation, he assumes an intentional subject prior to any engagement with the social. This a priori individual possesses a "character" which precedes and dictates the subject's encounter with the market.

Thornton does concede that the social milieu of the industrial city produces selfishness. He speaks of the "almost unlimited power the manufacturers had at the beginning of this century" and admits that "the men were rendered dizzy by it" (*NS* 124). However, he suggests that "by-and-by came a reaction; there were more factories, more masters; more men were wanted. The power of masters and men became more evenly balanced; and now the battle is pretty thoroughly waged between us" (*NS* 125). The abstract equality of male rights here produces an order of selfishness, but one which, through its "battle of all against all," will create progress and social amelioration.[46]

However, while Thornton understands an abstract equality of rights as the engine of civilization, he does not see social equality – equality of privilege or power – as the end result of such progress. While all participate in the "battle" of trade and production, it is the merchants and capitalists who are themselves "the great pioneers of civilization" in his view (*NS* 171). Thornton's conception of a regime of total selfishness, therefore, is based on the idea that the clash of self-interested agents in the marketplace will produce not only an orderly and "balanced" society, but also a cadre of industrial "pioneers." Mrs. Thornton, in teatime seminar 11, lectures Mr. Hale and Margaret about Thornton's position in society. She claims that her son's one desire is "to hold and maintain a high, honourable place among the merchants of this country – the men of his town . . . Go where you will – I don't say in England only but in Europe – the name of John Thornton of Milton is known and respected amongst all men of business" (*NS* 160). She seems perhaps only to be bragging about the achievement of her son, but we find out that an "honourable place" is precisely Thornton's aim, though one he is not always aware of.

At the end of the novel, faced with the prospect of losing his business, he worries not about the loss of money, but rather feels anxiety "acutely in his vulnerable point – his pride in the commercial character which he had established for himself" (*NS* 511). The passage continues:

Architect of his fortunes, he attributed this to no especial merit or qualities of his own, but to the power, which he believed that commerce gave to every brave, honest, and persevering man, to raise himself to a level from which he might see and read the great game of worldly success, and honestly, by such far-sightedness, command more power and influence than in any other mode of life. Far away, in the East and in the West, where his person would never be known, his name was to be regarded, and his wishes to be fulfilled, and his words passed like gold. (*NS* 511)

Thornton's faith is in the free rights of property and in the freedom of trade. That is, he believes in a society governed by economic principles, by the free circulation of money as the standard of wealth, and not in inherited privilege. Yet, he realizes in this passage that while he wants a society ruled by economy and not aristocracy, his vision of life in such a society is in fact a quasi-feudal one, a life where, his fortune already established, he will mount to the status of the aristocrat. His influence, power, and fame, he imagines, will become frozen at the highest point of his fortune. Regardless of any fluctuations in his actual net worth, he wishes his social position to be fixed, with all its privileges. He imagines, in a line that indicates quite precisely the atavism of his vision, that "his words" will pass "like gold." That is, he dreams that having once attained a certain wealth in pure money, his opinions and desires will gain a solidity beyond the risky arena of the marketplace. His speculations on paper in the commodities market will pass over into a realm of absolute – that is aristocratic – value, value which is locked to a conception of internal character, rather than dissociated from it. "That," we are told, "was the idea of merchant-life with which Mr. Thornton had started. 'Her merchants be like princes,' said his mother, reading the text aloud" (*NS* 511). The Bible passage (Isaiah 23:8) completes Gaskell's diagnosis of the incoherent and paradoxical conception of political economy that Thornton holds. He defends the democratic right to own and accumulate, yet he presumes that a system of social privilege will persist in such a society. He defends the equal right to property on the grounds of its fairness to every member of society, while at the same time secretly understanding the persistence of oppression this system will permit. What Gaskell makes clear, rounding out the critique launched in *Cranford*, is the secret romance within the supposedly rationalized system of capitalist trade. Democratic capitalism functions here in the occult promise that the honorable man can become a king.

What *North and South* shows, however, is that a society organized on the assumption of self-interested individualism produces neither orderly and balanced progress toward the good, nor the reward of neofeudal power for a chivalric class of merchant-princes. Rather it produces a kind of chaos. This is hinted at in a series of metaphors inaugurated at the moment that Margaret, in the beginning of the novel, must break the news to her mother that they will leave Helstone for Milton. Struggling to find the right words, "her eye caught on a bee entering a deep-belled flower: when that bee flew forth with his spoil she would begin – that should be the sign" (*NS* 78). Leaving the rural south will mean moving to a place where people behave like bees, moving with mechanical, inhuman regularity only in the attempt to accumulate "spoil." When they arrive in Milton, Mr. Hale remarks to Mrs. Thornton that the noise and smoke caused by the adjoining mill must prove annoying. She replies, "as for the continual murmur of the work-people, it disturbs me no more than the humming of a hive of bees" (*NS* 214). For Mrs. Thornton the hum of perpetual accumulation is significant only as "the source of [her] son's wealth and power" (*NS* 214). The factory system of Milton organizes its workers as labor-commodities, set into regular motion. However, we find that this system does not produce the orderly and geometric precision of the beehive, or the regular laying up of wealth. When the workers gather during the strike to protest the hiring of Irish replacement laborers, the crowd is described as "buzzing with excitement" (*NS* 226). Their sound increases like "the first long far-off roll of the tempest" (*NS* 226) and approaches with an "ominous gathering roar" (*NS* 227). The ambiguous character of the metaphor of bees, traditional in political economy since Mandeville's *Fable of the Bees*, is exploited in these passages. No longer as regular and predictable as the machines they work, the "bees" now develop a hostile power likened to the danger of larger and more ferocious animals, or to the chaotic violence of storms. These crowd descriptions that draw from natural images of violence may seem themselves somewhat ambiguous in character, readable as a pre-Darwinian characterization of the poor as animalistic, unevolved. Read with the understanding of the bee metaphor's relation to economic thought, however, the passage takes on a different character. It indicates that selfishness, based in the principle of abstract rights, will produce not a geometric "hive" of orderly accumulation and progress, but rather a violent and destructive chaos where some thrive and others starve. Treated like bees, the starving revolt.

The final confirmation of the chaos produced by the regime of self-interest descends upon Thornton when his mill fails. The market system deserts him here, and he sees that his personal "honour" and "bravery" in conducting business means nothing within an ultimately arbitrary market. Chapter 50, in which Thornton realizes the hypocrisy of his vision of himself as merchant-prince, sets the scene for this revelation as follows:

At Milton the chimneys smoked, the ceaseless roar and mighty beat, and dizzying whirl of machinery, struggled and strove perpetually. Senseless and purposeless were wood and iron and steam in their endless labours; but the persistence of their monotonous work was rivalled in tireless endurance by the strong crowds, who, with sense and with purpose, were busy and restless in seeking after – What? (*NS* 510)

The factories churn on here not in a grand teleology of civilization, but devoid of sense and purpose, and the inhabitants of Milton mime this perpetual motion. Their labor is driven not by a certain purpose, not even by self-interest; rather it takes on the chaotic and "dizzying" motion of the machine itself.

As with her diagnosis of the selfishness and inequality underpinning capitalist democracy, Gaskell's solution to this problem works in sympathy with Marx's. At the end of the first section of "On the Jewish Question," Marx concludes:

The actual individual man must take the abstract citizen into himself and, as an individual man in his empirical life, in his individual work and individual relationships become a species-being; man must recognize his own forces as social forces, organize them, and thus no longer separate social forces from himself in the form of political forces. Only when this has been achieved will human emancipation be completed.[47]

Marx proposes a reintegration of the two halves of human life separated by capitalist democratic societies. What he calls the "species-being" – that is, what we would call the social construction of human perception, desire, and thought – must be recombined, threaded back into that abstract citizen, who appears to be born fully grown, sprung completely from "his" own tastes, opinions, and ambitions, and responsible to no one but "himself." It is precisely such a reintegration that is theorized and enacted in the debates between John Thornton and Margaret Hale, a series of debates which functions as a courtship.

Within the capitalist democracy Marx argues, in the passage I quoted earlier, "none of the so-called rights of man goes beyond egoistic man."[48] He continues: "Far from the rights of man conceiving of man as a species-being, species-life itself, society, appears as a framework exterior to individuals, a limitation of their original self-sufficiency. The only bond that holds them together is natural necessity, need and private interest, the conservation of their property and egoistic person."[49] This is precisely the attitude which Gaskell diagnoses in Thornton. He conceives the success of his mill not as something made possible by a total system of social organization, but rather as something produced by himself out of whole cloth. Again in their first seminar over tea, he explains to Margaret and her father that all the manufacturers resent the "meddling" of Parliament in their business. "We will hardly submit," he says, ". . . to the interference of a meddler with only a smattering of the knowledge of the real facts of the case, even though that meddler may be the High Court of Parliament" (*NS* 125). Government can only appear to Thornton as a threat to his "original self-sufficiency." In seminar II, which takes place when the Hales return Mr. Thornton's visit, Margaret brilliantly opposes Thornton's position:

God has made us so that we must be mutually dependent. We may ignore our own dependence, or refuse to acknowledge that others depend upon us in more respects than the payment of weekly wages; but the thing must be, nevertheless. Neither you nor any other master can help yourselves. The most proudly independent man depends on those around him for their insensible influence on his character – his life. (*NS* 169)

In Marx's terms, Margaret opposes "species-being" with the abstract citizen of the political sphere. Moreover, she points out the contradiction of Thornton's position, in defending his right to dictate absolutely the fate of his workers, without explanation of the amount of work or the level of wages he provides. "I am trying to reconcile," she remarks, "your admiration of despotism with your respect for other men's independence of character" (*NS* 171). That is, while the "rights of man" posit an absolute equality and affirm a staunch independence, at the same time a political system founded on such rights permits and in fact presumes the continued power of "despotism" enabled by the accumulation of wealth and the absolute and irresponsible (male) right of property.

Thornton is embarrassed and baffled by Margaret's analysis of his position. However, in the end he is utterly persuaded by it, just as Margaret is ultimately persuaded of Thornton's commitment to a good society. The forum where this persuasion takes place, however, is not the drawing-room seminar on political economy, where the process begins, but rather in the interior world of feelings and sexual desire. Here the text moves from Margaret's religious politics, a critique of abstract individualism based on a community of faith, into a politics of character, one that recalls the debate between true speech and the artificiality of writing staged in *Mary Barton*. Whereas the Christian critique of capitalism suggests that humans will make the right political choices if they attend to the word of God, the politics of character argues that humans act in society's best interest when they listen to their "true heart." At the start of the novel Margaret is shown to be rigidly bound by the social conventions of the quasi-feudal south. She is unwilling to socialize with "shoppy people" (*NS* 50) and at first regards Thornton and the other mill owners simply as "tradesmen" (*NS* 102), not gentlemen. In the character of Fanny, Mr. Thornton's younger sister, the narrator ridicules people who rely on gossip or on judgments of others "for the rule of their feelings" (*NS* 219). But the text makes it equally clear that Margaret allows her feelings to be "ruled" in just this way.

Her true feelings for Thornton are first hinted at in the sexualized description of the crowd in the great strike scene at the center of the novel. Having insisted that Thornton face the mob of striking workers as they protest outside his house, Margaret looks on the scene from an upstairs window, sensing the impending violence of the crowd. "Margaret felt intuitively, that in an instant, all would be uproar; the first touch would cause an explosion . . . Mr. Thornton's life would be unsafe . . . in another instant the stormy passions would have passed their bounds, and swept away all barriers of reason, or apprehension of consequence" (*NS* 233). The "explosion" of "passions" that will ensue at "the first touch" is made clear to Margaret at the level of intuition. After the scene, Margaret realizes that she has become an object of gossip (*NS* 248–49), and that it appeared she defended Thornton because she was in love with him. Thornton, distinctly under this impression, proposes, and Margaret refuses indignantly. Embarrassed that she should be seen as attached to a man whom she considers to belong to an inferior class, she denies her feelings.

The force of these feelings, which the text suggests are at the base of Margaret's true character, persists mysteriously, without name, until Margaret is forced to yield to them. She wonders at one point "what strong feeling had overtaken her at last?" (*NS* 358). Caught by Thornton in a lie, in the plot relating to her exiled brother Frederick, Margaret later wonders, "why do I care what he [Thornton] thinks, beyond the mere loss of his good opinion as regards my telling the truth or not?" (*NS* 400). Her obligation to Thornton in this matter produces what she calls "this wild, strange, miserable feeling" (*NS* 407).

We find no evidence that this secret force of Margaret's character has become conscious until the very end of the novel, when Margaret "proposes" that she save Thornton from bankruptcy with the loan of money inherited from her godfather, Mr. Bell. Her money will enable Thornton to continue the experiment he has begun toward a new and more humane system of manufacturing. The system Thornton argues for is one itself based on a politics of authentic character. He explains:

I have arrived at the conviction that no mere institutions, however wise, and however much thought may have been required to organize and arrange them, can attach class to class as they should be attached, unless the working out of such institutions bring the individuals of the different classes into actual personal contact. Such intercourse is the very breath of life. (*NS* 525)

As in *Mary Barton*, the character and humanity of the laborers, when revealed and made clear to the manufacturers, will push class antagonism "beyond the mere 'cash nexus'" (*NS* 525), just as it brings the "species-being," the social connectedness of industrial society, into the system of clashing self-interest. These class interactions, where the revelation of character can take place, are "the very breath of life," embodying the "spirit" of living speech, here placed in opposition to the cold and artificial abstraction of the isolated individual. Margaret's money will underwrite this new system, this reintegration of the social and the individual, just as her reconciliation with Thornton reunites the alienated halves of her own character, the one ruled by social convention, and the one that possesses authentic feelings. Margaret's revelation of character is, in fact, only declared in her offer to capitalize Thornton's interests. It is only through Thornton's interpretation of her financial "proposal" that the love-plot is resolved and the marriage plans begun.

This closing scene, literally the last two pages of the novel, far from representing a retreat from the chaos and selfishness of the market, demands a radical restructuring of political and economic principles on which the concept of a market is based. Critics of the novel as early as Margaret Oliphant have condemned *North and South* for abandoning its political themes in headlong pursuit of a love-plot. Oliphant writes,

We are prepared . . . for the discussion of an important social question . . . [but] the story gradually slides off the public topic to pursue a course of its own . . . It is Mr. Thornton's fierce and rugged course of true love to which the author is most anxious to direct our attention; and we have little time to think of Higgins or his trade unions. (*NS* 346–47)

While this has become a standard way of understanding the industrial novel as a genre, it ignores *North and South*'s particular dynamic. There is no retreat here from public to private, but rather an insistent attempt to reintegrate the abstract subject of politics and economics with the private forces of character, responsibility, and belief.

But as may already be clear, the radical demands the novel advances under the headings of religious politics and the politics of character, as I have described them here, seem to acknowledge already their own limitations. Religious conviction, conscience, and personality have by the middle of the nineteenth century been corralled into the holding pen of democratic "freedoms." The democratic subject is free to choose any form of religious opinion, to feel any sort of feeling, because these opinions and feelings are irrelevant to and separate from the market, which proceeds with a force and logic entirely of its own. The novel's critique, based on these private-sphere convictions, thus contains and is already aware of its failure. Abstract individualism, as *North and South* shows, is already firmly entrenched at Milton and among the London set of the Lennoxes. The mere opinions of Margaret and John will carry no force beyond the strict limit of Margaret's eighteen thousand pounds. The scope of their radical politics is limited by the already self-contained market, and relegated to the slippery sphere of free opinion. Modern economics presumes an absolute equality among market agents, but it presupposes the continuing inequality of economic power.

Conclusion

In these chapters taken together, I have tried to chart the total reorientation of economic concepts which took place in the nineteenth century. The first section of the book presented a case for seeing the dominant theoretical model of contemporary economics, which emerged out of this shift, as an analogue to modern linguistic philosophy. The book's second section considered discrete examples of texts that contributed to this reorientation of ideas about the market and society. Given their direct engagement with theories of political economy, the treatments of the Irish disaster discussed in chapter 4 make this shift especially clear. There, books by Asenath Nicholson and Shafto Adair, both in different ways, are drawing from old and new modes of economic thought, blending these into distinctive theories of economic progress through inward exploration of character. But the novels by Charles Dickens and Elizabeth Gaskell discussed in chapters 3 and 5 likewise confront in clear ways the chaotic or threatening dimension of expanding capitalist markets. While they theorize the damage inflicted in the process of capitalist rationalization, they imagine a metaphysical compensation for these material losses, emphasizing images of home, nation, and character. In this way I have suggested that these fictional and non-fictional texts are engaged in the same enterprise. They are connected not simply through common metaphors, but through a common, though at this point still loose, set of assumptions. The major works I discussed here are all texts of protest, railing against the cruelty that could be justified by a mechanistic and rigidly progressive theory of capitalism. But the humanistic grounds of their critique helped to solidify the central assumptions of modern, neoclassical economics: the unique integrity of the subject and the authenticity of its behavior in the market.

I assemble these readings here in order to argue for a critique of the unexamined subjectivity of the consumer, as it structures the contemporary theory of capitalism and the current push toward economic globalization. Because at a basic level this study argues for a critique of the unified theory of the desiring subject, and the culture of individualism it supports, there is one final danger endemic to the project that I would like to note. Given the argument I make here, it may seem that the ultimate goal I have in mind is the dissolution of the perceiving agent, the "decentering" of the subject into a collection of material fragments. However, I make no easy association between radical politics and such a philosophical project. Indeed, I see no firm or inevitable political program that stems from an anti-essentialist or anti-foundationalist view of human perception. My discussion of Adam Smith makes this point: Smith's view of the subject is one that accounts for the "constructive" force of language and culture; it is, in broad terms, a kind of materialist history of human social activity. It is, however, a justification of accumulated wealth which, in its treatment of poverty, can be quite glib. Smith's theory may approximate a certain poststructuralist view of the subject, but it also leads Smith to conclude, in the passage I discussed in chapter 1, that "in ease of body and peace of mind, all the different ranks of life are nearly upon a level, and the beggar, who suns himself by the side of the highway, possesses that security which kings are fighting for."[1]

One important examination of this problem in contemporary literary theory is the recent reading of new corporate rhetoric begun by Romanticist Alan Liu. According to Liu, far from inaugurating an effective critique of capitalism, the poststructuralist theory of the subject was, in the high-spirited management theory of the 1990s, almost entirely absorbed by late-capitalist boosters. The global corporation, he argues from these readings, sees itself as a decentralized institution, a series of horizontally linked clusters, rather than a hierarchy of individuals taking orders from a "head man." The groups function as teams, effectively submerging the identities of individual members into a loose affiliation of idea-flows, moving with ultra-efficient speed in a network of electronic communication. The exuberance of 1980s poststructuralism receives a near-fatal corrective in this argument; the decentered subject here is not the left-handed agent of resistance but rather the perfect postmodern worker.[2]

What I do suggest, however, is that the seeming authenticity of consumer desire, the idea that purchasing is the clearest road toward personal expression, is still an unquestioned foundation of the late-capitalist marketplace, one where the romantic integrity of the perceiving subject is still presumed to be largely intact. I make no broader claims for the politics of theory here. But I do argue that, at this particular historical moment, the observation that the essence of commodities is purely social still has a potentially significant critical force.

Notes

INTRODUCTION

1. J.K. Gibson-Graham's *The End of Capitalism (As We Knew it)* (Oxford: Blackwell, 1996) points out the ubiquity of economic rhetoric in recent US electoral politics.

2. Stephen Gill, *Wordsworth and the Victorians* (Oxford: Clarendon, 1998) makes a powerful case for such diffuse literary and social influence. The impact of romanticism on economic behavior is confronted in Colin Campbell, *The Romantic Ethic and the Spirit of Modern Consumerism* (Oxford: Blackwell, 1987). However, Campbell's interest is not in the theory of economics but in a certain spirit of hedonistic indulgence he finds in modern consumerism. He attempts to trace this hedonistic spirit to the romantics.

3. W[illiam] Stanley Jevons, *The Theory of Political Economy*, 5th edn., ed. H. Stanley Jevons (1871; New York: Kelley & Millman, 1957), xiv.

4. *Ibid.*, vii.

5. On perceived connections between economics and the physical sciences in the nineteenth century, see Phillip Mirowski, *More Heat than Light: Economics as Social Physics: Physics as Nature's Economics* (Cambridge: Cambridge University Press, 1989).

6. Raymond Williams, *Culture and Society, 1780–1950* (New York: Columbia University Press, 1956), xviii.

7. *Ibid.*, xviii. Philip Connel makes the point in a somewhat different way:

   our inherited sense of the incompatibility between literary sensibility and economic science has obscured the extent to which early nineteenth-century political economy, and the debate on its legitimacy, scope, and function, played a formative role in the emergence of the idea of 'culture' itself, as a humanistic or spiritual resource resistant to the intellectual enervation produced by modern, commercial societies. (*Romanticism, Economics and the Question of "Culture"* [Oxford: Oxford University Press, 2001], 7)

8. Boyd Hilton, *The Age of Atonement: The Influence of Evangelicalism on Social and Economic Thought, 1795–1865* (Oxford: Clarendon, 1988). On the idea that Malthus trumps Adam Smith in the first half of the nineteenth century, see also Donald Winch, *Riches and Poverty: An Intellectual History of Political Economy in Britain, 1750–1834* (Cambridge: Cambridge University Press, 1996).

9. Quoted in *ibid.*, 6.
10. It is worth pointing out, as James Thompson does, that Gramsci explicitly mentions "specialists in political economy" in discussing his concept of the "organic intellectual" (Antonio Gramsci, *Selections from the Prison Notebooks*, ed. and trans. Quintin Hoare and Geoffrey Nowell Smith [New York: International, 1971], 5). Thompson's discussion of this passage is in *Models of Value: Eighteenth-Century Political Economy and the Novel* (Durham, NC: Duke University Press, 1996), 41.
11. Donald [Deirdre] McCloskey, *The Rhetoric of Economics* (Madison: University of Wisconsin Press, 1985).
12. Recent collections of work in this category include Arjo Klamer, ed., *The Value of Culture: On the Relationship Between Economics and Arts* (Amsterdam: Amsterdam University Press, 1996); Arjo Klamer, Donald [Deirdre] N. McCloskey, and Robert M. Solow, eds., *The Consequences of Economic Rhetoric* (Cambridge: Cambridge University Press, 1988); and Phillip Mirowski, ed., *Natural Images in Economic Thought: "Markets Read in Tooth and Claw"* (Cambridge: Cambridge University Press, 1994).
13. An introduction to feminist economics can be found in Marianne A. Ferber and Julie A. Nelson, *Beyond Economic Man: Feminist Theory and Economics* (Chicago: University of Chicago Press, 1993); and also in editor Diana Strassman's essay in the first number of *Feminist Economics* ("Creating a Forum for Feminist Economic Inquiry," *Feminist Economics* 1.1 [Spring 1995], 1–7). In its focus on the distortions inherent in the neoclassical model, and the universal subject at its center, the work of Susan Feiner is especially insightful. See "A Portrait of *Homo Economicus* as a Young Man," in *The New Economic Criticism: Studies at the Intersection of Literature and Economics*, ed. Martha Woodmansee and Mark Osteen (London: Routledge, 1999), 193–209; "Reading Neoclassical Economics: Toward an Erotic Economy of Sharing," in *Out of the Margin: Feminist Perspectives on Economics*, ed. Edith Kuiper and Jolande Sap (London: Routledge, 1995), 151–65; and with Bruce Roberts, "Slave Exploitation in Neoclassical Economics," in *The Wealth of Races: The Present Value of Benefits from Past Injustices*, ed. Richard F. America (New York: Greenwood Press, 1990), 139–49.
14. Recent Marxian economics in the *Rethinking* school would include Stephen A. Resnick and Richard D. Wolff, *Knowledge and Class: A Marxian Critique of Political Economy* (Chicago: University of Chicago Press, 1987); and Stephen Cullenberg, *The Falling Rate of Profit* (London: Pluto, 1994). Collections engaging the poststructuralist critique of Marxist economic and social theory include Antonio Callari and David Ruccio, eds., *Postmodern Materialism and the Future of Marxist Theory: Essays in the Althusserian Tradition* (Hanover, NH: University of New England Press, 1996); J.K. Gibson-Graham, Stephen A. Resnick, and Richard D. Wolff, eds., *Re/presenting Class: Essays in Postmodern Marxism* (Durham, NC: Duke University Press, 2001); and Berndt Magnus and Stephen Cullenberg, eds., *Whither Marxism?: Global Crises in International Perspective* (New York: Routledge, 1995). The latter volume

collects responses to Derrida's encounter with the Marxist tradition in Jacques Derrida, *Specters of Marx: The State of the Debt, the Work of Mourning, and the New International*, trans. Peggy Kamuf (London: Routledge, 1994).

15. See for example Jerry Mander and Edward Goldsmith, *The Case Against the Global Economy: And for a Turn Toward the Local* (San Francisco: Sierra Club, 1996). Arthur MacEwan, *Neo-Liberalism or Democracy? Economic Strategy, Markets, and Alternatives for the Twenty-first Century* (London: Zed, 1999); and Wolfgang Sachs, ed., *The Development Dictionary: A Guide to Knowledge as Power* (London: Zed, 1992) are representative popular-academic crossover offerings on globalization from Zed Press, which is dedicated to making work of this kind available.

16. See for example James Ferguson, *The Anti-Politics Machine* (Cambridge: Cambridge University Press, 1994); Bill Maurer, *Recharting the Caribbean: Land, Law, and Citizenship in the British Virgin Islands* (Ann Arbor: University of Michigan Press, 1997); Arturo Escobar, *Encountering Development: The Making and Unmaking of the Third World* (Princeton: Princeton University Press, 1995). Rethinking the nexus of culture and postmodern patterns of accumulation is also the project of the multi-disciplinary volume by Lisa Lowe and David Lloyd, eds., *Politics of Culture under the Shadow of Capital* (Durham, NC: Duke University Press, 1997).

17. For an overview of research on the money–language homology, beginning with the provocations of Goux and Shell, see Martha Woodmansee and Mark Osteen, "Taking Account of the New Economic Criticism: An Historical Introduction," in Woodmansee and Osteen, eds., *New Economic Criticism*, 3–50.

18. Another important contribution to the analysis of money and language is Jean Baudrillard, *For a Critique of the Political Economy of the Sign*, trans. and intr. Charles Levin (St. Louis: Telos, 1981), though this text has found few recent exponents. One salutary exception is Gerhard Joseph, "Commodifying Tennyson: The Historical Transformation of 'Brand Loyalty'," in Woodmansee and Osteen, eds., *New Economic Criticism*, 307–20.

19. In nineteenth-century studies, see John Sutherland, *Victorian Fiction: Writers, Publishers, Readers* (New York: St. Martin's, 1995); Norman Feltes, *Literary Capital and the Late Victorian Novel* (Madison: University of Wisconsin Press, 1993); Kevin McLaughlin, *Writing in Parts: Imitation and Exchange in Nineteenth-Century Literature* (Stanford, CA: Stanford University Press, 1995); Martha Woodmansee, *The Author, Art and the Market: Rereading the History of Aesthetics* (New York: Columbia University Press, 1994); Martha Woodmansee and Peter Jaszi, eds., *The Construction of Authorship: Textual Appropriation in Law and Literature* (Durham, NC: Duke University Press, 1994); John O. Jordan and Robert L. Patten, eds., *Literature in the Marketplace: Nineteenth-Century British Publishing and Reading Practices* (Cambridge: Cambridge University Press, 1995).

20. Jeff Nunokawa, *The Afterlife of Property: Domestic Security and the Victorian Novel* (Princeton: Princeton University Press, 1994).

21. Andrew H. Miller, *Novels Behind Glass: Commodity Culture and Victorian Narrative* (Cambridge: Cambridge University Press, 1995).
22. Thompson, *Models of Value.*
23. Christoper Herbert, *Culture and Anomie: Ethnographic Imagination in the Nineteenth Century* (Chicago: University of Chicago Press, 1991). See my discussion of this book in chapter 2, 56–57.
24. Jack Amariglio and David F. Rucio, "Literary/Cultural 'Economies,' Economic Discourse, and the Question of Marxism," in Woodmansee and Osteen, eds., *New Economic Criticism*, 385.
25. *Ibid.*, 386.
26. Regenia Gagnier and John Dupré, "Reply to Amariglio and Ruccio's 'Literary/Cultural "Economies," Economic Discourse, and the Question of Marxism'," in Woodmansee and Osteen, eds., *New Economic Criticism*, 404–05. Gagnier and Dupré demonstrate this tendency in reading Lawrence Birken, *Consuming Desires: Sexual Science and the Emergence of a Culture of Abundance, 1871–1914* (Ithaca, NY: Cornell University Press, 1988), which treats the expanding availability of consumer goods in the late nineteenth century as an indicator of increasing freedom.
27. Gagnier and Dupré, "Reply," 404–05.

NOTES TO PART I: OPENING

1. Immanuel Kant, *Critique of Pure Reason*, trans. Norman Kemp Smith (1781; New York: St. Martin's, 1929), 65; Jacques Derrida, *Of Grammatology*, trans. Gayatri Chakravorty Spivak (Baltimore: Johns Hopkins University Press, 1974).
2. David E. Mungello, *Curious Land: Jesuit Accommodation and the Origins of Sinology* (Stuttgart: Verlag, 1985), 183. I am grateful to Christopher L. Connery for this reference.
3. Quoted in *ibid.*, 204.
4. Derrida, *Of Grammatology*, 76. Whether Derrida himself diagnoses these errors of ethnocentrism correctly or not has continued to be a subject of some dispute. See Rey Chow, "How (the) Inscrutable Chinese Led to Globalized Theory," *PMLA* 116.1 (January 2001), 69–74; along with the responses it provoked: Arnold Bohm, Letter to Editor, *PMLA* 116.3 (May 2001), 657–58; Henry Staten, Letter to Editor, *PMLA* 116.3 (May 2001), 659–60. Chow's rejoinder is in the same number, *PMLA* 116.3 (May 2001), 660. In describing seventeenth-century European views of the Chinese language here, I have followed David Mungello, *Curious Land.*
5. Russell Fraser, *The Language of Adam: On the Limits and Systems of Discourse* (New York: Columbia University Press, 1977), 13.
6. Derrida, *Of Grammatology*, 11.
7. It is this concept of "the truth" that Derrida calls "logocentrism," the "metaphysics of phonetic writing" (*ibid.*, 3): "All the metaphysical determinations of truth . . . are more or less immediately inseparable from the instance of

the logos, or of a reason thought within the lineage of the logos . . . Within this logos, the original and essential link to the *phonè* has never been broken" (*ibid.*, 10–11).

8. While, like Leibniz, some seventeenth-century scholars interested in a universal language focused on inventing one, others sought clues to the existence of the primitive language of Eden, which they believed to be a perfect means of communication, bestowed by God. John Webb's *Historical Essay Endeavoring a Probability that the Language of the Empire of China is the Primitive Language* (London, 1669) is one example. See Mungello, *Curious Land*, chapter VI: "Proto-Sinology and the Seventeenth-Century European Search for a Universal Language." Fraser's *Language of Adam* surveys early modern theories of God's original language.

9. William Warburton, *The Divine Legation of Moses Demonstrated*, 10th edn., 2 vols. (1737–41; London: 1846), section IV.1.

10. Derrida indicates this when he argues that logocentrism functions as "nothing but the most original and powerful ethnocentrism" (Derrida, *Of Grammatology*, 3).

11. On the early history of the Bank of England, see Charles Poor Kindleberger, *A Financial History of Western Europe*, 2nd edn. (New York: Oxford University Press, 1993), 37–44, 53–56; and Pierre Villar, *A History of Gold and Money, 1450–1920* (1969; London: Verso, 1976), chapter 23.

12. "Financial revolution" is P. G. M. Dickson's phrase, in *The Financial Revolution in England: A Study in the Development of Public Credit, 1688–1756* (New York: St. Martin's, 1967).

13. Mungello, *Curious Land*, 204–05.

14. Derrida, *Of Grammatology*, 10.

15. "The first numeral forms of the Greeks seem to have been such upright strokes as were used in all Mediterranean countries, and perhaps represented the fingers" (David Eugene Smith, *History of Mathematics*, 2 vols. [New York: Ginn, 1923], II.47). Classical Greek mathematics, however, developed out of a system for indicating quantities by the first letter of their name. The quantity five, for example, was indicated by the symbol (Γ), an archaic form of the letter π (*pi*), first letter in the word πέντε (*pen'te*). Abbreviations like this for 5, 10, 100, etc., could be combined with upright markers (l, ll, etc.) to indicate any number (*ibid.*, II.50). By the second and third centuries, a system of alphabetic numerals was used both in Greek and Hebrew, where each letter indicated its cardinal place in the sequence. The origin of the Roman numerals is less certain. According to David Smith they derive from upright markers for single quantities, adaptations of Greek letters, and abbreviations of words: M for *mille* = 1,000, and perhaps C for *centum* = 100 (*ibid.*, II.54–58). Karl Menninger, in his supremely logocentric history of numbers, maintains that this correspondence between numeral and word for 1,000 and 100 developed "quite by coincidence!" (*Number Words and Number Symbols: A Cultural History of Numbers* [Cambridge, MA: MIT Press, 1969], 244). But coincidence or not, the correspondence between these numerals and their phonetically

spelled words is plain. It seems reasonable to conclude then that until the tenth century all systems of counting known in Europe bore some kind of link to phonetic writing.

Another way to trace the cultural impact of Hindu-Arabic mathematics in Europe is to examine the significance of the numeral zero, for which the Roman system had no equivalent, and the concept of "nothing" that it represents. This is the subject of Brian Rotman, *Signifying Nothing: The Semiotics of Zero* (New York: St. Martin's, 1987). Rotman also considers the status of mathematics as a system of writing in *Mathematics as Sign: Writing, Imagining, Counting* (Stanford, CA: Stanford University Press, 2000).

16. An early printed instructional manual, the *Treviso Arithmetic* (1478), translated by David E. Smith, is available in Frank J. Swetz, *Capitalism & Arithmetic: The New Math of the 15th Century* (La Salle, IL: Open Court, 1987). The text was designed for the use of "reckoning masters" who trained boys in the computational skills necessary for mercantile accounting (*ibid.*, 15–17).

17. Thomas Hill, *The Arte of Vulgar Arithmetic, Both in Integers and Fractions* (London, 1660), quoted in Patricia Cline Cohen, *A Calculating People: The Spread of Numeracy in Early America* (Chicago: University of Chicago Press, 1982), 15.

18. Mary Poovey, *A History of the Modern Fact: Problems of Knowledge in the Sciences of Wealth and Society* (Chicago: University of Chicago Press, 1998), 42, 30.

19. *Ibid.*, 55.

20. *Ibid.*

21. Ian Hacking, *The Emergence of Probability: A Philosophical Study of Early Ideas About Probability, Induction and Statistical Inference* (Cambridge: Cambridge University Press, 1975), 49–50. On the seventeenth-century interest in probabilities see also Lorraine Daston *Classical Probability in the Enlightenment* (Princeton: Princeton University Press, 1988); and Lorenz Krüger, Lorraine Daston and Michael Heidelberger, eds., *The Probabilistic Revolution.* 2 vols. (Cambridge, MA: MIT Press, 1987). Still of interest is Eric Temple Bell, *The Magic of Numbers* (New York: Whittlesey, 1946), a classic study of the interwoven histories of mathematics, metaphysics, and mysticism.

22. J. G. A. Pocock, *Virtue, Commerce, and History: Essays on Political Thought and History, Chiefly in the Eighteenth Century* (Cambridge: Cambridge University Press, 1985). See in particular chapter 3, "Authority and Property: The Question of Liberal Origins." Pocock's work has been central in redefining the role of finance in eighteenth-century English history. Where both left-wing and conservative accounts in the past had portrayed the century as characterized by the conflict between a growing merchant middle class and a waning aristocracy, Pocock suggests that the interests of these two groups, each essentially tied to property (land or fixed-capital investment), were much more closely aligned. It is the possibility of "fictional" property, created in speculation, that constituted the primary antagonist to traditional conceptions of power. Pocock details the redefinition of class and gender that results from these developments.

Also useful in this regard is Istvan Hont and Michael Ignatieff, eds., *Wealth and Virtue: The Shaping of Political Economy in the Scottish Enlightenment* (Cambridge: Cambridge University Press, 1983). In this volume see especially J. G. A. Pocock, "Cambridge Paradigms and Scotch Philosophers: A Study of the Relations Between the Civic Humanist and the Civil Jurisprudential Interpretation of Eighteenth-Century Social Thought," 235–52; and Istvan Hont and Michael Ignatieff, "Needs and Justice in *The Wealth of Nations*: An Introductory Essay," 1–44.

23. Pocock, "Cambridge Paradigms," 235–7; Pocock, *Virtue, Commerce, and History*, 113–14.
24. Hont and Ignatieff, "Needs and Justice," 2; Pocock, "Cambridge Paradigms," 240.

I. HISTORY AS ABSTRACTION

1. Adam Smith, "Considerations Concerning the First Formation of Languages" (1761), in *Lectures on Rhetoric and Belles Lettres* ed. J. C. Bryce (Oxford: Clarendon, 1983); Adam Smith "A Letter to the Authors of the Edinburgh Review" (1755) in *Essays on Philosophical Subjects*, ed. W. P. D. Wightman and J. C. Bryce (1795; Oxford: Clarendon, 1980).
2. See Hiroshi Mizuta, ed., *Adam Smith's Library: A Catalogue* (Oxford: Clarendon, 2000), 61–62; Condillac's (probably indirect) influence is also noted by J. C. Bryce (Smith, "First Formation of Languages," 203n) and Frans Plank ("Adam Smith: Grammatical Economist," in *Adam Smith Reviewed*, ed. Peter Jones and Andrew S. Skinner [Edinburgh: Edinburgh University Press, 1992], 24).
3. Etienne Bonnot de Condillac, *Essay on the Origin of Human Knowledge*, trans. and ed. Hans Aarsleff (1746; Cambridge: Cambridge University Press, 2001), 8. Until very recently the only readily available English edition of Condillac's *Essay* was a 1971 facsimile of Thomas Nugent's 1756 translation (Etienne Bonnot, Abbé de Condillac, *An Essay on the Origin of Human Knowledge: Being a Supplement to Mr. Locke's* Essay on the Human Understanding, trans. Thomas Nugent, ed. Robert G. Weyant, facsimile edn. [Gainesville, FL: Scholar's Facsimiles, 1971]). Aarsleff's edition corrects this problem, and I have used it here, with rare exceptions which are noted individually. His translation is direct and avoids the flourishes and syntactic innovations Nugent introduced.

    Prior to Aarsleff's edition, the only recent attempt to translate Condillac had been by Franklin Philip (*Philosophical Writings of Etienne Bonnot, Abbé de Condillac*, trans. Franklin Philip, 2 vols. [Hillsdale, NJ: Lawrence Erlbaum, 1982–7]). Philip omits eight chapters of the *Essay* that deal with the origin of language. He comments that this section

    consists of empirical speculation about the beginning of language in the nonverbal signs and pantomimic arts of primitive people. Although the themes of this section develop logically from [Condillac's] conception of analysis, the highly allusive and literary nature of the discussion are not in keeping with the interests of current scholarship and hence have been omitted from this translation. (II.ix–x)

This remark is characteristic of the marginalization of the theory of the sign in Condillac's work, a tendency shaped by the nineteenth century's dismissal of Enlightenment philosophies of language. See Hans Aarsleff, *From Locke to Saussure: Essays on the Study of Language and Intellectual History* (Minneapolis: University of Minnesota Press, 1982), on the Victorian reception of Condillac.

4. Condillac, *Essay*, trans. Aarsleff, 14. French text in Etienne Bonnot de Condillac, *Essai sur l'origine des connaissances humaines* (1746; Paris: Editions Alive, 1998), 31. The term "soul" here requires some comment. Condillac is working counter to the dualist tradition of Descartes, and his account of human cognition and awareness acknowledges no distinction between soul and body. The "soul" in this passage, for example, is the thing that receives and reflects upon the impressions of the senses, and it carries no prior or innate impressions. Nugent's translation of 1756 – the first English edition – consistently renders Condillac's word *"l'âme"* as "mind," probably to establish Condillac's allegiance to Locke's materialist psychology.

5. Condillac, *Essay*, trans. Aarsleff, 27.

6. *Ibid.*, 38–39.

7. *Ibid.*, 31, my emphasis.

8. *Ibid.*, 36.

9. *Ibid.*, 40.

10. *Ibid.*, 41.

11. *Ibid.*, 93.

12. Condillac, *Essay*, trans. Nugent, 2.

13. Condillac, *Essay*, trans. Aarsleff, 95.

14. *Ibid.*, 96.

15. *Ibid.*

16. *Ibid.*, 114.

17. *Ibid.*, 115.

18. *Ibid.*, 120.

19. *Ibid.*, 118.

20. *Ibid.*, 150.

21. *Ibid.*, 164, 228.

22. While I have drawn on Derrida's work above, my own account of Condillac differs significantly from his. See Jacques Derrida, *The Archeology of the Frivolous: Reading Condillac*, trans. and intr. John P. Leavey, Jr. (Lincoln: University of Nebraska Press, 1987).

23. Jean-Jacques Rousseau, *Discourse on the Origin and Foundations of Inequality among Men*, trans. Judith R. Masters, ed. Roger D. Masters (1755; New York: St. Martin's, 1964), 101. Further references are to this edition and will be cited within the text as *DO*.

24. Jean-Jacques Rousseau, *Discours sur l'origine et les fondements de l'inégalité parmi les hommes*, ed. Jean Starobinski, in *Oeuvres Complète*, 5 vols. (Paris: Gallimard, 1964), III.126.

25. *Ibid.*, 158.

26. A more recent adaptation of this view in a quasi-Marxist vein can be found in the work of Werner Sombart, who attributes the rise of consumer capitalism

to the vanity of women. See Maria Mies, *Patriarchy and Accumulation on a World Scale: Women in the International Division of Labor* (London: Zed, 1986), 101–03.

27. This is a term Derrida borrows from Rousseau's *Confessions*, in which he refers to masturbation as "*ce dangereux supplement.*" Rousseau describes masturbation as a temporary and partial source of pleasure, which can work in addition to heterosexual partnering, but which can also threaten to take over or substitute for it entirely.

   Rousseau's portrayal of masturbation corresponds exactly to the symbolic status of women in the second *Discourse*. Women are the destroyers of male self-sufficiency, luring young men into "many forms of excess at the expense of their health, strength, and, sometimes their life" (quoted in Derrida, *Of Grammatology*, trans. Gayatri Chakravorty Spivak [Baltimore: Johns Hopkins University Press, 1974], 150). Male auto-eroticism can preserve young men in a supposed state of innocence and purity of physical desire which would correspond to the first stage of civilization. But Rousseau sees auto-eroticism as a more direct expression of male physical desire, whereas the encounter with the woman would necessitate a reflection or diffusion of desire – a desire caught in the desire of the other. While Rousseau speaks of masturbation as "supplement," it seems in fact to take the place of or stand in for his primary idea of sex. Thus in attempting to preserve a primary stage of direct expression, Rousseau finds himself already plunged into that second stage where things are called upon to represent each other, where meaning operates in a chain of signs which stand for or "supplement" each other. In the parallel world of the voice,

   writing is dangerous from the moment that representation there claims to be presence and the sign of the thing itself. And there is a fatal necessity, inscribed in the very functioning of the sign, that the substitute makes one forget the vicariousness of its own function and makes itself pass for the plenitude of a speech whose deficiency and infirmity it nevertheless only *supplements*. (Derrida, *Of Grammatology*, 144).

28. *Ibid.*, 180, 245, 197.
29. *Ibid.*, 286–87.
30. Steven K. Land, "Adam Smith's 'Concerning the First Formation of Languages,'" *Journal of the History of Ideas* 38 (1977), 677.
31. Campbell and Skinner, *Adam Smith*, 71.
32. Land, "Adam Smith's 'Concerning,'" 690.
33. Adam Smith, "First Formation of Languages," 203. All further references are to this edition and will be cited within the text as FFL.
34. "Clown," *Oxford English Dictionay*, 2nd edn. (1989).
35. Plank, "Grammatical Economist," 25. Despite Plank's suggestive title, his central aim in the paper is "to appraise the significance of Smith's dissertation as a contribution to language typology" (23). He does hint at possible links between Smith's "Dissertation" and his later political economy (27, 30–31).
36. Rousseau, *Discourse on Inequality*, 120.

37. This is the historiographical model Jacques Derrida explores in "White Mythology" (Jacques Derrida, *Margins of Philosophy*, trans. Alan Bass [Chicago: University of Chicago Press, 1982], 209–71).

38. Condillac, *Essay*, trans. Aarsleff, 142.

39. *Ibid.*, 287–88, 288.

40. Jean-Jacques Rousseau, "Essay on the Origin of Languages," trans. John M. Moran, in *On the Origin of Language* (New York: Ungar, 1966), 5.

41. *Ibid.*, 38.

42. *Ibid.*, 32.

43. *Ibid.*, 45.

44. *Ibid.*, 46.

45. *Ibid.*, 49.

46. Adam Smith, *The Theory of Moral Sentiments*, ed. D. D. Raphael and A. L. Macfie (1759; Oxford: Clarendon, 1976), 9. Further references are all to this edition and will be cited in the text as *TMS*.

47. On this emerging eighteenth-century emphasis on the civilizing effects of trade, or what Montesquieu called "le doux commerce," see Colin Nicholson, *Writing and the Rise of Finance: Capital Satires of the Early Eighteenth Century* (Cambridge: Cambridge University Press, 1994).

48. See also Campbell and Skinner, *Adam Smith*, 94.

49. Karl Marx, *Capital: A Critique of Political Economy, Vol. 1*, trans. Ben Fowkes (New York: Vintage, 1977), 437–38.

50. The phrase "invisible hand" first appears in Smith's early "History of Astronomy," in *Essays on Philosophical Subjects*, 49.

51. Adam Smith, *An Inquiry into the Nature and Causes of the Wealth of Nations*, ed. R. H. Campbell, A. H. Skinner, and W. B. Todd, 2 vols. (1776; Oxford: Clarendon, 1976), 1.10. Further references are to this edition and will be cited within the text as *WN*.

52. Smith illustrates this idea by discussing the process of manufacturing pins (*WN* 3–4).

53. It is important to remember here that paper notes in eighteenth-century Britain could be issued privately by any bank, as markers on specific deposits. The standardization of paper currency through a central state bank begins only gradually with the Bank Charter Act of 1844. This is a subject I take up in chapter 3, pp. 81–86.

2. VALUE AS SIGNIFICATION

1. Adam Smith, *An Inquiry into the Nature and Causes of the Wealth of Nations*, ed. R. H. Campbell, A. S. Skinner, and W. B. Todd, 2 vols. (1776; Oxford: Clarendon, 1976), 1.44.

2. *Ibid.*, 47, 48.

3. Mark Blaug, *Ricardian Economics: A Historical Study* (New Haven: Yale University Press, 1958), 56.

4. Smith, *Wealth of Nations*, 50.

5. David Ricardo, *On the Principles of Political Economy and Taxation*, ed. Piero Sraffa (1817; Cambridge: Cambridge University Press, 1951), 5.
6. *Ibid.*, 100n.
7. *Ibid.*
8. The argument that popular conceptions of wealth and poverty, in combination with theoretical pronouncements of political economists, influenced British economic policy is Boyd Hilton's in *The Age of Atonement: The Influence of Evangelicalism on Social and Economic Thought, 1795–1865* (Oxford: Clarendon, 1988).
9. Blaug, *Ricardian Economics*, 6.
10. Ricardo, *Principles*, 72.
11. *Ibid.*, 70.
12. *Ibid.*, 43–44.
13. *Ibid.*, 73.
14. *Ibid.*, 13–14.
15. Michel Foucault, *The Order of Things: An Archaeology of the Human Sciences* (New York: Vintage, 1970), 223.
16. *Ibid.*, 224–25.
17. Gayatri Chakravorty Spivak, "Can the Subaltern Speak?" in *Marxism and the Interpretation of Culture*, ed. Cary Nelson and Lawrence Grossberg (Urbana: University of Illinois Press, 1988), 271–73, 281. My argument in this chapter is also indebted to Spivak's essay "Scattered Speculations on the Question of Value," *In Other Worlds* (New York: Methuen, 1987), 155–75.
18. Christopher Herbert, *Culture and Anomie: Ethnographic Imagination in the Nineteenth Century* (Chicago: University of Chicago Press, 1991), 29.
19. *Ibid.*, 74.
20. *Ibid.*, 95, emphasis original.
21. *Ibid.*, 97, 95.
22. *Ibid.*, 96.
23. Hans Aarsleff, *The Study of Language in England, 1780–1860* (Princeton: Princeton University Press, 1967), 46.
24. Stewart provides a biographical introduction to a late edition of Smith's *Moral Sentiments*, an edition that included the *Dissertation on the Origin of Languages*.
25. See also David Simpson, *Romanticism, Nationalism, and the Revolt against Theory* (Chicago: University of Chicago Press, 1993), 49.
26. Aarsleff, *Study of Language*, 99, 105.
27. *Ibid.*, 181–2.
28. Hans Aarsleff, *From Locke to Saussure: Essays on the Study of Language and Intellectual History* (Minneapolis: University of Minnesota Press, 1982), 7.
29. John Stuart Mill, "Coleridge," in *Collected Works of John Stuart Mill*, general ed. F. E. L. Priestly, 33 vols. (Toronto: University of Toronto Press, 1963–91), x. 129.
30. Aarsleff, *Study of Language*, 211. On the London Statistical Society and the many similar organizations in this period, see Theodore M. Porter, *The Rise of Statistical Thinking, 1820–1900* (Princeton: Princeton University Press, 1986),

31–37; and Mary Poovey, *A History of the Modern Fact: Problems of Knowledge in the Sciences of Wealth and Society* (Chicago: University of Chicago Press, 1998), 308–17.

31. T. R. Malthus, *Principles of Political Economy*, variorum edn., ed. John Pullen, 2 vols. (1820; Cambridge: Cambridge University Press, 1989), 1.53.
32. Quoted in Blaug, *Ricardian Economics*, 53.
33. *Ibid.*
34. René Wellek, *Immanuel Kant in England, 1793–1838*, reprint edn., with Giuseppe Micheli, *The Early Reception of Kant's Thought in England, 1785–1805* (London: Routledge/Thoemmes, 1993), v.
35. Quoted in Wellek, *Kant in England*, 84.
36. Quoted in Aarsleff, *Locke to Saussure*, 125. See also Wellek, *Kant in England*, 139–49.
37. Immanuel Kant, *Critique of Pure Reason*, trans. Norman Kemp Smith (1781; New York: St. Martin's, 1929), 65.
38. *Ibid.*, 365.
39. An overview of central texts can be found in Gary F. Langer, *The Coming of Age of Political Economy, 1815–1825* (New York: Greenwood, 1987), 68–71; and Blaug, *Ricardian Economics*, 129–39. Blaug focuses on Harriet Martineau's *Illustrations of Political Economy* and concludes that the "*Illustrations* impart an overwhelming air of finality to economic doctrines" (*ibid.*, 138). For a reading of Martineau's *Illustrations* in the context of the Unitarian debates on Providence and free will, see Catherine Gallagher, *The Industrial Reformation of English Fiction: Social Discourse and Narrative Form, 1832–1867* (Chicago: University of Chicago Press, 1985), 51–61. Gallagher's more nuanced approach allows her to notice the novels' ambivalence in response to the suffering that ensues when the working class fails to abide by the seemingly natural laws of wages, rent, and population.
40. S. J. Connolly. "Mass Politics and Sectarian Conflict, 1823–1830," in *A New History of Ireland, vol. v: Ireland Under the Union, 1: 1801–1870*, ed. W. E. Vaughan (Oxford: Clarendon, 1989), 105.
41. [Richard Whately], *Easy Lessons on Money Matters: For the Use of Young People*, 14th edn. (London: 1855), 28.
42. *Ibid.*, 30.
43. *Ibid.*, 32–33.
44. Thomas A. Boylan and Timothy P. Foley, *Political Economy and Colonial Ireland: The Propagation and Ideological Function of Economic Discourse in the Nineteenth Century* (London: Routledge, 1992), 79.
45. Quoted in *ibid.*, 79.
46. Quoted in Laurence Moss, *Mountifort Longfield: Ireland's First Professor of Political Economy* (Ottawa: Green Hill, 1976), 91.
47. Karl Marx, *Capital: A Critique of Political Economy, Vol. 1*, trans. Ben Fowkes (New York: Vintage, 1977), 436.
48. See my discussion of De Quincey in chapter 3, pp. 100–03.
49. Blaug, *Ricardian Economics*, 140–50.

50. *Ibid.*, 140. See also Ronald L. Meek, "The Decline of Ricardian Economics in England," in *Economics and Ideology and Other Essays: Studies in the Development of Economic Thought* (London: Chapman and Hall, 1967), 51–75.
51. Marx, *Capital 1*, 96. See the excellent discussion of this passage in Meek, "Decline of Ricardian Economics," 51.
52. The best discussion of the reaction against the political economy of the 1830s and 1840s is Hilton, *Age of Atonement*. See Chapter 2, "The Rage of Christian Economics, 1800–1840."
53. John Stuart Mill, "Auguste Comte and Positivism," in *Collected Works*, x.265–66.
54. Auguste Comte, *The Essential Comte*, ed. Stanislav Andreski (London: Croom Helm, 1974), 27. The case of Comte himself deserves more attention here. This first advocate of a strictly "positive" approach to social forms – in the take-off period of industrial capitalism in France – ended his life by attempting to establish a new "Religion of Humanity," of which he himself would serve as "Grand Priest" (Stanislav Andreski, "Comte's Place in the History of Sociology," in *ibid.*, 9). Comte by the end of his life, in the late 1850s, viewed himself as a mystic, with prophetic abilities. He seems thus to represent par excellence Deleuze and Guattari's notion of the schizophrenic: He flattened the densely over-coded text of early-nineteenth century French society to see social systems as mechanical flows, exchanges of desire and power. After a career of carefully "decoding" the social world, he was compelled to "recode" it in some intelligible way, and developed the paranoid delusion that in fact he was the spiritual center of creation, exerting invisible control over the entire world. Jacques Deleuze and Félix Guattari, *Anti-Oedipus: Capitalism and Schizophrenia*, trans. Robert Hurley, Mark Seem, and Helen R. Lane (Minneapolis: University of Minnesota Press, 1983).
55. John Stuart Mill, *A System of Logic*, in *Collected Works*, VIII.864.
56. *Ibid.*, VIII.873.
57. *Ibid.*, VIII.904; VIII.905.
58. Mill, "Coleridge," in *Collected Works*, x.128
59. John Stuart Mill, *Autobiography*, ed. Jack Stillinger (Boston: Houghton Mifflin, 1969), 148.
60. *Principles of Political Economy with some of their Applications to Social Philosophy*, in *Collected Works*, II.186.
61. *Ibid.*, 162.
62. *Ibid.*, 186.
63. *Ibid.*, See Regenia Gagnier, *The Insatiability of Human Wants: Economics and Aesthetics in Market Society* (Chicago: University of Chicago Press, 2000), 28–29.
64. Mill, *Political Economy*, 199.
65. *Ibid.*, 164, my emphasis.
66. Aarsleff, *Locke to Saussure*, 207.
67. Mary Jean Corbett, *Allegories of Union in Irish and English Writing, 1790–1870: Politics, History, and the Family from Edgeworth to Arnold* (Cambridge: Cambridge University Press, 2000), 171–73.

68. W[illiam] Stanley Jevons, *The Theory of Political Economy*, 5th edn., ed. H. Stanley Jevons (1871; New York: Kelley & Millman, 1957), 14.
69. *Ibid.*, xiv.
70. *Ibid.*, 4, 5.
71. *Ibid.*, 5, my emphasis.
72. *Ibid.*, 92.
73. *Ibid.*, 11, emphasis original.
74. *Ibid.*, 34.
75. *Ibid.*, 35.

NOTES TO PART II: OPENING

1. W[illiam] Stanley Jevons, *The Theory of Political Economy*, 5th edn., ed. H. Stanley Jevons (1871; New York: Kelley & Millman, 1957), 5.
2. Gillian Beer, *Darwin's Plots: Evolutionary Narrative in Darwin, George Eliot and Nineteenth-Century Fiction*, 2nd edn. (1983; Cambridge: Cambridge University Press, 2000). George Levine, *Darwin and the Novelists: Patterns of Science in Victorian Fiction* (Cambridge, MA: Harvard University Press, 1988).
3. Elizabeth Gaskell, *Mary Barton: A Tale of Manchester Life*, ed. and intr. Stephen Gill (London: Penguin, 1970), 38.
4. Eric Hobsbawm, *The Age of Capital, 1848–1875* (New York: Scribner, 1975), 2.
5. Walter Bagehot, "Investments," in *The Collected Works of Walter Bagehot*, ed. Norman St. John-Stevans, 13 vols. (London: *The Economist*, 1978), IX.274.

3. MARKET INDICATORS: BANKING AND HOUSEKEEPING IN *BLEAK HOUSE*

1. Walter Bagehot, "Charles Dickens," in *The Collected Works of Walter Bagehot*, ed. Norman St. John-Stevas, 13 vols. (London: *The Economist*, 1978), II.87. Further references are to this edition of the article and will be cited in the text as CD. All references to Bagehot's *Collected Works* are to this edition.
2. Walter Benjamin, "Theses on the Philosophy of History," in *Illuminations*, ed. Hannah Arendt, trans. Harry Zohn (New York: Schocken, 1969), 261. This idea of a temporality of modernization is important for Benedict Anderson's study of nationalism, *Imagined Communities* (London: Verso, 1983). It also informs a number of theoretical works on politics and representation including Homi K. Bhabha, "DissemiNation: Time, Narrative, and the Margins of the Modern Nation," in *Nation and Narration*, ed. Bhabha (London: Routledge, 1990); and Derrida's concept of "spectrality" in Jacques Derrida, *Specters of Marx: The State of the Debt, the Work of Mourning, and the New International*, trans. Peggy Kamuf (London: Routledge, 1994).
3. Charles Dickens, *Bleak House*, ed. Norman Page (Harmondsworth: Penguin, 1971), 272. Further references are to this edition and will be cited in the text as *BH*.
4. J. Hillis Miller, Introduction to *Bleak House*, in *BH* 33.

5. D. A. Miller, "Discipline in Different Voices: Bureaucracy, Police, Family, and *Bleak House*," in *The Novel and the Police* (Berkeley: University of California Press, 1988), 58–107.

6. Bruce Robbins, "Telescopic Philanthropy: Professionalism and Responsibility in *Bleak House*," in *Nation and Narration*, ed. Bhabha, 213–330.

7. Karl Polanyi, *The Great Transformation* (New York: Rinehart, 1944), 139.

8. *Ibid.*, 131.

9. J. G. A. Pocock, *Virtue, Commerce, and History: Essays on Political Thought and History, Chiefly in the Eighteenth Century* (Cambridge: Cambridge University Press, 1985); Istvan Hont and Michael Ignatieff, eds., *Wealth and Virtue: The Shaping of Political Economy in the Scottish Enlightenment* (Cambridge: Cambridge University Press, 1983).

10. G. M. Young, *Victorian England: Portrait of an Age*, 2nd edn. (1953; Oxford University Press, 1980), 67.

11. Bagehot, "Investments," in *Collected Works*, IX.274.

12. *Ibid.*, IX.274. Bagehot draws here on an emerging theory of the trade cycle. For a reading of *Great Expectations* in this light, see Susan Walsh, "Bodies of Capital: *Great Expectations* and the Climacteric Economy," *Victorian Studies* 37 (Autumn 1993), 73–98.

13. The mortality rate for these years in Ireland has been extensively debated. Here I follow the estimate of Joel Mokyr's econometric history *Why Ireland Starved: A Quantitative and Analytical History of the Irish Economy, 1800–1850* (London: Allen & Unwin, 1983), 266.

14. The sense of mission with which English liberals attempted to bring political economy to Ireland is made clear in [Charles Trevelyan], "The Irish Crisis," *Edinburgh Review* 87.176 (January 1848), 229–320; and [Richard Whately], *Easy Lessons on Money Matters: For the Use of Young People*, 14th edn. (London: 1855). On Whately see Thomas A. Boylan and Timothy P. Foley, *Political Economy and Colonial Ireland: The Propagation and Ideological Function of Economic Discourse in the Nineteenth Century* (London: Routledge, 1992). I look briefly at Whately's school text in chapter 2, pp. 61–62, and at Trevelyan in chapter 4, pp. 119–22.

15. Boyd Hilton, *The Age of Atonement: The Influence of Evangelicalism on Social and Economic Thought, 1795–1865* (Oxford: Clarendon, 1988), 248–51.

16. David Morier Evans, *The Commercial Crisis of 1847–48*, 2nd edn. (London: 1849), 84; House of Lords, *Report from the Secret Committee of the House of Lords Appointed to Inquire into the Causes of the Distress*, in *Monetary Policy and Commercial Distress: Session 1847–48*, vol. III of 4, Irish University Press Series of British Parliamentary Papers (Shannon, Ireland: Irish University Press, 1968), viii.

17. An overview of the Bank Charter Act and the debates surrounding it can be found in Charles Poor Kindleberger, *A Financial History of Western Europe*, 2nd edn. (New York: Oxford University Press, 1993), 86–96. For more specific commentary from a contemporary observer, see Walter Bagehot, *Lombard Street* (1873), in *Collected Works*, IX.48–233. See also the various histories of

the Bank of England: John Clapham, *The Bank of England: A History*, 2 vols. (Cambridge: Cambridge University Press, 1958); W. Marston Acres, *The Bank of England from Within, 1694–1900* (London: Oxford University Press, 1931); A. Andréadès, *History of the Bank of England, 1640 to 1903* (1909; New York: Kelly, 1966); John Francis, *History of the Bank of England, its Times and Traditions*, 2 vols. (London: Willoughby, 1848).

18. Karl Marx, *A Contribution to the Critique of Political Economy*, ed. Maurice Dobb (Moscow: International Press, 1970), 100.

19. *Ibid.*

20. Karl Marx, *Capital: A Critique of Political Economy, Vol. III*, trans. David Fernbach (New York: Vintage, 1981), 516. In this particular passage, the anonymous International Press translation is somewhat more direct: "it appears . . . as though interest were the typical product of capital" (Karl Marx, *Capital: A Critique of Political Economy, Vol. III*, [New York: International Press, 1967], 392).

21. Marx, *Capital III*, trans. Fernbach, 515.

22. See also Patrick Brantlinger's discussion of "fetish capital" in *Fictions of State: Culture and Credit in Britain, 1694–1994* (Ithaca, NY: Cornell University Press, 1996), 149.

23. Quoted in Marx, *Capital III*, trans. Fernbach, 521.

24. Kindleberger, *Financial History*, 64.

25. Francis, *Bank of England*, II.197.

26. *Ibid.*

27. Kindleberger, *Financial History*, 195.

28. David Kynaston, *The City of London*, 2 vols. (London: Chatto & Windus, 1994), 1.153; Evans, *Commercial Crisis*, 80; Andréadès, *Bank of England*, 334.

29. Quoted in John Clapham, *An Economic History of Modern Britain: The Early Railway Age, 1820–1850*, vol. 1 of 2 (Cambridge: Cambridge University Press, 1959), 525.

30. Peter Gray, *Famine, Land and Politics: British Government and Irish Society, 1843–1850* (Dublin: Irish Academic Press, 1999), 108.

31. Statistics on price fluctuations and a complete list of firms that failed are provided in Evans, *Commercial Crisis*, 61.

32. House of Commons, *First Report from the Secret Committee on Commercial Distress*, in *Monetary Policy and Commercial Distress: Session 1847–48*, vol. 1 of 4, Irish University Press Series of British Parliamentary Papers (Shannon, Ireland: Irish University Press, 1968), v; Evans, *Commercial Crisis*, 95.

33. Quoted in Clapham, *Economic History*, 534.

34. House of Commons, *First Report*, iv.

35. House of Lords, *Report from the Secret Committee*, iii.

36. Clapham, *Economic History*, 529.

37. Quoted in Evans, *Commercial Crisis*, 73.

38. Quoted in *ibid.*, 99.

39. Marx, *Capital III*, trans. Fernbach, 694.

40. Adam Smith, *Inquiry into the Nature and Causes of the Wealth of Nations*, ed. R. H. Campbell, A. H. Skinner, and W. B. Todd, 2 vols. (Oxford: Clarendon, 1976), 1.321.
41. Roland Barthes, *S/Z: An Essay*, trans. Richard Howard (New York: Hill and Wang, 1974), 40.
42. Miller, Introduction to *Bleak House*, 25.
43. Nancy Armstrong, *Desire and Domestic Fiction: A Political History of the Novel* (New York: Oxford University Press, 1987), 73.
44. David Trotter, *Circulation: Defoe, Dickens, and the Economics of the Novel* (Basingstoke: Macmillan, 1988). Trotter follows the metaphor of circulating blood in a number of Dickens novels and reads Krook's death in this context. For another approach see Daniel Hack, " 'Sublimation Strange': Allegory and Authority in *Bleak House*," *ELH* 66 (1999), 129–56.
45. Marx, *Contribution to the Critique*, 27; Karl Marx, *Capital: A Critique of Political Economy, Vol. 1*, trans. Ben Fowkes (New York: Vintage, 1977), 125.
46. Marx, *Capital 1*, 163.
47. David Fitzpatrick, "Emigration, 1801–1870," in *A New History of Ireland, vol. v: Ireland Under the Union, 1: 1801–70*, ed. W. E. Vaughan (Oxford: Clarendon, 1989), 577; Henry Mayhew's chapter on "The Street Irish" records his observations in London during the early 1850s (*London Labour and the London Poor* [1861; New York: Dover, 1968], 1.104–20).
48. Charles Dickens, "Post Office Money Orders," *Household Words* 5.104 (March 20, 1852), 1–5; Charles Dickens, "Two Chapters on Bank Note Forgeries: Chapter II," *Household Words* 1.26 (September 21, 1850), 615–20. See "Potato Money" in chapter 4 below.
49. Marx, *Capital 1*, 207.
50. In fact, as will become clear in chapter 4 below, it is important to understand that Ireland was certainly not outside the systems of English-language publishing and British capital, no matter how exotic and distant the island and its inhabitants sometimes appeared. The system of National Schools set up throughout Ireland in the period following the Act of Catholic Emancipation in 1829 caused the illiteracy rate in Ireland to fall below that of many other European countries. In 1841 the Irish illiteracy rate was 53 percent, in 1851 47 percent (Oliver MacDonagh, "The Economy and Society, 1830–45," in *Ireland Under the Union*, ed. Vaughan, 234). However, Irish settlers and migrants in English cities probably were disproportionately illiterate (Fitzpatrick, "Emigration, 1801–1870," 577), and in any case English perception of Irish ignorance, if not illiteracy, was widespread. On the politics of literacy in Ireland 1840–60 see Mary Castelyan, *A History of Literacy and Libraries in Ireland* (Aldershot: Gower, 1984).
51. Jacques Derrida, *Of Grammatology*, trans. Gayatri Chakravorty Spivak (Baltimore: Johns Hopkins University Press, 1974), 90.
52. The preceding analysis leads to a useful position in the debate about the extent to which the Irish economy was monetized in the nineteenth century. Patrick Lynch and John Vaizey's book *Guiness's Brewery in the Irish Economy, 1759–1876*

(Cambridge: Cambridge University Press, 1960) argued provocatively that the western regions of the country relied almost exclusively on a neo-feudal exchange of crops and livestock produce for rent and household needs, suggesting the possibility that Irish agricultural communities lived beyond the scope of the economic sign, untouched by the language of Chancery. More recently historians have questioned Lynch and Vaisey's thesis, confirming the sense of things suggested in Dickens and Marx: the market as system circulates even where wage labor is not practiced or where the nearest bank is several days' walk. (See in particular Mokyr, *Why Ireland Starved*; and Cormac Ó Gráda, *Ireland: A New Economic History, 1780–1939*, [Oxford: Clarendon, 1994].) This is not to argue that radically different forms of individual and communal identification do not exist within such a system; Lynch and Vaisey's argument continues to have value in the way it stresses the unevenness of an economic development which conceives itself as total. Marx himself, we might note, speculates on the consciousness of the peasant in "The Eighteenth Brumaire of Louis Napoleon," hinting at an analysis of metonymically organized peasant communities within the metaphorical narrative of the nation (*Selected Writings*, ed. David McLellan [Oxford: Oxford University Press, 317–18). Gayatri Spivak's "Can the Subaltern Speak" (in *Marxism and the Interpretation of Culture*, ed. Cary Nelson and Lawrence Grossberg [Urbana: University of Illinois Press, 1988], 271–313) and David Lloyd's "Violence and the Constitution of the Novel" (in *Anomalous States: Irish Writing and the Post-Colonial Moment* [Durham, NC: Duke University Press, 1993], 125–62) are examples of work in this tradition.

53. Martin A. Danahay, "Housekeeping and Hegemony in *Bleak House*," *Studies in the Novel* 23.4 (Winter 1991), 416–31. Danahay reads the treatment of domesticity in the novel alongside a number of recent social histories of housework and the economics of women's labor. For a discussion of housework in a global economic context, see Maria Mies, *Patriarchy and Accumulation on a World Scale: Women in the International Division of Labor* (London: Zed, 1986).

54. Armstrong, *Desire and Domestic Fiction*, 95.

55. "Finance" and "Revenue," both in *Oxford English Dictionary*, 2nd edn. (1989).

56. Wills's official title was "sub-editor." His working relationship with Dickens is explored in Fred Kaplan, *Dickens: A Biography* (New York: Morrow, 1988), 265–68; and in Stone's Introduction to Harry Stone, ed., *Charles Dickens' Uncollected Writings from Household Words 1850–1859*, 2 vols. (Bloomington: Indiana University Press, 1968), 1.36–43.

57. Charles Dickens, "The Old Lady of Threadneedle Street," *Household Words* 1.15 (July 6, 1850), 337 ("the honour," "Hall"), 338 ("parlour," "a long table"). Further references are all to this edition and will be cited in the text as OLT.

58. For a discussion of the position of the daughter in this novel, see Hilary M. Schor "*Dombey and Son*: The Daughter's Nothing," in *Dickens and the Daughter of the House* (Cambridge: Cambridge University Press, 2000).

59. Stone, Introduction, in *Uncollected Writings*, 1.151.

60. "Economy," in *Oxford English Dictionary*, 2nd edn. (1989).

61. William Shakespeare, *Henry V*, IV.iii.51. The line, attributed to Shakespeare, appeared as an epigraph at the head of each weekly number of *Household Words*.

62. Jacques Derrida, "White Mythology," in *Margins of Philosophy*, trans. Alan Bass (Chicago: University of Chicago Press, 1982), 270

63. J. C. Loudon, *The Suburban Gardener and Villa Companion* (1838; New York: Garland, 1982), 1.

64. Jean Baudrillard, *For a Critique of the Political Economy of the Sign*, trans. and intr. Charles Levin (St. Louis: Telos, 1981), 92.

65. *Ibid.*, 93.

66. See Bhabha, "DissemiNation," 291: "The nation fills the void left in the up-rooting of communities and kin, and turns that loss into the language of metaphor."

67. Thomas De Quincey, *The Logic of Political Economy*, in *Collected Writings*, enlarged edn., ed. David Masson, 14 vols. (Edinburgh, 1899–90), IX.119.

68. *Ibid.*, 118.

69. *Ibid.*, 132.

70. *Ibid.*, 156, emphasis original.

71. Smith, *Wealth of Nations*, 1.44–45.

72. *Ibid.*, 1.47.

73. Ibid. 1.191.

74. De Quincey, *Logic*, 145.

75. *Ibid.*, 154, emphasis original.

76. *Ibid.*

77. See Thomas De Quincey, "Malthus on the Measure of Value" and "Dialogues of Three Templars on Political Economy," both in vol. IX of *Collected Writings*.

78. De Quincey, *Logic*, 155.

79. *Ibid.*, 150, 190.

80. The most complete assessment of De Quincey's political economy to date can be found in Josephine McDonagh, *De Quincey's Disciplines* (Oxford: Clarendon, 1994). Although McDonagh notes that in *The Logic of Political Economy* "value is deemed to be caused not by labour . . . but by the desires of a consumer" (60), her analysis focuses on connections between the political economy and De Quincey's opium writings, through what she calls "the economy of addiction" (60), and not on the importance of his argument for modern economic thought.

Attention to De Quincey in standard histories of economic thought is often slight. His treatment in Joseph Schumpeter's *History of Economic Analysis* (ed. Elizabeth Boody Schumpeter [New York: Oxford University Press, 1954]) is symptomatic of Schumpeter's own attempt to narrate the triumph of liberalism. He notes De Quincey's "delight in refined logic" but argues that De Quincey "touched economics only peripherally" (477). No doubt this would thoroughly offend De Quincey, who thought he was getting to the heart of the matter in a way no one else had attempted. Schumpter does not wholly ignore the metaphysical problem of value as it was debated in this era, but he assigns the position I have given here to De Quincey – that is, the construction of a realm of essential value in conservative reaction to the discontinuous force of industrial capital – to Marx. "For Marx," he writes, "the quantity of labor embodied in products did not merely 'regulate' their value. It *was* (the 'essence' or 'substance' of) their value" (596). Given an awareness of these philosophical backgrounds, it is difficult to understand why Schumpeter misses De Quincey's attempt to specify the "substance" of the commodity, unless he prefers to assign the nostalgic reaction to the left.

81. Schumpeter does suggest that in privileging a supply–demand theory of value, "Malthus adopted the line that won out ultimately" (*ibid.*, 482).

82. See Regenia Gagnier's discussion of this point in *The Insatiability of Human Wants: Economics and Aesthetics in Market Society* (Chicago: University of Chicago Press, 2000), 42–43.

83. Bagehot, *Lombard Street, Collected Works*, IX.118; "Investments," *Collected Works*, IX.273; "Monetary Schemes," *Collected Works*, IX.300.

84. Bagehot, Letter to Emily Davies, 1867 (no date), in *Collected Works*, VIII.622.

85. Bagehot, "Investments," 274.

86. *Ibid.*, 274, 275.

87. Bagehot, "Monetary Schemes" 302.

88. Bagehot, "Principles of Political Economy," *Collected Works*, IX.193.

89. Two recent works on Bagehot, while stressing different aspects of his work than those I highlight here, regard Bagehot as pivotal figure in the transformation of economic and financial theory in the late nineteenth century: Timothy Alborn, "Economic Man, Economic Machine: Images of Circulation in the Victorian Money Market," in *Natural Images in Economic Thought: "Markets Read in Tooth and Claw,"* ed. Phillip Mirowski (Cambridge: Cambridge University Press, 1994), 173–96); Christopher Herbert, *Culture and Anomie: Ethnographic Imagination in the Nineteenth Century* (Chicago: University of Chicago Press, 1991).

90. Acres, *Bank of England*, 368.

91. Eve Kosofsky Sedgewick, *Between Men: English Literature and Male Homosocial Desire* (New York: Columbia University Press, 1985).

92. Compare Helena Michie's reading of these passages in " 'Who is this in Pain?': Scarring, Disfigurement, and Female Identity in *Bleak House* and *Our Mutual Friend*," *Novel: A Forum on Fiction* 22 (1989), 199–218.

4. ESOTERIC SOLUTIONS: IRELAND AND THE COLONIAL CRITIQUE
OF POLTICAL ECONOMY

1. [Anonymous Diary], ms. 194, National Library of Ireland, 1837, 27.

2. On this series of associations, linking the Irish and their potato food to dirt, see Catherine Gallagher and Stephen Greenblatt, *Practicing New Historicism* (Chicago: University of Chicago Press, 2000), 113–17.

3. Thomas A. Boylan and Timothy P. Foley, *Political Economy and Colonial Ireland: The Propagation and Ideological Function of Economic Discourse in*

the Nineteenth Century (London: Routledge, 1992). In *Allegories of Union*, Mary Jean Corbett traces a similar process on the other side of the Irish Sea. Examining representations of the Irish in the condition of England debate, she shows that while writers in the 1820s and 1830s assumed the Irish would be assimilated into English economy and society, post-Famine texts portray the Irish as a fundamentally alien people (Mary Jean Corbett, *Allegories of Union in Irish and English Writing, 1790–1870: Politics, History, and the Family from Edgeworth to Arnold* [Cambridge: Cambridge University Press, 2000], 82–84.) S. B. Cook also charts the rising importance of cultural nationalism in nineteenth-century economic thought in *Imperial Affinities: Nineteenth-Century Analogies and Exchanges Between India and Ireland* (New Delhi: Sage, 1993). Cook compares colonial economic policy in Ireland and India and, like Boylan and Foley, stresses the transition from the universal laws of Enlightenment thought toward a racialized sense of national particularity.

4. L. M. Cullen, *An Economic History of Ireland since 1660* (New York: Barnes & Nobel, 1972), 12.

5. Kevin Whelan, *The Killing Snows: Cultural Change in Nineteenth-Century Ireland* (Cork, Ireland: Cork University Press, forthcoming*)*, 5. Further evidence of the relationship between English market demand and Irish economic development is offered by Raymond Crotty, in his correlation between eighteenth-century population trends in Ireland and levels of pig production: "Ireland's population, between 1712 and 1831, increased or decreased almost precisely by 6.88 persons (or, say, one family) for every increase or decrease of one pig exported" (Raymond Crotty, *Ireland in Crisis: A Study in Capitalist Colonial Undevelopment* [Dingle, Ireland: Brandon, 1986], 42–43).

6. Discussion of this system of land leasing is provided in Oliver MacDonagh, "The Economy and Society, 1830–1845," in *A New History of Ireland, vol. v: Ireland Under the Union 1: 1801–1870*, ed. W. E. Vaughan (Oxford: Clarendon, 1989), 218–41; Gearóid Ó Tuathaigh, *Ireland Before the Famine, 1798–1848* (Dublin: Gill & Macmillan, 1972); Cormac Ó Gráda, *Ireland: A New Economic History, 1780–1939* (Oxford: Clarendon, 1994); and James S. Donnelly, *The Land and the People of Nineteenth-Century Cork: The Rural Economy and the Land Question* (London: Routledge, 1975).

7. Crotty, *Ireland in Crisis*, 48.

8. Cormac Ó Gráda, "Industry and Communications, 1801–45," in *Ireland Under the Union*, ed. Vaughan, 154.

9. Boyd Hilton, *Cash, Corn, and Commerce: The Economic Policies of the Tory Governments 1815–1830* (Oxford: Oxford University Press, 1977), 3–4.

10. Boylan and Foley, *Political Economy and Colonial Ireland*, 77. See also D. H. Akenson, "Pre-University Education, 1782–1870," in *Ireland Under the Union*, ed. Vaughan, 532.

11. Boylan and Foley, *Political Economy and Colonial Ireland*, 4.

12. MacDonagh, "Economy and Society," 214.

13. *Ibid.*, 214.

14. R. V. Comerford, "Ireland 1850–70: Post-Famine and Mid-Victorian," in *Ireland Under the Union*, ed. Vaughan, 390.

15. J. H. Andrews, *A Paper Landscape: The Ordnance Survey in Nineteenth-Century Ireland* (Oxford: Clarendon, 1975).

16. T. W. Freeman, "Land and People, *c.* 1841," in *Ireland Under the Union*, ed. Vaughan, 249–50.

17. "The English Pale" was the name given in the fourteenth century to the territory under English military control, hence the phrase "beyond the pale." My understanding of the diffuse power exercised by the modern state derives from Benedict Anderson, *Imagined Communities* (London: Verso, 1983); ideological features of this process in Ireland are discussed in Terry Eagleton, "Ascendency and Hegemony," in *Heathcliff and the Great Hunger: Studies in Irish Culture* (London: Verso, 1995), 27–103.

18. John Locke, *Diary of John Locke, Valuer, Limerick*, ms. 3566, National Library of Ireland, March 27, 1848.

19. Boyd Hilton, *The Age of Atonement: The Influence of Evangelicalism on Social and Economic Thought, 1795–1865* (Oxford: Clarendon, 1988), 6.

20. Peter Gray, *Famine, Land and Politics: British Government and Irish Society, 1843–1850,* (Dublin: Irish Academic Press, 1999), 98–99.

21. *Clachan* is the term for the clustering of houses on an area of leased land, which would be used communally. See Kevin Whelan, "The Modern Landscape," in *Atlas of the Irish Rural Landscape*, ed. F. H. A. Aalen, Kevin Whelan, and Matthew Stout (Toronto: University of Toronto Press, 1997), 79–89.

22. R. D. Collison Black, *Economic Thought and the Irish Question, 1817–1870* (Cambridge: Cambridge University Press, 1960), 107–11; Christine Kinealy, *This Great Calamity: The Great Irish Famine, 1845–52* (Dublin: Gill & Macmillan, 1994), 18–20.

23. [Charles Trevelyan], "The Irish Crisis," *Edinburgh Review* 87.176 (January 1848), 255. Further references will be cited with the text as IC.

24. Despite this bluff rhetoric, Peel's approach and Trevelyan's were near cousins. Peel, once out of office, never criticized the cessation of food aid, and Peelites and evangelical Whigs agreed in supporting free trade in land (Gray, *Famine, Land and Politics*, 230, 196–97).

25. John Forster, *The Life of Charles Dickens*, 2 vols. (1872–74; London: Dent, 1927), 1.407.

26. Quoted in *ibid.*, 1.407–08.

27. On the lazy-bed system of cultivation see Kevin Whelan, "Pre- and Post-Famine Landscape Change," in *The Great Irish Famine*, ed. Cathal Pórtéir (Dublin: Mercier, 1995); and Whelan, *Killing Snows*.

28. Adam Smith, *An Inquiry into the Nature and Causes of the Wealth of Nations*, ed. R. H. Campbell, A. S. Skinner, and W. B. Todd, 2 vols. (Oxford: Clarendon, 1976), 1.10, 37.

29. Gray, *Famine, Land and Politics*, 253–54.

30. Isaac Butt, *A Voice for Ireland: The Famine in the Land* (Dublin, 1847), 11. See the discussion of this passage in Black, *Economic Thought*, 118.

31. Black, *Economic Thought*, 120–21; Gray, *Famine, Land and Politics*, 238–39.
32. Shafto Adair, *The Winter of 1846-7 in Antrim, with Remarks on Outdoor Relief and Colonization* (London, 1847), 27, 16. Further references are all to this edition and will be cited in the text as *W*. I am grateful to Kevin Whelan for bringing this book to my attention.
33. On the increasing prevalence of New Testament motifs after 1850, see Hilton, *Age of Atonement*, chapter 8: "Incarnational Social Thought and its Intellectual Context."
34. I use the term "occult" primarily to mean "hidden from view," but also to suggest a contrast between the rhetoric of the nation here in Adair's account and that of Franz Fanon, in his famous notion of the "zone of occult instability" developed in *The Wretched of the Earth* (trans. Constance Farrington [New York: Grove Weidenfeld, 1963], 227). Whereas for Adair the hidden will become absolutely known, for Fanon the "occult" arena of the people will always escape both imperial and native bourgeois historiographies.
35. Homi Bhabha, "DissemiNation: Time, Narrative, and the Margins of the Modern Nation," in *Nation and Narration*, ed. Bhabha (London: Routledge, 1990), 291.
36. Charles Dickens, "The Old Lady of Threadneedle Street," *Household Words* 1.15 (July 6, 1850), 337.
37. Jasper W. Rogers, *Employment of the Irish Peasantry: The Best Means to Prevent the Drain of Gold from England* (London: 1847), 5–6, emphasis original.
38. *Ibid.*, 7.
39. *Ibid.*, 6.
40. *Ibid.*, 4, 5.
41. Jonathan Pim, *The Conditions and Prospects of Ireland* (Dublin, 1848), 124.
42. Karl Marx, *Capital: A Critique of Political Economy, Vol. III*, trans. David Fernbach (New York: Vintage, 1981), 515.
43. *Ibid.*, 516.
44. *Ibid.*
45. See Marx's famous play on words in the chapter on commodity fetishism, *Capital: A Critique of Political Economy, Vol. I*, trans. Ben Fowkes (New York: Vintage, 1977), 163.
46. Gallagher and Greenblatt, *Practicing New Historicism*, 128.
47. *Ibid.*, 129.
48. See Cormac Ó Gráda's evaluation of this controversy in *New Economic History*, 40–43.
49. *Digest of Evidence taken before Her Majesty's Commissioners of Inquiry into the State of the Law and Practice in respect to the Occupation of Land in Ireland*, Part I (Dublin: 1847). See chapter 5, "Capital," which includes testimony from a number of regions on the loaning of money for rent.
50. Gray, *Famine, Land and Politics*, 77.
51. Thomas Campbell Foster, *Letters on the Condition of the People of Ireland* (London, 1846), 314.
52. Quoted in *ibid.*, 392.

53. *Ibid.*

54. Charles Dickens, "Two Chapters On Banknote Forgeries: Chapter II," *House-hold Words* 1.26 (September 21, 1850), 619.

55. *Ibid.*

56. *Ibid.*, 620.

57. Samuel Lover, *Handy Andy: A Tale of Irish Life* (1842; London: Henry Lea, n.d.), 9–12.

58. 'An Irish gentleman (who had left his hod at the door) recently applied in Aldersgate Street for an order for five pounds on a Tipperary Post-office: for which he tendered (probably congratulating himself on having hit upon so good an investment) sixpence! It required a lengthened argument to prove to him that he would have to pay the five pounds into the office, before his friend could receive that small amount in Tipperary; and he went away, after all, evidently convinced that his not having this order was one of the personal wrongs of Ireland.' (Charles Dickens, "Post Office Money Orders," *Household Words* 5.104 [March 20, 1852], 5)

59. Quoted in Foster, *Letters*, x.

60. Maureen Murphy, Introduction to *Annals of the Famine*, by Asenath Nicholson (Dublin: Liliput, 1998), 10.

61. A[senath] Nicholson, *Ireland's Welcome to the Stranger, or An Excursion Through Ireland in 1844 & 1845 for the Purpose of Personally Investigating the Condition of the Poor* (New York: Baker and Scribner, 1847), iii.

62. *Ibid.*, iv.

63. See Pedro Schwartz, *The New Political Economy of J. S. Mill* (London: London School of Economics, 1968), chapter 1.

64. Nicholson, *Ireland's Welcome*, 39.

65. Asenath Nicholson, *Lights and Shades of Ireland* (London: Houlston and Stone-man, 1850), 253, 254, 254. A discussion of Nicholson's practices of visiting can be found in Margaret Kelleher, "The Female Gaze: Asenath Nicholson's Famine Narrative," in *Fearful Realities: New Perspectives on the Famine*, ed. Chris Morash and Richard Hayes (Dublin: Irish Academic Press, 1996), 119–30.

66. Nicholson, *Lights and Shades*, 250.

67. *Ibid.*, 251–52.

68. *Ibid.*, 217.

69. *Ibid.*, 218, emphasis original.

70. *Ibid.*, 218–19.

71. *Ibid.*, 220.

72. See especially Nicholson's discussion of Swift and eighteenth-century economic history in *ibid.*, 99–104.

73. *Ibid.*, 253.

74. Kathryn Kish Sklar, Introduction to *A Treatise on Domestic Economy*, by Catherine Beecher (1841; New York: Schocken, 1977), vi.

75. Catherine Gallagher, *The Industrial Reformation of English Fiction: Social Discourse and Narrative Form, 1832–1867* (Chicago: University of Chicago Press,

1985). The concept of metonymy is developed in Part II of this volume, "The Family Versus Society," especially in the discussion of Dickens's *Hard Times*.

76. Nicholson, *Lights and Shades*, 7.
77. Nicholson, *Ireland's Welcome*, 187.
78. Seamus Deane, *Strange Country: Modernity and Nationhood in Irish Writing since 1790* (Oxford: Clarendon, 1997), 56, 70–71. Deane's analysis begins with Gerald Griffin's *The Collegians* (1829) and concludes with a dazzling retake on Stoker's *Dracula* (1897).
79. Nicholson, *Lights and Shades*, 272.
80. *Ibid.*, 428.
81. *Ibid.*, 427.
82. *Ibid.*, 206.
83. Davis's pivotal articulation of a cultural nationalism is first laid out in "The Young Irishman of the Middle Classes" (in *Essays of Thomas Davis*, ed. D. J. O'Donoghue [New York: Lemma, 1974], 1–51), a talk delivered to the under-graduate Historical Society at Trinity College, 1840.
84. David Lloyd, *Nationalism and Minor Literature: James Clarence Mangan and the Emergence of Irish Cultural Nationalism* (Berkeley: University of California Press, 1987), 3, 76.
85. For this program, see Thomas Osborne Davis, "Udalism and Feudalism," in *Essays of Thomas Davis*, ed. O'Donoghue, 52–89.
86. Quoted in Boylan and Foley, *Political Economy and Colonial Ireland*, 138.
87. Whelan, *Killing Snows*, 10.
88. An interpretation of Celtic society that emphasizes the communal holding of land was proposed in James Connolly, *Labor in Irish History* (New York: Don-nelly, 1919). Connolly's position is unique among the anti-colonial rereadings of Irish history which were produced at the turn of the twentieth century, in that Connolly stresses the community over the nuclear family as the basic economic unit of Irish life.
89. Ó Gráda, *New Economic History*, 18–23.
90. *Ibid.*, 83–84.

5. TOWARD A SOCIAL THEORY OF WEALTH: THREE NOVELS
BY ELIZABETH GASKELL

1. Raymond Williams, *Culture and Society, 1780–1950* (1958; New York: Columbia University Press, 1983), 87–91.
2. *Ibid.*, 89.
3. Rosemarie Bodenheimer, "Private Grief and Public Acts in Mary Barton," *Dickens Studies Annual* 9 (1981), 196.
4. Hilary M. Schor, *Scheherezade in the Marketplace: Elizabeth Gaskell and the Victorian Novel* (New York: Oxford University Press, 1992), 15.
5. Joseph Childers, *Novel Possibilities: Fiction and the Formation of Early Victo-rian Culture* (Philadelphia: University of Pennsylvania Press, 1995), 169–72;

Jonathan Grossman, *The Art of Alibi: English Law Courts and the Novel* (Baltimore: Johns Hopkins University Press, 2002), 109–18; Mary Poovey, *Making a Social Body: British Cultural Formation, 1830–1864* (Chicago: University of Chicago Press, 1995), 149.

6. Elizabeth Gaskell, *Mary Barton: A Tale of Manchester Life*, ed. and intr. Stephen Gill (London: Penguin, 1970), 150. Further references are to this edition and will be noted in the text as *MB*.

7. The only sustained look at the novel's representation of dialect is Gunnel Melchers, "Mrs. Gaskell and Dialect," in *Studies in English Philology, Linguistics and Literature*, ed. Mats Ryden and Lennart A. Bjork (Stockholm: Almqvist & Wiksell, 1978), 112–24. He argues that it strengthens the reader's sympathy for Gaskell's factory-worker characters.

8. For a discussion of Esther and the broader theme of women in public in the novel, though one that does not consider Esther's role in the solution to the murder, see Deirdre D'Albertis, "Wild Night Wanderings," in *Dissembling Fictions: Elizabeth Gaskell and the Victorian Social Text* (New York: St. Martin's, 1997).

9. "Racy," *Oxford English Dictionary*, 2nd edn. (1989).

10. For more on this significant piece of paper, see Grossman, *Art of Alibi*. He links the valentine to other circulating texts in the novel and considers this evidence as one of the ways "Gaskell uses her story to raise consciousness of its textual materiality" (114).

11. On valentines in the early Victorian period, see J. Hillis Miller, "Sam Weller's Valentine," in *Literature in the Marketplace: Nineteenth-Century British Publishing and Reading Practices*, ed. John O. Jordan and Robert L. Patten (Cambridge: Cambridge University Press, 1995), 93–122.

12. The significance of this essay by Carlyle was first made clear to me in a talk by Hilary Schor called "The Stupidest Novel in London" (Strouse Memorial Lecture, McHenry Library, University of California, Santa Cruz, January 18, 1995).

13. Thomas Carlyle, "Biography," *English and Other Critical Essays* (New York: Dutton, 1950), 66.

14. *Ibid.*, 67–68.

15. *Ibid.*, 68.

16. *Ibid.*, 69.

17. *Ibid.*

18. Hans Aarsleff, *The Study of Language in England, 1780–1860* (Princeton: Princeton University Press, 1967), 235.

19. Richard Chevenix Trench, *On the Study of Words*, reprinted with *English Past and Present*, Everyman Library 788 (London: Dent, 1927), 22.

20. *Ibid.*, 23.

21. Richard Chevenix Trench, *English Past and Present*, reprinted with *On the Study of Words*, Everyman Library 788 (London: Dent, 1927), 8.

22. William Wordsworth, "The Recluse," in *Selected Poems and Prefaces*, ed. Jack Stillinger (Boston: Houghton Mifflin, 1965), 1.805–06; William

Wordsworth, *The 1805 Prelude*, in *The Prelude: 1799, 1805, 1850*, ed. Jonathan Wordsworth, M. H. Abrams, and Stephen Gill (New York: Norton, 1979), XIII.226.

23. Compare Joseph Childers's account of Barton and working-class struggle in *Novel Possibilities*. Childers links Gaskell's work with that of Engels and other urban social investigators, arguing that the poor in Gaskell's novel take on the Hegelian role of "the universally negated" (162).

24. Poovey, *Social Body*, 149.

25. *Ibid.*, 147.

26. Quoted in Elizabeth Gaskell, "The Last Generation in England," in Elizabeth Gaskell, *Cranford*, ed. Elizabeth Porges Watson (Oxford: Oxford University Press, 1972), 161.

27. Gaskell, "Last Generation," 161.

28. Schor, *Scheherezade*, 91.

29. Elizabeth Gaskell, *Cranford*, ed. Elizabeth Porges Watson (Oxford: Oxford University Press, 1972), 42. Further references to *Cranford* are all to this edition and will be cited within the text as *C*.

30. Andrew H. Miller, "Subjectivity Ltd.: The Discourse of Liability in the Joint Stock Companies Act of 1865 and Gaskell's *Cranford*," *ELH* 61 (1994), 149. Miller considers the novel's understanding of financial responsibility alongside the Parliamentary debate over the limitation of corporate liability.

31. See also *ibid.*, 153.

32. W[illiam] Stanley Jevons, *The Theory of Political Economy*, 5th edn., ed. H. Stanley Jevons (1871; New York: Kelley & Millman, 1957), 14.

33. For a different reading of fantastic animals in the novel, see Rowena Fowler, "*Cranford*: Cow in Grey Flannel or Lion *Couchant*?" *SEL* 24.4 (1984), 717–29.

34. Jacques Derrida, *Specters of Marx: The State of the Debt, the Work of Mourning, and the New International*, trans. Peggy Kamuf (London: Routledge, 1994), 12.

35. John Francis, *History of the Bank of England, its Times and Traditions*, 2 vols. (London: Willoughby, 1848), II.103.

36. Elizabeth Gaskell, *North and South*, ed. Dorothy Collin (London: Penguin, 1970), 66, 67. Further references are to this edition and will be cited within the text as *NS*.

37. Quoted in Karl Marx, "On the Jewish Question," in *Karl Marx: Selected Writings*, ed. David McLellan (Oxford: Oxford University Press, 1977), 42.

38. Quoted in *ibid.*, 42.

39. *Ibid.*, 41.

40. *Ibid.*, 43.

41. *Ibid.*, 52.

42. *Ibid.*, 53.

43. *Ibid.*, 45.

44. *Ibid.* I have not attempted a complete reading of Marx's text here, but rather focused on the critique of abstract rights in Part 1 of the review. For broader consideration of the essay, including the charges of anti-semitism it has

consistently provoked, see Regenia Gagnier, *The Insatiability of Human Wants: Economics and Aesthetics in Market Society* (Chicago: University of Chicago Press, 2000), 74–75.

45. Edward Norman, "Church and State since 1800," in *A History of Religion in Britain: Practice and Belief from Pre-Roman Times to the Present*, ed. Sheridan Gilley and W. J. Sheils (Oxford: Blackwell, 1994), 278.

46. Friedrich Engels, *The Condition of the Working Class in England* (1845; Moscow: Progress, 1973), 103.

47. Marx, "Jewish Question," 57.

48. *Ibid.*, 54.

49. *Ibid.*

CONCLUSION

1. Adam Smith, *The Theory of Moral Sentiments*, ed. D. D. Raphael and A. L. Macfie (1759; Oxford: Clarendon, 1976), 185.

2. Alan Liu, "Managing History: The Downsizing of Knowledge and the Future of Literary History in the Information Age," keynote address, *Information, Technology, and the Humanities*, Western Humanities Conference, University of California, Riverside, October 17, 1997; Alan Liu, *The Laws of Cool: The Culture of Information* (University of Chicago Press, forthcoming).

Bibliography

[Anonymous Diary]. ms. 194. National Library of Ireland. 1837.

Aalen, F. H. A., Kevin Whelan, and Matthew Stout, eds. *Atlas of the Irish Rural Landscape*. Toronto: University of Toronto Press, 1997.

Aarsleff, Hans. *From Locke to Saussure: Essays on the Study of Language and Intellectual History*. Minneapolis: University of Minnesota Press, 1982.

The Study of Language in England, 1780–1860. Princeton: Princeton University Press, 1967.

Acres, W. Marston. *The Bank of England from Within, 1694–1900*. London: Oxford University Press, 1931.

Adair, Shafto. *The Winter of 1846–7 in Antrim, with Remarks on Outdoor Relief and Colonization*. London, 1847.

Akenson, D. H. "Pre-University Education, 1782–1870." *A New History of Ireland, vol. v: Ireland Under the Union, 1: 1801–1870*. Ed. W. E. Vaughan. Oxford: Clarendon, 1989. 523–37.

Alborn, Timothy L. "Economic Man, Economic Machine: Images of Circulation in the Victorian Money Market." *Natural Images in Economic Thought: "Markets Read in Tooth and Claw."* Ed. Phillip Mirowski. Cambridge: Cambridge University Press, 1994. 173–96.

Amariglio, Jack and David F. Ruccio. "Literary/Cultural 'Economies,' Economic Discourse, and the Question of Marxism." *The New Economic Criticism: Studies at the Intersection of Literature and Economics*. Ed. Martha Woodmansee and Mark Osteen. London: Routledge, 1999. 381–400.

Anderson, Benedict. *Imagined Communities*. London: Verso, 1983.

Andréadès, A. *History of the Bank of England, 1640 to 1903* (1909). New York: Kelly, 1966.

Andreski, Stanislav. "Introduction: Comte's Place in the History of Sociology." *The Essential Comte*. Ed. Andreski. London: Croom Helm, 1974. 7–18.

Andrews, J. H. *A Paper Landscape: The Ordnance Survey in Nineteenth-Century Ireland*. Oxford: Clarendon, 1975.

Armstrong, Nancy. *Desire and Domestic Fiction: A Political History of the Novel*. New York: Oxford University Press, 1987.

Ashley, W. J. Introduction. Mill, *Principles of Political Economy with their Applications to Social Philosophy* (1848). Ed. Ashley. London: Longmans, 1915.

Bagehot, Walter. *The Collected Works of Walter Bagehot*. Ed. Norman St. John-Stevas. 13 vols. London: *The Economist*, 1978.

Barthes, Roland. *S/Z: An Essay*. Trans. Richard Howard. New York: Hill and Wang, 1974.

Baudrillard, Jean. *For a Critique of the Political Economy of the Sign*. Trans. and intr. Charles Levin. St. Louis: Telos, 1981.

Beecher, Catherine. *A Treatise on Domestic Economy* (1841). New York: Schocken, 1977.

Bell, Eric Temple. *The Magic of Numbers*. New York: Whittlesey, 1946.

Benjamin, Walter. "Theses on the Philosophy of History." *Illuminations*. Ed. Hannah Arendt. Trans. Harry Zohn. New York: Schocken, 1969. 253–64.

Beer, Gillian. *Darwin's Plots: Evolutionary Narrative in Darwin, George Eliot and Nineteenth-Century Fiction* (1983). 2nd edn. Cambridge: Cambridge University Press, 2000.

Bhabha, Homi K. "DissemiNation: Time, Narrative, and the Margins of the Modern Nation." *Nation and Narration*. Ed. Bhabha. London: Routledge, 1990. 291–322.

Birken, Lawrence. *Consuming Desires: Sexual Science and the Emergence of a Culture of Abundance, 1871–1914*. Ithaca, NY: Cornell University Press, 1988.

Black, R. D. Collison. *Economic Thought and the Irish Question, 1817–1870*. Cambridge: Cambridge University Press, 1960.

Blaug, Mark. *Ricardian Economics: A Historical Study*. New Haven: Yale University Press, 1958.

Bodenheimer, Rosemarie. "Private Grief and Public Acts in Mary Barton." *Dickens Studies Annual* 9 (1981), 195–216.

Bohm, Arnold. Letter to Editor. *PMLA* 116.3 (May 2001), 657–58.

Boylan, Thomas A., and Timothy P. Foley. *Political Economy and Colonial Ireland: The Propagation and Ideological Function of Economic Discourse in the Nineteenth Century*. London: Routledge, 1992.

Brantlinger, Patrick. *Fictions of State: Culture and Credit in Britain, 1694–1994*. Ithaca, NY: Cornell University Press, 1996.

Butt, Isaac. *A Voice for Ireland: The Famine in the Land*. Dublin, 1847.

Callari, Antonio and David Ruccio, eds. *Postmodern Materialism and the Future of Marxist Theory: Essays in the Althusserian Tradition*. Hanover, NH: University of New England Press, 1996.

Campbell, Colin. *The Romantic Ethic and the Spirit of Modern Consumerism*. Oxford: Blackwell, 1987.

Campbell, R. H., and A. S. Skinner. *Adam Smith*. London: Croom Helm, 1982.

Carlyle, Thomas. "Biography." *English and Other Critical Essays*. New York: Dutton, 1950. 65–79.

Sartor Resartus and Selected Prose. New York: Holt, Reinhart and Winston, 1970.

Castelyan, Mary. *A History of Literacy and Libraries in Ireland*. Aldershot: Gower, 1984.

Childers, Joseph. *Novel Possibilities: Fiction and the Formation of Early Victorian Culture*. Philadelphia: University of Pennsylvania Press, 1995.

Chow, Rey. "How (the) Inscrutable Chinese Led to Globalized Theory." *PMLA* 116.1 (January 2001), 69–74.

Letter to Editor. *PMLA* 116.3 (May 2001), 660.

Clapham, John. *The Bank of England: A History*. 2 vols. Cambridge: Cambridge University Press, 1958.

An Economic History of Modern Britain: The Early Railway Age, 1820–1850. Vol. 1 of 2. Cambridge: Cambridge University Press, 1959.

"Clown," *Oxford English Dictionary*. 2nd edn. 1989.

Cohen, Patricia Cline. *A Calculating People: The Spread of Numeracy in Early America*. Chicago: University of Chicago Press, 1982.

Comerford, R. V. "Ireland 1850–70: Post-Famine and Mid-Victorian." *A New History of Ireland, vol. v: Ireland Under the Union, 1: 1801–1870*. Ed. W. E. Vaughan. Oxford: Clarendon, 1989. 372–95.

Comte, Auguste. *The Essential Comte*. Ed. Stanislav Andreski. London: Croom Helm, 1974.

Condillac, Etienne Bonnot, Abbé de. *An Essay on the Origin of Human Knowledge: Being a Supplement to Mr. Locke's* Essay on the Human Understanding (1756). Trans. Thomas Nugent. Ed. Robert G. Weyant. Facsimile edn. Gainesville, FL: Scholar's Facsimiles, 1971.

Essai sur l'origine des connaissances humaines (1746). Paris: Editions Alive, 1998.

Essay on the Origin of Human Knowledge (1746). Trans. and ed. Hans Aarsleff. Cambridge: Cambridge University Press, 2001.

Philosophical Writings of Etienne Bonnot, Abbé de Condillac. Trans. Franklin Philip. Hillsdale, NJ: Lawrence Erlbaum, 1982–87.

Connel, Philip. *Romanticism, Economics and the Question of "Culture."* Oxford: Oxford University Press, 2001.

Connolly, James. *Labour in Irish History*. New York: Donnelly, 1919.

Connolly, S. J. "Mass Politics and Sectarian Conflict, 1823–1830." *A New History of Ireland, vol. v: Ireland Under the Union, 1: 1801–1830*. Ed. W. E. Vaughan. Oxford: Clarendon, 1989. 74–107.

Cook, S. B. *Imperial Affinities: Nineteenth-Century Analogies and Exchanges Between India and Ireland*. New Delhi: Sage, 1993.

Corbett, Mary Jean. *Allegories of Union in Irish and English Writing, 1790–1870: Politics, History, and the Family from Edgeworth to Arnold*. Cambridge: Cambridge University Press, 2000.

Crotty, Raymond. *Ireland in Crisis: A Study in Capitalist Colonial Undevelopment*. Dingle, Ireland: Brandon, 1986.

Cullen, L. M. *An Economic History of Ireland since 1660*. New York: Barnes & Nobel, 1972.

Cullenberg, Stephen. *The Falling Rate of Profit*. London: Pluto, 1994.

D'Albertis, Deirdre. *Dissembling Fictions: Elizabeth Gaskell and the Victorian Social Text*. New York: St. Martin's, 1997.

Danahay, Martin A. "Housekeeping and Hegemony in *Bleak House*." *Studies in the Novel* 23.4 (Winter 1991), 416–31.

Daston, Lorraine. *Classical Probability in the Enlightenment*. Princeton: Princeton University Press, 1988.

Davis, Thomas Osborne. *Essays of Thomas Davis*. Ed. D. J. O'Donoghue. New York: Lemma, 1974.

"Dazzle." *Oxford English Dictionary*. 2nd edn. 1989.

De Quincey, Thomas. *Collected Writings*. New and enlarged edn. 14 vols. Ed. David Masson. Edinburgh, 1889–90.

Deane, Seamus. *Strange Country: Modernity and Nationhood in Irish Writing since 1790*. Oxford: Clarendon, 1997.

Deleuze, Jacques and Félix Guattari. *Anti-Oedipus: Capitalism and Schizophrenia*. Trans. Robert Hurley, Mark Seem, and Helen R. Lane. Minneapolis: University of Minnesota Press, 1983.

Derrida, Jacques. *The Archeology of the Frivolous: Reading Condillac*. Trans. and intr. John P. Leavey, Jr. Lincoln: University of Nebraska Press, 1987.

Of Grammatology. Trans. Gayatri Chakravorty Spivak. Baltimore: Johns Hopkins University Press, 1974.

Specters of Marx: The State of the Debt, the Work of Mourning, and the New International. Trans. Peggy Kamuf. London: Routledge, 1994.

"White Mythology." *Margins of Philosophy*. Trans. Alan Bass. Chicago: University of Chicago Press, 1982. 209–71.

Dickens, Charles. *Bleak House*. Ed. Norman Page. Harmondsworth: Penguin, 1971.

"The Old Lady of Threadneedle Street." *Household Words* 1.15 (July 6, 1850), 337–42.

"Post Office Money Orders." *Household Words* 5.104 (March 20, 1852), 1–5.

"Two Chapters on Bank Note Forgeries: Chapter II." *Household Words* 1.26 (September 21, 1850), 615–20.

Dickson, P. G. M. *The Financial Revolution in England: A Study in the Development of Public Credit, 1688–1756*. New York: St. Martin's, 1967.

Digest of Evidence taken before Her Majesty's Commissioners of Inquiry into the State of the Law and Practice in respect to the Occupation of Land in Ireland. Part 1. Dublin, 1847.

Donnelly, James S. *The Land and the People of Nineteenth-Century Cork: The Rural Economy and the Land Question*. London: Routledge, 1975.

Eagleton, Terry. *Heathcliff and the Great Hunger: Studies in Irish Culture*. London: Verso, 1995.

Engels, Friedrich. *The Condition of the Working Class in England* (1845). Moscow: Progress, 1994.

Escobar, Arturo. *Encountering Development: The Making and Unmaking of the Third World*. Princeton: Princeton University Press, 1995.

Evans, David Morier. *The Commercial Crisis of 1847–48*. 2nd edn. London, 1849.

Fanon, Frantz. *The Wretched of the Earth*. Trans. Constance Farrington. New York: Grove Weidenfeld, 1963.

Feiner, Susan. "A Portrait of *Homo Economicus* as a Young Man." *The New Economic Criticism: Studies at the Intersection of Literature and Economics*. Ed. Martha Woodmansee and Mark Osteen. London: Routledge, 1999. 193–209.

"Reading Neoclassical Economics: Toward an Erotic Economy of Sharing." *Out of the Margin: Feminist Perspectives on Economics.* Ed. Edith Kuiper and Jolande Sap. London: Routledge, 1995. 151–65.

Feiner, Susan and Bruce Roberts. "Slave Exploitation in Neoclassical Economics." *The Wealth of Races: The Present Value of Benefits from Past Injustices.* Ed. Richard F. America. New York: Greenwood Press, 1990. 139–49.

Feltes, Norman. *Literary Capital and the Late Victorian Novel.* Madison: University of Wisconsin Press, 1993.

Ferber, Marianne A., and Julie A. Nelson. *Beyond Economic Man: Feminist Theory and Economics.* Chicago: University of Chicago Press, 1993.

Ferguson, James. *The Anti-Politics Machine.* Cambridge: Cambridge University Press, 1994.

Fitzpatrick, David. "Emigration, 1801–1870." *A New History of Ireland, vol. v: Ireland Under the Union, 1: 1801–1870.* Oxford: Clarendon, 1989. 562–622.

Forster, John. *The Life of Charles Dickens* (1872–74). 2 vols. London: Dent, 1927.

Foster, Thomas Campbell. *Letters on the Condition of the People of Ireland.* London, 1846.

Foucault, Michel. *The Order of Things: An Archaeology of the Human Sciences.* New York: Vintage, 1970.

Fowler, Rowena. "*Cranford*: Cow in Grey Flannel or Lion *Couchant?*" *SEL* 24.4 (1984), 718–29.

Francis, John. *History of the Bank of England, its Times and Traditions.* 2 vols. London: Willoughby, 1848.

Fraser, Russell. *The Language of Adam: On the Limits and Systems of Discourse.* New York: Columbia University Press, 1977.

Freeman, T. W. "Land and People, *c.* 1841." *A New History of Ireland, vol. v: Ireland Under the Union, 1: 1801–1870.* Ed. W. E. Vaughan. Oxford: Clarendon, 1989. 242–71.

Gagnier, Regenia. "On the Insatiability of Human Wants: Economic and Aesthetic Man." *Victorian Studies* 36 (1993), 125–53.

   The Insatiability of Human Wants: Economics and Aesthetics in Market Society. Chicago: University of Chicago Press, 2000.

Gagnier, Regenia and John Dupré. "Reply to Amariglio and Ruccio's 'Literary/Cultural "Economies," Economic Discourse, and the Question of Marxism'." *The New Economic Criticism: Studies at the Intersection of Literature and Economics.* Ed. Martha Woodmansee and Mark Osteen. London: Routledge, 1999. 401–07.

Gallagher, Catherine. *The Industrial Reformation of English Fiction: Social Discourse and Narrative Form, 1832–1867.* Chicago: University of Chicago Press, 1985.

Gallagher, Catherine and Stephen Greenblatt. *Practicing New Historicism.* Chicago: University of Chicago Press, 2000.

Gaskell, Elizabeth. *Cranford.* Ed. Elizabeth Porges Watson. Oxford: Oxford University Press, 1972.

   Mary Barton: A Tale of Manchester Life. Ed. Stephen Gill. London: Penguin, 1970.

North and South. Ed. Dorothy Collin. London: Penguin, 1970.

Gibson-Graham, J. K. *The End of Capitalism (As We Knew It).* Oxford: Blackwell, 1996.

Gibson-Graham, J. K., Stephen A. Resnick, and Richard D. Wolff, eds. *Re/presenting Class: Essays in Postmodern Marxism.* Durham, NC: Duke University Press, 2001.

Gill, Stephen. *Wordsworth and the Victorians.* Oxford: Clarendon, 1998.

Gramsci, Antonio. *Selections from the Prison Notebooks.* Trans. and ed. Quintin Hoare and Geoffrey Nowell Smith. New York: International Press, 1971.

Gray, Peter. *Famine, Land and Politics: British Government and Irish Society, 1843–1850.* Dublin: Irish Academic Press, 1999.

Grossman, Jonathan. *The Art of Alibi: English Law Courts and the Novel.* Baltimore: Johns Hopkins University Press, 2002.

Hack, Daniel. "'Sublimation Strange': Allegory and Authority in *Bleak House,*" *ELH* 66 (1999), 129–56.

Hacking, Ian. *The Emergence of Probability: A Philosophical Study of Early Ideas About Probability, Induction and Statistical Inference.* Cambridge: Cambridge University Press, 1975.

Herbert, Christoper. *Culture and Anomie: Ethnographic Imagination in the Nineteenth Century.* Chicago: University of Chicago Press, 1991.

Hilton, Boyd. *The Age of Atonement: The Influence of Evangelicalism on Social and Economic Thought, 1795–1865.* Oxford: Clarendon, 1988.

  Cash, Corn, and Commerce: The Economic Policies of the Tory Governments 1815–1830. Oxford: Oxford University Press, 1977.

Hobsbawm, E. J. *The Age of Capital: 1848–1875.* New York: Scribner, 1975.

Hont, Istvan and Michael Ignatieff, eds. *Wealth and Virtue: The Shaping of Political Economy in the Scottish Enlightenment.* Cambridge: Cambridge University Press, 1983.

House of Commons. *First Report from the Secret Committee on Commercial Distress. Monetary Policy and Commercial Distress: Session 1847–48.* 4 vols. Irish University Press Series of British Parliamentary Papers. Shannon, Ireland: Irish University Press, 1968. Vol. 1 of 4.

House of Lords. *Report from the Secret Committee of the House of Lords Appointed to Inquire into the Causes of the Distress. Monetary Policy and Commercial Distress: Session 1847–48.* 4 vols. Irish University Press Series of British Parliamentary Papers. Shannon, Ireland: Irish University Press, 1968. Vol. III of 4.

Jevons, W[illiam] Stanley. *The Theory of Political Economy* (1871). 5th edn. Ed. H. Stanley Jevons. New York: Kelley & Millman, 1957.

Jordan, John O. and Robert L. Patten, eds. *Literature in the Marketplace: Nineteenth-Century British Publishing and Reading Practices.* Cambridge: Cambridge University Press, 1995.

Joseph, Gerhard. "Commodifying Tennyson: The Historical Transformation of 'Brand Loyalty.'" *The New Economic Criticism: Studies at the Intersection of Literature and Economics.* Ed. Martha Woodmansee and Mark Osteen. London: Routledge, 1999. 307–20.

Kant, Immanuel. *Critique of Pure Reason* (1781). Trans. Norman Kemp Smith. New York: St. Martin's, 1929.

Kaplan, Fred. *Dickens: A Biography*. New York: Morrow, 1988.

Kelleher, Margaret. "The Female Gaze: Asenath Nicholson's Famine Narrative." *Fearful Realities: New Perspectives on the Famine*. Ed. Chris Morash and Richard Hayes. Dublin: Irish Academic Press, 1996. 119–30.

Kindleberger, Charles Poor. *A Financial History of Western Europe*. 2nd edn. New York: Oxford University Press, 1993.

Kinealy, Christine. *This Great Calamity: The Great Irish Famine, 1845–52*. Dublin: Gill & Macmillan, 1994.

Klamer, Arjo, ed. *The Value of Culture: On the Relationship Between Economics and Arts*. Amsterdam: Amsterdam University Press, 1996.

Klamer, Arjo, Donald [Deirdre] N. McCloskey, and Robert M. Solow, eds. *The Consequences of Economic Rhetoric*. Cambridge: Cambridge University Press, 1988.

Krüger, Lorenz, Lorraine Daston, and Michael Heidelberger, eds. *The Probabilistic Revolution*. 2 vols. Cambridge, MA: MIT Press, 1987.

Kynaston, David. *The City of London*. 2 vols. London: Chatto & Windus, 1994.

Land, Steven K. "Adam Smith's 'Concerning the First Formation of Languages'." *Journal of the History of Ideas* 38 (1977), 677–90.

Langer, Gary F. *The Coming of Age of Political Economy, 1815–1825*. New York: Greenwood, 1987.

Levine, George. *Darwin and the Novelists: Patterns of Science in Victorian Fiction*. Cambridge, MA: Harvard University Press, 1988.

Liu, Alan. *The Laws of Cool: The Culture of Information*. University of Chicago Press, forthcoming.

"Managing History: The Downsizing of Knowledge and the Future of Literary History in the Information Age." Keynote address. *Information, Technology, and the Humanities*: Western Humanities Conference. University of California, Riverside. October 17, 1997.

Lloyd, David. *Nationalism and Minor Literature: James Clarence Mangan and the Emergence of Irish Cultural Nationalism*. Berkeley: University of California Press, 1987.

"Violence and the Constitution of the Novel." *Anomalous States: Irish Writing and the Post-Colonial Moment*. Durham, NC: Duke University Press, 1993. 125–62.

Locke, John. *Diary of John Locke, Valuer, Limerick*. ms. 3566. National Library of Ireland, Dublin. 1840–49.

Loudon, J. C. *The Suburban Gardener and Villa Companion* (1838). New York: Garland, 1982.

Lover, Samuel. *Handy Andy: A Tale of Irish Life* (1842). London: Henry Lea, n.d.

Lowe, Lisa and David Lloyd, eds. *Politics of Culture under the Shadow of Capital*. Durham, NC: Duke University Press, 1997.

Lynch, Patrick and John Vaizey. *Guiness's Brewery in the Irish Economy, 1759–1876*. Cambridge: Cambridge University Press, 1960.

MacDonagh, Oliver. "The Economy and Society, 1830–45." *A New History of Ireland, vol. v: Ireland Under the Union, 1: 1801–1870*. Ed. W. E. Vaughan. Oxford: Clarendon, 1989. 218–41.

MacEwan, Arthur. *Neo-Liberalism or Democracy? Economic Strategy, Markets, and Alternatives for the Twenty-First Century*. London: Zed, 1999.

Magnus, Berndt and Stephen Cullenberg, eds. *Whither Marxism?: Global Crises in International Perspective*. New York: Routledge, 1995.

Malthus, T. R. *Principles of Political Economy* (1820). Variorum edn. Ed. John Pullen. 2 vols. Cambridge: Cambridge University Press, 1989.

Mander, Jerry, and Edward Goldsmith. *The Case Against the Global Economy: And for a Turn Toward the Local*. San Francisco: Sierra Club, 1996.

Marx, Karl. *Capital: A Critique of Political Economy, Vol. 1* (1867). Trans. Ben Fowkes. New York: Vintage, 1977.

Capital: A Critique of Political Economy, Vol. III (1894). New York: International Press, 1967.

Capital: A Critique of Political Economy, Vol. III (1894). Trans. David Fernbach. New York: Vintage, 1981.

A Contribution to the Critique of Political Economy (1859). Ed. Maurice Dobb. Moscow: International Press, 1970.

Selected Writings. Ed. David McLellan. Oxford: Oxford University Press, 1977.

Maurer, Bill. *Recharting the Caribbean: Land, Law, and Citizenship in the British Virgin Islands*. Ann Arbor: University of Michigan Press, 1997.

Mayhew, Henry. *London Labour and the London Poor* (1861). 4 vols. New York: Dover, 1968.

McCloskey, Donald [Deirdre]. *The Rhetoric of Economics*. Madison: University of Wisconsin Press, 1985.

McDonagh, Josephine. *De Quincey's Disciplines*. Oxford: Clarendon, 1994.

McLaughlin, Kevin. *Writing in Parts: Imitation and Exchange in Nineteenth-Century Literature*. Stanford, CA: Stanford University Press, 1995.

Meek, Ronald L. "The Decline of Ricardian Economics in England." *Economics and Ideology and Other Essays: Studies in the Development of Economic Thought*. London: Chapman and Hall, 1967. 51–75.

Melchers, Gunnel. "Mrs. Gaskell and Dialect." *Studies in English Philology, Linguistics and Literature*. Ed. Mats Ryden and Lennart A. Bjork. Stockholm: Almqvist & Wiksell, 1978. 112–24.

Menninger, Karl. *Number Words and Number Symbols: A Cultural History of Numbers*. Cambridge, MA: MIT Press, 1969.

Michie, Helena. "'Who is this in Pain?': Scarring, Disfigurement, and Female Identity in *Bleak House* and *Our Mutual Friend*." *Novel: A Forum on Fiction* 22 (1989), 199–218.

Mies, Maria. *Patriarchy and Accumulation on a World Scale: Women in the International Division of Labor*. London: Zed, 1986.

Mill, John Stuart. *Autobiography*. Ed. Jack Stillinger. Boston: Houghton Mifflin, 1969.

Collected Works of John Stuart Mill. General ed. F. E. L. Priestly. 33 vols. Toronto: University of Toronto Press, 1963–91.

Miller, Andrew H. *Novels Behind Glass: Commodity Culture and Victorian Narrative.* Cambridge: Cambridge University Press, 1995.

"Subjectivity Ltd. The Discourse of Liability in the Joint Stock Companies Act of 1856 and Gaskell's *Cranford.*" *ELH* 61 (1994), 139–57.

Miller, D. A. "Discipline in Different Voices: Bureaucracy, Police, Family, and *Bleak House.*" *The Novel and the Police.* Berkeley: University of California Press, 1988. 58–107.

Miller, J. Hillis. Introduction. *Bleak House.* By Charles Dickens. Ed. Norman Page. Harmondsworth: Penguin, 1971. 11–34.

"Sam Weller's Valentine." *Literature in the Marketplace: Nineteenth-Century British Publishing and Reading Practices.* Ed. John O. Jordan and Robert L. Patten. Cambridge: Cambridge University Press, 1995. 93–122.

Mirowski, Phillip. *More Heat than Light: Economics as Social Physics, Physics as Nature's Economics.* Cambridge: Cambridge University Press, 1989.

Mirowski, Phillip, ed. *Natural Images in Economic Thought: "Markets Read in Tooth and Claw."* Cambridge: Cambridge University Press, 1994.

Mizuta, Hiroshi, ed. *Adam Smith's Library: A Catalogue.* Oxford: Clarendon, 2000.

Mokyr, Joel. *Why Ireland Starved: A Quantitative and Analytical History of the Irish Economy, 1800–1850.* London: Allen & Unwin, 1983.

Moss, Laurence. *Mountifort Longfield: Ireland's First Professor of Political Economy.* Ottawa: Green Hill, 1976.

Mungello, David E. *Curious Land: Jesuit Accommodation and the Origins of Sinology.* Stuttgart: Verlag, 1985.

Murphy, Maureen. "Introduction." *Annals of the Famine.* By Asenath Nicholson. Ed. Maureen Murphy. Dublin: Liliput, 1998. 5–19.

Nicholson, A[senath]. *Ireland's Welcome to the Stranger, or An Excursion Through Ireland in 1844 & 1845 for the Purpose of Personally Investigating the Condition of the Poor.* New York: Baker and Scribner, 1847.

Lights and Shades of Ireland. London: Houlston and Stoneman, 1850.

Nicholson, Colin. *Writing and the Rise of Finance: Capital Satires of the Early Eighteenth Century.* Cambridge: Cambridge University Press, 1994.

Norman, Edward. "Church and State since 1800." *A History of Religion in Britain: Practice and Belief from Pre-Roman Times to the Present.* Ed. Sheridan Gilley and W. J. Sheils. Oxford: Blackwell, 1994. 277–90.

Nunokawa, Jeff. *The Afterlife of Property: Domestic Security and the Victorian Novel.* Princeton: Princeton University Press, 1994.

Ó Gráda, Cormac. "Industry and Communications, 1801–45." *A New History of Ireland, vol. v: Ireland Under the Union, 1: 1801–1870.* Ed. W. E. Vaughan. Oxford: Clarendon, 1989. 137–57.

Ireland: A New Economic History, 1780–1939. Oxford: Clarendon, 1994.

"Poverty, Population, and Agriculture, 1801–1845." *A New History of Ireland, vol. v: Ireland Under the Union, 1: 1801–1870.* Ed. W. E. Vaughan. Oxford: Clarendon, 1989. 108–33.

Ó Tuathaigh, Gearóid. *Ireland Before the Famine, 1798–1848*. Dublin: Gill & Macmillan, 1972.

Oliphant, Margaret. "Modern Novelists – Great and Small." *Elizabeth Gaskell: The Critical Heritage*. Ed. Angus Easson. London: Routledge, 1991.

Pim, Jonathan. *The Conditions and Prospects of Ireland*. Dublin, 1848.

Plank, Frans. "Adam Smith: Grammatical Economist." *Adam Smith Reviewed*. Ed. Peter Jones and Andrew S. Skinner. Edinburgh: Edinburgh University Press, 1992. 21–55.

Pocock, J. G. A. "Cambridge Paradigms and Scotch Philosophers: A Study of the Relations Between the Civic Humanist and the Civil Jurisprudential Interpretation of Eighteenth-Century Social Thought." *Wealth and Virtue: The Shaping of Political Economy in the Scottish Enlightenment*. Ed. Istvan Hont and Michael Ignatieff. Cambridge: Cambridge University Press, 1983. 235–52.

Virtue, Commerce, and History: Essays on Political Thought and History, Chiefly in the Eighteenth Century. Cambridge: Cambridge University Press, 1985.

Polanyi, Karl. *The Great Transformation*. New York: Rinehart, 1944.

Poovey, Mary. *A History of the Modern Fact: Problems of Knowledge in the Sciences of Wealth and Society*. Chicago: University of Chicago Press, 1998.

Making a Social Body: British Cultural Formation, 1830–1864. Chicago: University of Chicago Press, 1995.

Porter, Theodore M. *The Rise of Statistical Thinking, 1820–1900*. Princeton: Princeton University Press, 1986.

Resnick, Stephen and Richard Wolff. *Knowledge and Class: A Marxian Critique of Political Economy*. Chicago: University of Chicago Press, 1987.

Ricardo, David. *On the Principles of Political Economy and Taxation* (1817). Ed. Piero Sraffa. Cambridge: Cambridge University Press, 1951.

Rogers, Jasper W. *Employment of the Irish Peasantry: The Best Means to Prevent the Drain of Gold from England*. London, 1847.

Rotman, Brian. *Mathematics as Sign: Writing, Imagining, Counting*. Stanford, CA: Stanford University Press, 2000.

Signifying Nothing: The Semiotics of Zero. New York: St. Martin's, 1987.

Rousseau, Jean-Jacques. *Discours sur l'origine et les fondements de l'inégalité parmi les hommes* (1755). Ed. Jean Starobinski. *Oeuvres Complètes*. 5 vols. Paris: Gallimard, 1964. III.109–237.

Discourse on the Origin and Foundations of Inequality among Men (1755). Trans. Judith R. Masters. Ed. Roger D. Masters. New York: St. Martin's, 1964.

"Essay on the Origin of Languages." Trans. John M. Moran. *On the Origin of Language*. New York: Ungar, 1966. 5–74.

Sachs, Wolfgang, ed. *The Development Dictionary: A Guide to Knowledge as Power*. London: Zed, 1992.

Scally, Robert James. *The End of Hidden Ireland: Rebellion, Famine, and Emigration*. Oxford University Press, 1995.

Schor, Hilary M. *Dickens and the Daughter of the House*. Cambridge: Cambridge University Press, 2000.

Scheherezade in the Marketplace: Elizabeth Gaskell and the Victorian Novel. New York: Oxford University Press, 1992.

"The Stupidest Novel in London." Strouse Memorial Lecture. McHenry Library, University of California, Santa Cruz. January 18, 1995.

Schumpeter, Joseph A. *History of Economic Analysis*. Ed. Elizabeth Boody Schumpeter. New York: Oxford University Press, 1954.

Schwartz, Pedro. *The New Political Economy of J. S. Mill*. London: London School of Economics, 1968.

Sedgewick, Eve Kosofsky. *Between Men: English Literature and Male Homosocial Desire*. New York: Columbia University Press, 1985.

Simpson, David. *Romanticism, Nationalism, and the Revolt against Theory*. Chicago: University of Chicago Press, 1993.

Sklar, Kathryn Kish. Introduction. *A Treatise on Domestic Economy* (1841). Catherine Beecher. New York: Schocken, 1977. v–xviii.

Smith, Adam. "Considerations Concerning the First Formation of Languages" (1761). *Lectures on Rhetoric and Belles Lettres*. Ed. J. C. Bryce. Oxford: Clarendon, 1983. 201–26.

Essays on Philosophical Subjects (1795). Ed. W. P. D. Wightman and J. C. Bryce. Oxford: Clarendon, 1980.

Inquiry into the Nature and Causes of the Wealth of Nations (1776). Ed. R. H. Campbell, A. H. Skinner, and W. B. Todd. 2 vols. Oxford: Clarendon, 1976.

The Theory of Moral Sentiments (1759). Ed. D. D. Raphael and A. L. Macfie. Oxford: Clarendon, 1976.

Smith, David Eugene. *History of Mathematics*. 2 vols. New York: Ginn, 1923.

Spivak, Gayatri Chakravorty. "Can the Subaltern Speak?" *Marxism and the Interpretation of Culture*. Ed. Cary Nelson and Lawrence Grossberg. Urbana: University of Illinois Press, 1988. 271–313.

"Scattered Speculations on the Question of Value." *In Other Worlds*. New York: Methuen, 1987. 155–75.

Staten, Henry. Letter to Editor. *PMLA* 116.3 (May 2001), 659–60.

Stone, Harry, ed. *Charles Dickens' Uncollected Writings from Household Words 1850–1859*. 2 vols. Bloomington: Indiana University Press, 1968.

Strassman, Diana. "Editorial: Creating a Forum for Feminist Economic Inquiry." *Feminist Economics* 1.1 (Spring 1995), 1–7.

Sutherland, John. *Victorian Fiction: Writers, Publishers, Readers*. New York: St. Martin's, 1995.

Swetz, Frank J. *Capitalism & Arithmetic: The New Math of the 15th Century*. La Salle, IL: Open Court, 1987.

Thompson, James. *Models of Value: Eighteenth-Century Political Economy and the Novel*. Durham, NC: Duke University Press, 1996.

Trench, Richard Chevenix. *On the Study of Words* and *English Past and Present*. Everyman Library 788. London: Dent, 1927.

[Trevelyan, Charles.] "The Irish Crisis." *Edinburgh Review* 87.176 (January 1848), 229–320.

Trotter, David. *Circulation: Defoe, Dickens, and the Economics of the Novel.* Basingstoke: Macmillan, 1988.

Vaughan, W. E., ed. *A New History of Ireland, vol. v: Ireland Under the Union, 1: 1801–1870.* Oxford: Clarendon, 1989.

Villar, Pierre. *A History of Gold and Money, 1450–1920* (1969). London: Verso, 1976.

Walsh, Susan. "Bodies of Capital: *Great Expectations* and the Climacteric Economy." *Victorian Studies* 37 (Autumn 1993), 73–98.

Warburton, William. *The Divine Legation of Moses Demonstrated* (1737–41). 10th edn. 2 vols. London: 1846.

Webb, John. *An Historical Essay Endeavoring a Probability that the Language of the Empire of China is the Primitive Language.* London, 1669.

Wellek, René. *Immanuel Kant in England, 1793–1838.* Reprint edn., with Giuseppe Micheli, *The Early Reception of Kant's Thought in England, 1785–1805.* London: Routledge/Thoemmes, 1993.

[Whately, Richard]. *Easy Lessons on Money Matters: For the Use of Young People* (1832). 14th edn. London, 1855.

Whelan, Kevin. *The Killing Snows: Cultural Change in Nineteenth-Century Ireland.* Cork, Ireland: Cork University Press, forthcoming.

"The Modern Landscape." *Atlas of the Irish Rural Landscape.* Ed. F. H. A. Aalen, Kevin Whelan, and Matthew Stout. Toronto: University of Toronto Press, 1997. 67–103.

"Pre- and Post-Famine Landscape Change." *The Great Irish Famine.* Ed. Cathal Póirtéir. Dublin: Mercier, 1995.

Williams, Raymond. *Culture and Society, 1780–1950* (1958). New York: Columbia University Press, 1983.

Winch, Donald. *Riches and Poverty: An Intellectual History of Political Economy in Britain, 1750–1834.* Cambridge: Cambridge University Press, 1996.

Woodmansee, Martha. *The Author, Art and the Market: Rereading the History of Aesthetics.* New York: Columbia University Press, 1994.

Woodmansee, Martha and Peter Jaszi, eds. *The Construction of Authorship: Textual Appropriation in Law and Literature.* Durham, NC: Duke University Press, 1994.

Woodmansee, Martha and Mark Osteen, eds. *The New Economic Criticism: Studies at the Intersection of Literature and Economics.* London: Routledge, 1999.

Wordsworth, William. *The Prelude: 1799, 1805, 1850.* Ed. Jonathan Wordsworth, M. H. Abrams, and Stephen Gill. New York: Norton, 1979.

"The Recluse." *Selected Poems and Prefaces.* Ed. Jack Stillinger. Boston: Houghton Mifflin, 1965.

Young, G. M. *Victorian England: Portrait of an Age* (1953). 2nd edn. Oxford University Press, 1980.

Index

Aarsleff, Hans 58, 59, 190–191n
abstraction, as principle of history; in Adair,
    Shafto 124; in Condillac, Etienne Bonnot
    21–23, 45, 50, 118–119; in Rousseau,
    Jean-Jacques 26, 27; in Smith, Adam 30–33,
    39, 43–47, 50, 63, 118–119; in Trevelyan,
    Charles 119–120, 121, 144
Acres, W. Marston 106, 199n
Adair, Shafto 123–127, 144, 182; on abstraction
    124; on empire 126–127; on feudalism 125; on
    national character 123, 125–126; on potatoes
    124; representation of writing 125–126; and
    Trevelyan, Charles 123–124
Akenson, D. H. 204n
Alborn, Timothy 203n
Amariglio, Jack 8
Anderson, Benedict 197n, 205n
Andréadès, A. 198n, 199n
Armstrong, Nancy 94
Arnold, Matthew 133

Babbage, Charles 136
Bagehot, Walter 75, 80, 103–105, 113; on
    Bank Charter Act of 1844 103, 198n;
    "Charles Dickens" 77–78, 86, 98, 105; and
    gender 98, 104–105, 110; *Lombard Street* 103
Bailey, Samuel 60, 115
Bank of England 15, 95–100; Bank Charter Act
    of 1844 81–86, 87, 96, 110, 193; Dickens,
    Charles on 80, 94–99, 100, 127; as "Old Lady
    of Threadneedle Street" 98, 106, 127; Sara
    Whitehead, "The Bank Nun" 106; Francis,
    John on 166
Barthes, Roland 88–89, 107
Baudrillard, Jean 99, 186n
Bauer, Bruno 167, 173
Beecher, Catherine 138
Beer, Gillian 75, 197n
Bell, Eric Temple 189n
Benjamin, Walter 77, 197n; *see also*
    "homogeneous, empty time"

Bentham, Jeremy 66
Bhabha, Homi 126, 197n
Black, R. D. Collison 205n
Blaug, Mark 51, 195n
Bodenheimer, Rosemay 145
Bohm, Arnold 187n
Bouvet, Joachim 16
Boylan, Thomas 112, 198n
Brantlinger, Patrick 199n
Butt, Isaac 4, 123

Cairnes, John Elliot 113
Callari, Antonio 185n
Campbell, Collin 184n
Carlyle, Thomas 4; "Biography" 151–152, 154;
    Sartor Resartus 151
Castelyan, Mary 200n
castration, as trope; in Rousseau, Jean-Jacques
    39; in Smith, Adam 39, 47–48, 63–64; *see also*
    masculinity, gender
Chaucer, Geoffrey 146
Childers, Joseph 208n, 210n
Chow, Rey 187n
Clapham, J. C. 85–98, 199n
Clifford, James 6
Cohen, Patricia Cline 189n
Coleridge, Samuel Taylor 4, 60, 66, 75
colonialism, *see under* empire
Comerford, R. V. 204n
Comte, Auguste 65–67, 152, 196n
Condillac, Etienne Bonnot, Abbé de 19–23, 58,
    152, 190–191n; on abstraction 21–23, 71; on
    imagination 20–21; and Locke, John 19; on
    memory 20; and Mill, John Stuart 59;
    nineteenth-century reception 59; on
    reminiscence 20; and Rousseau, Jean-Jacques
    19, 23–27, 33–34, 35; on signs 19–22, 45; and
    Smith, Adam 19, 23, 28–30, 36, 37,
    45–49; theory of history 22–23, 50,
    118–119
Connel, Philip 184n

CAMBRIDGE STUDIES IN NINETEENTH-CENTURY
LITERATURE AND CULTURE

General editor
Gillian Beer, *University of Cambridge*

Titles published